UNIVERSITY OF NORTH C.
STUDIES IN THE GERMANIC I
AND LITERATURES

Franz Grillparzer's Portraiture Of Men

BY

FREDERIC E. COENEN

CHAPEL HILL

NUMBER FOUR

1951

Printed in United States

by

THE ORANGE PRINTSHOP

IN MEMORY OF

MY TWO BROTHERS

Hans Coenen

*March 9, 1908 at Unna-Königsborn †April 24, 1945 at
Potsdam-Rehbrücke

AND

Ernst Ferdinand Coenen

*May 25, 1915 at Unna-Königsborn †February 21, 1943 at Kiev

PREFACE

Many Grillparzer scholars have approached the study of his works with the preconception that the artist's own experiences, emotions, and sentiments must be reflected in his creations, thereby denying from the start that he was able to raise his work above the personal to the higher level of the symbolical. Other critics were determined to discover in Grillparzer's works certain characteristics and weaknesses which they believed to have discerned in the artist himself. It is clear that the procedure of both groups is prejudicial to a fair evaluation of the dramas as works of art with lives of their own. Out of the endeavor—laudable in itself—to fathom the soul of the artist which itself is considered a work of art, there has been too much probing and guessing in regard to Grillparzer's life on the basis of his plays, on the one hand, and too much emphasis on the dramatist's personality in the criticisms of his plays, on the other. The resulting controversies among critics are worthless and lead nowhere inasmuch as both sides of the arguments appear with ample "proofs" and "Belege."

This investigation treats Grillparzer's dramas as independent works which, like all true works of art, began their own lives the moment they were launched on the world. The emphasis lies, of course, where it ought to lie in the study of dramatic characters, on characterization, motivation, and viability. Grillparzer's purpose in writing his dramas is taken into consideration wherever it is positively known.

—It is encouraging to note that a revaluation of Grillparzer's life in the light of "modern psychology" is also undertaken by recent critics. We quote one of them. Max Mell, in his preface to a special edition of DER ARME SPIELMANN, DAS KLOSTER BEI SENDOMIR, and Grillparzer's SELBSTBIOGRAPHIE (1947), has this to say:

> Nun wird gegen ihn [Grillparzer]geltend gemacht, es habe ihm eben ein männlicher Geist der Auflehnung, ja des Aufruhrs gemangelt, der auch unter Opfern jeder Art zur Herbeiführung eines besseren Zustandes der öffentlichen Dinge hinzuwirken hätte, und als wäre es Schwäche gewesen, die ihn hinderte, sein Leben anders zu gestalten. Dieses Urteil kommt nicht aus tiefer Kenntnis dieser Seele. Ein anderer und keineswegs minder männlicher Geist war in ihm, dem hohen bildenden verschwistert, und das ist der der Ordnung und des Begreifens, wie in der Ordnung, die er vorfand und in der er sich aufgenommen fühlte, ein Höheres von weither wirksam ist: Grillparzer bewährt in seinem Beharren einen Glauben und sein Glauben ruht eben in dieser Geborgenheit im Vaterland, im Kaisertum und in dem Auftrag der Gerechtigkeit, den diese beiden haben. . . .

I am deeply indebted to Dr. E. A. Zucker, Head of the Modern Language Department and the Humanities Division of the University of Maryland at College Park, for his scholarly guidance and encouragement.

For a grant in partial support of this publication I thank the North Carolina Center of the Carnegie Foundation for the Advancement of Teaching, at the University of North Carolina.

F. E. C.

Chapel Hill, N. C.

CONTENTS

INTRODUCTION

The purpose of this study is two-fold. In its analysis of the men-characters in the thirteen completed dramas of Austria's greatest dramatist, it, first, represents a counterpart to Francis Wolf-Cirian's GRILLPARZERS FRAUENGESTALTEN. Secondly, it examines critically the often repeated assertion that Franz Grillparzer was incapable of creating or reluctant to create "manly men."

In 1888 Johannes Volkelt published *Grillparzer als Dichter des Tragischen*,[1] a work in which he revalued to some extent the tragedies of the Austrian dramatist. He summarizes what such critics as Gervinus, Joseph Hillebrand, Wolfgang Menzel, and others[2] had said about Grillparzer and adds: "Damit aber doch der arme erschrockene Dichter nicht vollig zerschmettert dastehe, so wird hie und da gnadig und vornehm von oben herab ein dürftiges Lobspruchlein eingestreut."[3]

In his turn Volkelt sees in Grillparzer certain weaknesses which he criticises especially "eine gewisse Scheu vor der Darstellung der reifen, gediegenen Mannlichkeit mit ihrem klaren, hellstrebenden Charakter."[4] Following Volkelt's lead the phrase "Typus der dem Leben nicht gewachsenen Innerlichkeit" is quoted directly by Reich, Bulthaupt, and Kaderschafka,[5] while the same general idea is repeated by almost all critics who have subsequently written on Grillparzer. Typical of such statements is the following quotation from E. J. Williamson:[6]

> Grillparzer's characters correspond excellently to Schlegel's demand for "sanfte Mannlichkeit" and "selbstandige Weiblichkeit." Sappho, Medea, Esther, Libussa, and Rahel are the leading spirits of the dramas in which they play a role, and are infinitely greater than any of the men-characters in the same. On the other hand, Jaromir, Phaon, Leander, Rustan, Rudolf the Second, Bancbanus, Alfonso, and even Jason and Ottokar all belong to the männlich-weiblich type. Like the persons in the various romantic novels they are "unstät und wankelmütig" and either lack the power to act or fail to maintain their manly dignity when fortune ceases to smile upon them.

A glance at the Grillparzer literature of recent years shows that the myth of his preference of the "weak hero" (1948) still has its disciples, even among the younger generation of scholar-critics. Among the latter, certain fallacies and inconsistencies become especially glaring when they speak, on the one hand, of "modern psychology," "Freudian implications," "Nervenmensch," the "abnormal, a familiar trait of the moderns," in connection with Grillparzer's plays, and, on the other hand, fail to interpret the dramatist's characters in the light of the "new knowledge" of our age. Great dramatists—and Franz Grillparzer is one of them—are far ahead of ordinary mortals in their knowledge of the human soul. They portray, in their characters, the human soul in eternally valid types and individuals. It would be almost laboring the point to call to mind the fact that Heinrich von Kleist's PRINZ FRIEDRICH VON HOMBURG (1810) could not be performed at the time he wrote his drama because a man and soldier simply did not show abject fear in the face of death, while today few people hesitate to admit that they have been afraid in the face of death and fewer still would call them cowards.

It seems imperative to subject Volkelt's judgment, which has been repeated so often, to a detailed examination to see whether it in turn is not ready for a new evaluation.

The standards and laws applied by Volkelt and the other critics are usually not consistent with the author's intentions. By way of illustration: Grillparzer believes and expresses dramatically that *he* is a strong man who remains a loyal subject although he has suffered injustice and although it is in his power to take the law into his own hands. The critic— living in the days of Bismarck, in an age which knows nothing of the horrors of a violent revolution and its aftermath—may consider the victim of injustice a weakling if he does not take the law into his own hands when he has the opportunity to do so. His criticism of Grillparzer's work would fail of complete understanding simply because he does not approach it with the same background as the author who lived through the days of Napoleon and the Revolution of 1848. Other critics attack Grillparzer's works with a preconceived philosophic scheme which they "prove" by selecting passages which seem suitable for their main ideas, but with no regard for the plan and the thought of the drama as a whole.[7] Such investigations, interpretations, and analyses seem doubly unfair when they are used as the basis for conclusions concerning the author's own character. A sounder judgment is expressed by George O. Curme[8] in discussing Grillparzer's lyric productions, epigrams, his esthetical, religious, and philosophical studies, and his dramas:

> In the dramas not only the artistic expression is finer, but the thought is milder, clearer, and higher. These dramas are, as it were, the products of those blessed moments when he had attained for a time spiritual elevation high above pain and care. This simple fact destroys the common view of his biographers, who are wont to speak of his broken spirit and dreary life. Scholars have heeded too much his cries of pain and have overlooked the blessed moments of sovereign calm that rewarded the poet and enriched the world.

This study analyzes the men-characters in Franz Grillparzer's dramas. The interpretations are based on the text as well as on the statements the author made concerning his characters and his dramas. The analysis, further, attempts to show whether or not Grillparzer was capable of portraying "manly men", whether or not he avoided the portraiture of such men, and whether or not the woman-characters in *Libussa* and *Die Judin von Toledo* (cf. E. J. Williamson's statement, quoted above) are infinitely greater than the men-characters in the dramas that bear their names. —Summaries of the thirteen dramas are appended.

All quotations from Grillparzer's dramas are from the *Historisch-kritische Gesamtausgabe im Auftrage der Stadt Wien*, herausgegeben von August Sauer und Reinhold Backmann, referred to as "W. A. (Wiener Ausgabe), Wien (1909ff).

CHAPTER ONE

DIE AHNFRAU

Die Ahnfrau was first produced on January 31, 1817. The "Fate Drama" then dominated the German stage. The problem of whether this early work of a budding dramatist is a fate drama of the Werner and Müllner type or whether it is a non-fatalistic redemption tragedy (Hans M. Wolff) has been amply discussed.[1] *Die Ahnfrau* suffers from too many literary influences and, moreover, the young dramatist undertook changes upon Schreyvogel's suggestion.

The main characters of *Die Ahnfrau* are Graf Zdenko von Borotin, his daughter Bertha, his son Jaromir, and the ghost of the ancestress, all four the tragic sufferers in this drama. There are several minor figures: Boleslaw, the romantic robber who kidnapped Jaromir and trained him for his ignoble profession, Günther the old superstitious servant of the count's family, the Captain of a company of soldiers, and servants. We are here concerned with Jaromir and the count.

The legend of the ancestress represents the background of this tragedy. The wife of one of the ancestors of the Borotins had been forced into marriage against her will.[2] One day her husband found her with her lover and stabbed her to death with a dagger that was later to hang on the wall in the hall of the castle. Since the son of the unfortunate wife was the offspring of this clandestine affair, her ghost must restlessly haunt the castle until the death of the last Borotin. Only then can she find rest in the grave. Her dramatic suffering consists of the conflict between two desires. The one is her love of life and the wish to see herself perpetuated in her descendents; this impulse obliges her to appear and give warning whenever danger is impending. The other desire is her craving for rest in the grave which can only come with the death of the last member of the family.

Jaromir

In Jaromir Grillparzer has created a most phantastic figure. A malicious chance throws the child among people whose only aim in life is violence and destruction. The young nobleman becomes one of the robbers. His strength, his courage, and his passionate nature secure for him the rank of a leader. But there is another side to his nature. He always feels that his innermost self has nothing in common with his associates. In moments of reflection he is appalled by his existence. He longs for peace of the soul, for quiet happiness. He suffers as an outcast of society and welcomes an opportunity to escape his present life. Yet he is so much a part of his world that he is unable to renounce it when the test comes. His passionate nature makes him resort to violence whenever he finds the road to his desires blocked. This leads ultimately to his destruction. It is the passionate, irrational will to live that forces him to use his weapon against his pursuers. And it is the irrational, almost insane demand to possess Bertha that prevents flight and drives him ultimately into the arms of the ghost, *i.e.* into the arms of death.

In view of the many literary influences briefly referred to above and the changes suggested by Schreyvogel it is not surprising that the portraiture of Jaromir is not perfect. He combines the chief characteristics of the young hero, *i.e.* bravery in fighting, even though in an anti-social cause, with the chivalry and dash of the lover. Somehow the nefariousness of his cause is minimized in the reader's eyes by the moral courage Jaromir shows in defending the robbers before the very soldiers who are hunting them down. Jaromir is in imminent danger of his own life when he shows that to some extent the robbers are victims of society. When later on he gives up his safe refuge in the castle to fight with and for his companions, one sees the qualities that led to his selection as the captain of the band. All of a piece with these winning traits is his manner of facing his own unspeakably cruel fate, brought upon him suddenly with a cunning malice that seems like a wanton boy's torturing of an insect: Jaromir does not cringe, he does not repent in tearful contrition as do the victims of other fate tragedies; but he places the blame on fate where every modern reader no doubt feels that it belongs. Unfortunately the portrait of this virile, sympathetic youth is made a great deal less life-like and unconvincing by the literary traditions superimposed on it, namely that of the "noble robber" of Romanticism and of the lover of a vampyrish corpse derived from Goethe's *Braut von Korinth.*

Count Borotin

Graf Zdenko von Borotin is a man whom grief has aged before his time. He shows most of the characteristics which make a nobleman. He is proud of his family whose fame is based on courageous deeds on the battlefield. This pride augments his grief at not having a son who will follow his bier, and at having to take the much-used family sword into his grave with him.

The opening scene presents Count Borotin in a mood of dejection. He has received word of the death of a cousin who died without an heir. The belief becomes stronger to him:

> Dass das Schicksal hat beschlossen,
> Von der Erde auszustossen
> Das Geschlecht der Borotin.

In his youth he lost his three brothers. He lost his wife after she had given him a son and a daughter. He lost the only heir when the child was drowned in the pond of the castle, so, at least, the father thought. He cannot help thinking of the old legend of the "Ahnfrau", though, of course, he does not believe in it. But the events which follow during that night lead him from doubt to conviction.

The Count is very ready to accept Jaromir as his son-in-law, which seems rather strange at first glance, considering the fact that the young man is unknown to him. Of course, Borotin had good reason to be grateful, for Jaromir had saved the life of the only child left to him. His words of gratitude show Borotin as a generous, broadminded, and frank nobleman (666-680). However, this indebtedness to the stranger does not explain the Count's readiness to give to him the hand of his daughter in marriage.

The second act throws a better light on the situation. Mindful of his "hallucination" when he hears of the terror Jaromir had experienced in the house, the last Borotin exclaims:

> Zahlt man dich schon zu den Meinen?
> Ist's in jenen dunkeln Orten
> Also auch schon kund geworden,
> Sohn, dass du mir teuer bist?

As he seems to believe already that the legend concerning his house is true and that the mysterious power is determined to ruin his family, the Count's sense of honor even dictates to him to sound a warning to the eager young man:

> Flieh, mein Sohn, weil es noch Zeit:
> Nur ein Tor baut seine Hütte
> Hin auf jenes Platzes Mitte,
> Den der Blitz getroffen hat.

Little wonder that—under such circumstances—Borotin does not stop to consider the character of a man who is ready to share his misfortune.

When the captain of the soldiers calls, we have occasion to note Borotin's courage and his loyalty to the king. No one can dissuade him from participating in the hunt for the robbers outside the castle:

> Kommt mein Herr, und sagt dem König,
> Dass ich, Graf von Borotin,
> Kein Genoss der Rauber bin.

Why this eagerness? Was it prompted by his great loyalty to his king? Or by the captain's demand to be allowed to search the castle? Or had the count already become suspicious of Jaromir? The count's touchiness at the captain's demand that a search of the castle be made, which seems symptomatic of an exaggerated sense of honor, is perhaps also due to a sensitiveness prompted by the count's uncertainty concerning the honor of his ancestors.

In the fourth act the count is brought in, mortally wounded in the fight with the robbers. He knows that death is near. But he, nevertheless, shows a zestful love of life, if not a touch of hedonism:

> Lass mich . . . .
> Noch zum letztenmale schlürfen
> Aus dem bittersussen Becher—
> Und dann, Schicksal, nimm ihn hin.

But he is not to enjoy this pleasant mood for long. Boleslaw appears. And Count Borotin lives to learn that his son is alive, that his son is the robber who stabbed his own father:

> Seht des Schicksals gift'gen Hohn!
> Seht, ich *habe* einen Sohn,
> Es erhielt ihn mild am Leben,
> Mir den Todesstreich zu geben!

The Count discovers the dagger with which he was stabbed and recognizes the old family weapon. Now he is convinced that fate has a hand in the misfortune of his family:

> Das hat nicht mein Sohn getan !
> Tiefverhüllte, finstre Mächte
> Lenkten seine schwanke Rechte!

But he does not spend his last breath in cursing his unfortunate son. After a long speech reviewing the gloomy history of his house, Count Borotin dies, his last words bespeaking his pride in the house of Borotin.

The count did not become a pessimist. He had lost his brothers, his wife, his son; and the grief over his misfortune had darkened his life and turned him into a melancholy old man who had aged much too soon. Nevertheless, a deep love for life, engendered when in youthful energy he fought loyally for his king and gained the honors in which he takes deep satisfaction, still survives in him and rounds out his portrait.

CHAPTER TWO

SAPPHO

The simple plot was derived from a legend according to which Sappho, the "tenth muse," a contemporary of Alcaeus, Stesichorus, and Pittacus (about 600 B. C.), leaped from the Leucadian rock because of her unrequited love for Phaon, the kind old ferryman who had been rejuvenated by a salve given him by Aphrodite. Grillparzer used the figures of Sappho and Phaon, the motive, and the catastrophe. Otherwise his drama is entirely his own creation.[1]

To what an extent *Sappho* must be considered an "artist-tragedy" or merely a drama of general human import continues to be an intriguing question among Grillparzer enthusiasts.[2] This discussion will, of course, go on inasmuch as Grillparzer, in the course of his long life, contradicted himself concerning his intentions in writing *Sappho*.

There are only three main characters in *Sappho*: Sappho, Phaon, and Melitta. The minor figures are: Eucharis, Sappho's servant, Rhamnes, a slave, a peasant, servants of both sexes, and peasants. The characters of Phaon and Rhamnes are here analyzed.

Phaon

The gulf between Sappho and Phaon is apparent from the very beginning. While she is arrayed in precious clothes, a golden lyre in her hand and a laurel wreath on her head, Phaon accompanies her in simple attire (43). This contrast is too obvious to escape attention. And Sappho feels herself that she owes an introduction and an explanation to the festive crowd which welcomes her home. He is a youth of quality, she says; although young, he has shown himself to be a man. She emphasizes the usefulness of the new citizen of Lesbos: they will find him a good warrior, orator, and even a poet. Did she believe Phaon to possess these qualities? Or did she feel self-conscious because she favored a stranger rather than a Lesbian? At any rate, Phaon, knowing his limitations and mindful of his humble origin, can only say:

> Du spottest Sappho eines armen Jünglings!
> Wodurch hätt' ich so reiches Lob verdient
> Wer glaubt so Hohes von dem Unversuchten?

Indeed, how could he have been tried? To be sure, he had been victorious in the chariot race (480). But aside from that there is nothing in the drama to indicate that Phaon had distinguished himself in any other field such as war, oratory, or poetry.

We soon learn from Phaon himself about his life. He speaks of the quiet lowliness of his home (133, 165). He and his family, like many Greek families, have enjoyed and appreciated Sappho's songs (168 ff). The imagination of Phaon, his sisters and his friends had been occupied with the person of Sappho. It is of interest that Grillparzer wishes to portray this youth as a child of nature whose poetic appreciation seems to be linked with nature. When the others describe readily and freely how they picture Sappho to themselves, Phaon goes out into the night. We hear him say:

> Dort an den Pulsen der süss schlummernden Natur,
> In ihres Zaubers magisch-mächt'gen Kreisen,
> Da breitet' ich die Arme nach dir aus;
> Und wenn mir dann der Wolken Flocken-Schnee,
> Des Zephyrs lauer Hauch, der Berge Duft,
> Des bleichen Mondes silberweisses Licht
> In Eins verschmolzen um die Stirne floss,
> Dann warst du mein, dann fuhlt' ich deine Nähe
> Und Sapphos Bild schwamm in den lichten Wolken!

An image in the clouds, an ideal which filled Phaon with veneration and awe. This is what Sappho was to him. And then his dream was realized. His enthusiasm for the games is lost in anticipation of seeing Sappho and, indeed, he is fortunate enough to witness her victory. As her lyre dropped from her hand, Phaon rushed to pick it up and their eyes met. He stood "stumm und schüchtern" (249). Sappho bade him follow her.

These events form the background before their arrival in Lesbos. That Phaon has never been at ease with Sappho is evident from his replies. What he feels for her is the same veneration and awe which he felt for the image in the clouds his imagination had created. This uneasiness becomes manifest in the answers he finds. The great poetess who was known for her pride, who had rejected many suitors, among them kings, bared her soul to him, the soul of a woman who had been humbled by her love, every fibre tense with the anticipation of Phaon's love. And all Phaon finds to say is "Erhabne Frau" (131). For him she has always been and always will be a "hohes Gotterbild" (164). The replies Phaon gives are indeed such as an awe-stricken mortal may find for his God:

> Wer glaubte auch, dass Hellas' erste Frau
> Auf Hellas' letzten Jüngling würde schauen.

and:

> Was kannst du sagen, holde Zauberin,
> Das man für wahr nicht hielte, da du's sagst?

and again:

> Wie kann ich so viel Güte je bezahlen?
> Stets wachsend fast erdrückt mich meine Schuld!

Bewildered and confused, Phaon wants to be alone, alone with himself and nature. Being the guileless person he is, it seems quite natural that he should be averse to muddled issues. He wishes to think and gain clearness:

> Um ganz zu sein, was ich zu sein begehre!

It seems a happy choice on Grillparzer's part that he presents Phaon alone in his next appearance—at the beginning of the second act. He has left the banquet which Sappho has prepared to celebrate her reunion with her people. Phaon is still struggling for clarity. His past seems far away. He recalls that only a short time before he had been willing to give his life for a glance, for a kind word from Sappho, and now

> Da meiner Wünsche winterliche Raupen
> Als goldne Schmetterlinge mich umspielen,
> Jetzt frag' ich noch und steh' und sinn' und zaudre!

The idealistic youth is gaining experience: he is learning that fulfillment of one's wishes does not necessarily bring the anticipated happiness.

And now, his thoughts return to his family. He has not sent them any news, and he is seized by apprehension concerning the attitude of his family toward his journey to Lesbos. His remarks afford an illuminating insight into the ethics which prevail in his home. Is Phaon quite free from his home influence? Has he ever before questioned his pious father's prejudice against "freche Zitherspielerinnen" (510)? But how could any one dare mention his goddess Sappho in the same breath with the gay musicians scorned by his stern parent? Yet the thought that at home they might know that he is Sappho's lover causes him consirable discomfort. His defiant attitude is partly an outgrowth of this distress:

> Wer wagt es sie zu schmähn!
> Der Frauen Zier, die Krone des Geschlechts!
> Mag auch des Neides Geifer sie bespritzen,
> Ich steh' für sie, sei's gegen eine Welt!

When Phaon hears footsteps he retreats to a near-by grotto, for the thought of meeting any one in his present mood is "widerlich" to him (513). Melitta, Eucharis, and other slaves appear. They have been gathering flowers to adorn Sappho's home. Melitta has been rather sad and listless; her companions depart. Phaon in the grotto overhears her sad soliloquy. The beautiful young slave had fallen in love with Phaon at first sight though she is unaware of her feeling. She reveals that she now feels her slavery as a burden; she regrets that she has no relatives or friends. Phaon, whose interest has been aroused, leaves his hiding place and gallantly offers his friendship to this beautiful child of nature. But when he beholds her face, he realizes that they have met before. We are struck by the change in the attitude, bearing, and tone of the timid, silent companion of the great Sappho. With a patronizing air he speaks:

> Ei sieh! Du bist wohl gar der kleine Mundschenk,
> Der statt des Gasts den blanken Estrich tränkte.
> Darum so bang? Nicht doch!

This difference in manner seems psychologically motivated, for Phaon is now speaking to his inferior. We are surprised somewhat by what follows:

> Es hat der Unfall
> So mich als die Gebieterin belustigt.

This lack of finer insight, of tact, must be ascribed to Phaon's youth and inexperience. He not only failed to see the real reason for Melitta's awkwardness in serving wine to the man to whom she was so irresistably attracted, but he is even tactless enough to embarrass her again by reminding her of Sappho's and his own amusement over this incident.

Phaon, however, realizes his crudeness as he observes the effect of his words on Melitta. He cannot bear to see her suffer. Now he becomes aware that he had paid more than casual attention to the young slave during the banquet:

> Die jungfräuliche Stille glanzte lieblich
> Durch all den wilden Taumel des Gelags.

He wishes to know why Melitta is a slave. Chivalrous and generous, Phaon is ready to secure Melitta's freedom from Sappho if that will make the young girl happy. They are soon engaged in an animated conversation. Phaon displays unusual interest in Melitta's past and succeeds in cheering her up. The charm of the scene which shows the attraction of these kindred souls betrays the hand of the master. Phaon gives Melitta a rose and offers his friendship. A similar token he asks of her. She wishes to give him a rose picked by her own hand. But the only one left is out of reach. In attempting to break it from a nearby bush, Melitta slips and is prevented from falling by the embrace of Phaon who presses a kiss on the girl's lips.

The spell is broken when Sappho appears. She had been a witness of the flirtatious scene. Tortured by jealously and doubts, Sappho tells Phaon that she had missed him at the banquet. But what happens to the gallant and dashing young swain of a moment ago? Forgetful or ignorant of all social graces, Phaon explains his absence from the banquet by saying he likes neither wine nor noisy merriment. His attitude and his abrupt replies to Sappho remind us of a school boy caught stealing apples by a severe mother and eager to leave her presence in order to avoid uncomfortable questions. His youth, his inexperience, his self-centredness his lack of sensitiveness render him wholly unable to cope with the situation. When Sappho asks: "Ich sah dich mit Melitten scherzen—" (737), he can only stammer:

> Melitta? Wer? Ei ja ganz recht! Nur weiter!

He is so confused and occupied with himself that he does not even listen to what Sappho has to say, which is quite evident from his answers:

> Recht schón, recht schön.

and:

> Wie sagtest du?

Sappho finally notices his distraction; she is quite willing to postpone the discussion. She retreats into the grotto where she is wont to devote herself to her art. Again Phaon shows no regard for his hostess; he makes no move toward reconciliation.

Phaon is left alone; his thoughts are with Melitta. He drops on the bench where Melitta had sat and, his head on his hands, peacefully falls asleep.

Sappho, still tormented by her doubts, finds Phaon in the same position, still sleeping—at the beginning of the third act. She embraces him and kisses his forehead in the hope of hearing her name from the lips of the awakening Phaon. But, alas! half unconscious, Phaon calls: "Melitta!" (858)

His sleep and his dream seem to have put him into a pleasanter mood. He is kinder to Sappho:

> Sei gegrüsst! Ich wusst' es wohl
> Dass Holdes mir zur Seite stand, darum
> War auch so hold des Traumes Angesicht!

But we are bitterly disappointed in the assumption that he will smooth things over and reassure Sappho of his love for her. He crowns his previous crudities by telling her naively of his dream in which he saw her image replaced by that of a child, of Melitta. Now convinced that she has lost Phaon, Sappho dismisses him.

But Phaon is soon called to the scene again—in the sixth scene of the third act. Hearing Melitta shout for help, he rushes forward and finds Sappho threatening her slave with a dagger. He learns that Melitta had refused to surrender her rose to Sappho who, enraged and blinded by her jealousy, had lost her self-control and drawn her dagger against her favorite slave. But while Sappho is momentarily carried away by her passion, Phaon's subsequent action is determined by his passion for Melitta. Or are the wild accusations which he hurls at Sappho in part a result of a feeling of guilt toward his benefactress?

> O weine nicht Melittion!
> Hast diese Tränen Du auch mitbezahlt,
> Als du sie von dem Sklavenmäkler kauftest?

and further:

> Mir diesen Stahl! Ich will ihn tragen
> Hier auf der warmen, der betrognen Brust, . . .

Twice (1174, 1665) he calls Sappho a Circe under whose spell he had been until the sight of Melitta had broken it. He seems to revel in the satisfaction of having found something that he can hold against the greatest poetess of Greece; and when later he rejoices at having the dagger he took from her: "Du gabst mir selber Waffen gegen dich!" (1407), he unwittingly gives expression to what he does not realize himself: a joy over having found a reason for turning against Sappho with such violence.

In the fifth scene of the fourth act the open conflict between Phaon and Sappho begins. Rhamnes had received orders from Sappho to take Melitta secretly to the island of Chios. But the girl, who senses the situation, calls for help. The courage, boldness, and resourcefulnes we see Phaon display suit perfectly the character of the impetuous youth as far as we know it from his previous conduct. His determination to get the truth from Rhamnes, his plan to flee with Melitta—made and executed immediately —suggested by the mere mention of a boat, his force when he drives Rhamnes to accompany him and Melitta to the shore in order to prevent the old slave from alarming the Lesbians before he and Melitta can escape, make us forget completely—for a while, at least—the heroine of the drama.

The fifth act, too, gives evidence of the tremendous courage which culminates in a fearlessness that knows no prudence. The two elopers have been captured and are brought before Sappho. In the third scene Phaon

and Melitta appear in the midst of the incensed Lesbians. Phaon is the
first to speak:

> Ha wag' es keiner Diese zu berühren!
> Nicht wehrlos bin ich, wenn auch gleich entwaffnet!
> Zu ihrem Schutz wird diese Faust zur Keule,
> Und jedes meiner Glieder wird ein Arm!

Phaon's rage had been increased because Melitta had been struck by an
oar in the heat of the struggle. Proudly presuming on the fact that he
is a free man, he demands to see Sappho in order to exact an explanation. One of the Lesbians points out that Phaon has broken the law by
trying to kidnap a slave. But the proud Greek reproaches them for aiding
in the revenge of a woman, saying: "*Mir* steht bei, denn Unrecht wider-
fahrt mir!" (1636)

He forces his way through the hostile crowd and finds Sappho on the
steps of the altar of Aphrodite. When Sappho sullenly declares that he is
free to leave, but that she is not willing to give up Melitta, not even for
ransom, Phaon is again carried away by his wrath:

> Zerbrich die Leier, gifterfullte Schlange!
> Die Lippe tone nimmerdar Gesang,
> Du hast verwirkt der Dichtung goldne Gaben!

But his recollections of a gentler Sappho make him doubtful of her de-
pravity. Glancing at her, he believes that he sees the old Sappho again. His
account of what had happened to him shows that he has learned to distin-
guish between the admiration he had for Sappho and his passionate love
for Melitta. He is also quite ready to admit that he was wrong in 'the
wild accusations he hurled at Sappho:

> Du warst—zu *niedrig* glaubte dich mein Zorn,
> Zu *hoch* nennt die Besinnung dich—für meine Liebe.

But Sappho is not willing to forgive the two. Again Phaon's pride
and defiance flare up while Melitta prefers to prevail upon Sappho by ap-
pealing to the better nature of the woman who for fifteen years had been
a kind mother to her. Now Phaon kneels before Sappho at Melitta's side
and makes his appeal:

> Den Menschen Liebe und den Göttern Ehrfurcht,
> Gib uns was unser, und nimm hin was dein!
> Bedenke was du tust, und wer du bist!

While Sappho leaves without committing herself, Phaon takes again his
defiant attitude, only to find in both Melitta and Rhamnes ardent defenders
of the great poetess. We gain the impression that Phaon's role has suddenly been reduced to that of a stubborn child who is receiving a cur-
tain-lecture from his elder Rhamnes. And Rhamnes' tirade seems to convince
Phaon that he had wronged Sappho:

> Wer rettet mich aus dieser Qual!

Thus—in the sixth scene of the fifth act—the transfigured Sappho
meets a changed, a repentant Phaon who is eager to be forgiven. Sappho,

meanwhile, has risen to a higher level of serenity where love and hatred are unknown. She returns to her gods, parting as a friend from Phaon and Melitta.

In Phaon Grillparzer has created a delightfully youthful figure. Coming from a middle class family with Puritan ideas—to express it in modern terms—he is well-built, strong, courageous, chivalrous, determined. He likes sports, shows appreciation for nature, enjoys poetry and music, but usually in connection with nature as we have seen. Phaon is more than a young man who is skillful in handling horses.[3] His very enthusiasm for Sappho's poetic achievements prove that. Nevertheless, he would have remained unnoticed, for he is one of many, an average youth, unsophisticated and unfamiliar with the ways of the world, were it not for his association with Greece's greatest woman poet. We have occasion to observe Phaon grow, to see the enthusiastic youth develop into a man who learns a few facts about life and its dynamic forces which are stronger than all reason. His force, his straightforwardness, his lack of hypocrisy, of polish, and urbanity, which he displays as soon as his heart is involved are indeed refreshing.[4]

Rhamnes

In Rhamnes, Sappho's teacher-slave, Grillparzer has drawn a loyal servant. His position in Sappho's house is that of a major-domo. He is proud and jealous of his position; little wonder that his zeal makes him officious at times.

Rhamnes has learned of Sappho's victory in the Olympic contest. Feverishly he has been looking forward to her arrival: and now she is approaching. In his excitement he stirs up the entire household to receive the mistress:

> Heraus ihr faulen Mädchen! Zögert ihr?

But as soon as he hears that Sappho is accompanied by a stranger, he turns into a kill-joy, a stickler for form. He sends the girls back to their work:

> Der *Mann* mag das Geliebte laut begrüssen,
> Geschäftig für sein Wohl liebt still das *Weib*.

The zealous slave plunges into the crowd, hailing Sappho, most eager to be noticed by her: "Heil Sappho, teure Frau!" (43) and: "Sei mir gegrüsst, gegrüsst, Du Herrliche!" (62). Sappho finally notices him; but her words of greeting are very short. "Mein treuer Rhamnes sei gegrüsst!" (63) she says and turns to the Lesbians, calling many of them by their names.

But Rhamnes experiences a great surprise when—in the fourth scene of the first act—Sappho introduces Phaon as their new master to Rhamnes and the household. Astonished, Rhamnes murmurs "Herrn?" (302). But Sappho's "Wer spricht hier? Was willst du sagen?" (302-303) puts him back into his place: "Nichts!" (303) the slave replies.

That Rhamnes' feeling toward the newcomer is not too friendly is natural. The servant welcomes an opportunity to outwit Phaon when the former receives orders to take Melitta secretly to Chios under the cover of night. The harsh treatment he meets with from the hands of Phaon when the latter forces him at the point of a dagger to accompany him and Melitta to the shore does not serve to make Rhamnes any more favorably disposed toward Phaon. The capture of the two fugitives is due to Rhamnes' zeal (1483-1493).

To be sure, Sappho declares Phaon a free man; but Rhamnes gets at least a verbal revenge (1812-1892). Praising Sappho, her teacher-slave tells Phaon that the only stain in her life had been her love for him,

> Die undankbare Schlange (meaning Phaon) . . . .
> Die nun mit gift'gem Zahn ihr Herz zerfleischt.

Even his pride and his spite, Rhamnes goes on, was given to Phaon by the fact that Sappho had looked at him, the most forgotten of all forgotten ones. And what he loved in Melitta was the spirit of Sappho who had reared the child. Phaon would find no rest on this earth; the Eumenides, the black messengers of the Goddess of revenge, would haunt him and drive him, the murderer of Sappho, to an early grave.

Rhamnes perhaps more than any of those who know Sappho appreciates the poetic art of Greece's greatest poetess, whose name and songs will survive even the graves of any of her contemporaries. Proud of his pupil, the noble teacher becomes her defender in the most eloquent and poetic language:

> Hoch an den Sternen hat sie ihren Namen
> Mit diamantnen Lettern angeschrieben
> Und mit den Sternen nur wird er verlöschen!

Through this lyrical speech the major-domo and teacher of Sappho is raised above the status of a typical servant.

CHAPTER THREE

DAS GOLDENE VLIESS

Grillparzer gave the subtitles *Der Gastfreund, Die Argonauten,* and *Medea* to the subdivisions of his trilogy. The sources, influences, and history have been discussed most thoroughly by Reinhold Backmann.[1] Suffice it to say here that Grillparzer used the traditional Medea material (derived chiefly from Euripides' *Medea*) to express his psychological interest in the woman who killed her own children and who—at first glance—seemed to lack all those human feelings which we attribute to a mother. By portraying Medea also as a happy huntress and priestess before her meeting with Jason, by showing the struggles of her soul in the face of the inevitable tragic happenings which precede her apparently inhuman act, Grillparzer succeeded in a measure in vindicating and enobling the barbarian princess. Realizing that the material was too abundant to be pressed into a conventional five-act drama, he decided on the tripartition. This psycho-analysis of Medea was the author's main motive. A second motive, almost equally strong, was the destructive power of the lust for gold and fame, symbolized by the lust for the golden fleece that brought ruin to all who possessed it. The portrayal of the contrast between the barbarians of Colchis and the more highly civilized Greeks was a third, not unimportant motive.

The main characters of *Der Gastfreund* are Aietes, Medea, and Phryxus. To these are added Absyrtus, Aietes' son; Jason in *Die Argonauten;* and Kreon and his daughter Kreusa in *Medea.* We are here discussing Phryxus, Jason, Aietes, Absyrtus, and Kreon. It must not be forgotten that Medea had the dramatist's chief attention throughout the trilogy, and that all other characters, even Jason, were less important to Grillparzer than Medea.

Phryxus

Phryxus claimed the gods of Hellas as his ancestors (265). His stepmother, however, "ein niedrig Weib" (273), had incited his father (Athamas, according to history) against the youth and thus forced the proud Greek to seek his fortune elsewhere. In Delphi he had prayed to Apollo for help and advice. Overcome by fatigue, Phryxus had fallen asleep in the sanctuary. In a dream he had seen the marble image of Peronto, the god of the people of Colchis, which stood in the temple among other statues. Peronto had smiled at the fugitive, saying "Nimm Sieg und Rache hin" (299) while handing him the golden fleece. Awakening, Phryxus had perceived the statue of his dream in the light of the morning sun, the golden fleece attached to its shoulders. The persecuted youth had let his imagination be his guide and interpreted the dream in his own way. He had snatched the fleece from the shoulders of the statue.

It is of the greatest interest that the fleece actually assisted Phryxus in the beginning. As he held it before him on a lance, he saw his father's men, sent to capture or kill him, likewise the priests and a thousand enemies (320) on their knees, bowing to the treasure. After he had em-

barked, the fleece on the mast of his ship protected Phryxus against the
ocean, the wind, and hell, which had conspired to sink him (324-325).

Phryxus' miraculous escape and sea-voyage serve well to motivate his
boldness when he addresses the king of Colchis, upon whose coast he had
landed by chance or by the will of the gods:

> Nimm auf mich und die Meinen in dein Land,
> Wo nicht so fass' ich selber Sitz und Statte
> Vertrauend auf der Gotter Beistand, die
> Mir *Sieg und Rache* durch dies Pfand verliehn!

Malicious Aietes, as we know, had planned to murder Phryxus, who through
his impudent threat now plays into the hands of the king by giving him
at least the semblance of a justification for his underhanded procedure.
The optimistic Greek, however, adds another imprudence. Struck by the
appearance of Medea, "das holde Kind" (354), Phryxus gives up his sword.

When he finally becomes aware of the situation, it is too late. "Ihr
Götter! Was ist das? Ich ahne Schreckliches." (408) He notices the furtive
behaviour of the natives. The Greeks are falling asleep, lulled by a sleep-
ing-draught. Phryxus sees only one way out: flight to the boat with the
rest of his men. However, the next moment shows that his men have already been overpowered. Phryxus rushes to the altar of Peronto, clinging
to it:

> Nun denn, du Hoher, der mich hergefuhrt,
> Bist du ein Gott, so schirme deinen Schützling!

Accused of treachery by Phryxus ("Du auch hier Schlange?" 431), Medea
attempts to give a sword to the doomed victim of her father's cunning,
but is stopped by Aietes. Phryxus knows now that he must die; he still believes in the "unbekannte Macht" (442), which promised him victory and
revenge:

> Hab' ich den *Sieg* durch eigne Schuld verwirkt,
> Das Haupt darbietend dem Verräternetz
> Und blind dem Schicksal trauend statt mir selber
> So lass doch *Rache* wenigstens ergehn
> Und halte deines Wortes zweite Hälfte!

Phryxus gives his most valued possession, the fleece, to his "host," whose
greed leads him to take it. However, the barbarian is frightened by his
victim's threat:

> Und gibst du's nicht zurücke, Unbeschädigt
> Nicht mir dem Unbeschadigten zurück
> So treffe dich der Gotter Donnerfluch
> Der über dem rollt, der die Treue bricht.

Aietes wishes to return the fleece to his guest, and, enraged by the latter's refusal, thrusts his sword into the breast of the unarmed Phryxus,
but cannot prevent him from uttering a terrible curse (484-495).

In Phryxus Grillparzer has portrayed a proud, straightforward Greek
youth forced by the unfortunate circumstances in his father's home to
seek his happiness elsewhere. Anyone sailing for unknown lands takes his

chances. Phryxus' dream, giving him too much assurance, precipitates injudicious acts of such magnitude that he fails and has no choice but to die. He meets death like a man, however, admitting his fault of credulity and expressing confidence in the revenge of the gods. Phryxus as well as the other male figures so far discussed certainly do not support the statement of Johannes Volkelt who speaks of the "Scheu vor dem spezifisch Männlichen in Mann"[2] in the portraiture of Grillparzer's characters.

Jason

In his discussion of Grillparzer's *König Ottokars Glück und Ende* Volkelt says: "Es muss auffallen, wie isoliert das tragische Thema des Ottokar bei Grillparzer dasteht. In keinen anderen seiner zahlreichen Tragödien hat er einen Helden gezeichnet, der nach Macht und Herrschaft strebt und kühn und rücksichtslos der Welt seinen Willen aufzwingen will. Sämtliche Themen der übrigen Tragödien liegen weit davon ab. Ja auch einen ganzen Mann wird man unter seinen übrigen Helden vergebens suchen."[3] This critic adds: "Aber auch an den Personen zweiten Ranges tritt bei Grillparzer nirgends ausser an Rudolf von Habsburg in unserem Stucke ein gewaltiger Herrscherwille hervor."[4] Did Volkelt forget the Jason of *Die Argonauten* when he made this statement? E. J. Williamson goes a step farther and gives Jason a place among the "männlich-weiblich" characters[5] who "correspond excellently to Schlegel's demand for 'sanfte Mannlichkeit.' "[6] Our analysis of the Jason of *Die Argonauten* is greatly facilitated by the definition Volkelt gives of manliness: "Das wahrhaft männliche Wollen geht in dem klaren Lichte des Bewusstseins vor sich, es hat zu Bedingungen weiten und freien Blick, bewegliche, gewandte Reflexion, kritisches, ungeniertes, bis zu gewissem Grade respektloses Denken."[7] We shall see that this definition suits Jason perfectly.

In every respect Jason's figure is the ruling one in *Die Argonauten*. "Veni, vidi, vici," he could have said when he boarded his ship at the end of the fourth act.

> Ruhmvoller Tod für ruhmentblösstes Leben
> Mag's tadeln wer da will, mich lockt der Tausch!

Even if Jason's uncle Pelias, the ruler of Thessalia, who had deprived him of his father's throne, had not treacherously sent him to Colchis to recover the fleece, he would have come to avenge the" Gottersohn Phryxus" (299) and to cover himself with immortal glory. His courage and brutal determination linked with shrewdness know only this one aim.

Jason's superior strength could not have been brought out better than by his conquest of an opponent almost equalling him in vigor—Medea. Upon encountering her for the first time in the tower where she is endeavouring to conjure up the gods of death, he wounds her arm in the darkness; her beauty prevents him from killing "das doppeldeutige Geschöpf" (438), whom he has just seen practicing her magic. A moment later she saves him from Absyrtus' sword, thinking that the intruder is the god of death, Heimdar. Jason's leadership is best shown in the second act. He has not been missing for more than twenty-four hours, and already

the Argonauts are losing heart. Jason returns in time to keep them from
surrendering to Aietes. As he discovers that fright has been their motive,
we hear the fearless Greek say to one of them:

> Sprich nicht!
> Mach' nicht, dass ich mich schäme vor mir selbst!
> Denn, o nicht ohne Tränen konnt' ich schauen
> In ein von Scham gerotet Mannerantlitz.
> Ich will's vergessen, wenn ich kann.

At the next moment Jason meets the king of Colchis; and the Greek's
language is that of a man who knows no fear in his determination to
force his will upon his opponent. Jason has soon sized up Aietes, who
unwittingly belies his denial that the fleece is in his possession. Shrewdly
Phryxus' avenger employs the most effective argument he could have
found to impress his primitive foe:

> Schwachsinniger Barbar, und darauf stützest
> Du deiner Weigrung unhaltbaren Trotz?
> Du glaubst zu siegen, weil in deiner Hand—
> Nicht gut nicht schlimm ist, was die Gotter geben
> Und der Empfanger erst macht das Geschenk.
> So wie das Brot, das uns die Erde spendet,
> Den Starken stärkt, des Kranken Siechtum mehrt,
> So sind der Götter hohe Gaben alle,
> Dem Guten gut, dem Argen zum Verderben.
> In meiner Hand fuhrt jenes Vliess zum Siege,
> In deiner sichert's dir den Untergang.
> Sprich selbst, wirst du es wagen zu berühren
> Besprutzt wie's ist mit deines Gastfreunds Blut, —

In the third act Jason again proves his mettle when he is trying to
force his way to Medea's tent. He finally has to retreat with his twelve
men when they find themselves opposed by a hundred barbarians. Later,
after chance had placed Medea in his power, we have occasion to admire
Jason's *modus operandi* in his wooing of the proud Colchian girl, which
is so well adapted to her character that its success is not to be wondered
at. Only a man of Jason's calibre could defeat this "herbe Jungfräulichkeit"
in such a short time. He had seen her only twice before, and twice, according to his own words, she had saved his life (914-915). Thus he knew
her feelings toward him. On his part he had been impressed by her personality and her beauty. Seeing how she fought against her love for him,
Jason found his interest growing into an infatuation for her and a mad
desire to force an admission of her love from her lips. Medea is in his
power; he has shattered her lance; but she still has a dagger. Very sure
of himself, Jason throws away his arms. "Töte mich Medea, wenn du
kannst," (1152) he repeats. She cannot kill him. And now he resorts to
gentle persuasion. His long speech— quite a lyrical passage (1178-1218)—
might lead us to believe that he really loves her. But all along he does
not forget the purpose of his adventurous journey. He begins his eloquent
plea of love with these words:

> Zwar geb' ich leicht dem Vater dich nicht wieder,
> Ein teures Unterpfand ist mir sein Kind.

Still Medea resists. They wrestle. "Mich lüstet deines Starrsinns Mass zu kennen!" (1227) Medea is forced to her knees. "Erkenne deinen Meister, deinen Herrn!" (1229)[8].

Jason is unrelenting. Medea's eyes and behaviour finally give proof of her love for him. Ostensibly angered by her refusal to say the three words "ich liebe dich," Jason sends the proud Colchian princess back to her father, who happens to appear at this juncture. Again Jason takes his leave with shrewdly chosen words:

> Du siehst mich nimmermehr auf dieser Erde.
> Leb' wohl Medea, leb' auf ewig wohl!

Now Medea's resistence is completely overcome. She leaves her father for Jason. A moment later she throws herself between the enraged Aietes and Jason, who has just pronounced her his wife without her contradicting him: "Vater, tot' ihn nicht! Ich lieb' ihn!" (1336) A lover would have been delighted at this confession. Jason has won, but what does he say? "*Er* konnte dir's entreissen und ich nicht!" (1337)

Disowned and cursed by her father, Medea soon learns what she can expect from a man whose determination stops at nothing. He must obtain the fleece: "Kam ich hierher und fürchtete den Tod?" (1438) As no manner of entreaty avails, Medea decides to go and die with him in the attempt to wrest the fleece from the poisonous dragon. She is certainly aware that Jason does not love her; how could she have expressed her feelings more fittingly at this time than by the words she utters:

> Die Liebkosungen lass
> Ich habe sie erkannt!—O Vater! Vater!

The fourth act offers another proof of Jason's failure to reciprocate Medea's affection. As a last resort, in the cave where the dragon guards the fleece, she has snatched Jason's sword from his side, threatening to kill herself rather than see him go to a certain death. Jason's words are not those of a lover:

> Beweinen kann ich dich, ruckkehren nicht.
> Mein Hochstes fur mein Wort und war's dein Leben!

The harrowing experiences in the cave make Jason fiercer than ever. With Medea he is very harsh:

> Komm her mein Weib, mir angetraut
> Bei Schlangenzischen unterm Todestor.

And he is in the mood for fighting (1682). He wounds Absyrtus who demands the fleece. Again we are struck by Jason's determination to rule and to be obeyed (1723). Aietes and the Colchians are approaching, and Jason decides to take Absyrtus to his ship as a hostage, hoping thus to insure a safe escape. Of course, he had not counted on Absyrtus' fatal step.

It is perhaps his fabulous success which elicits from Jason his haughty statement to the grief-stricken Aietes:

> Als Werkzeug einer höheren Gewalt
> Steh ich vor dir.

Jason has much in common with Phryxus. Both are of noble descent; both are driven to their unusual ventures by discord in their families. The doomed Phryxus comes to the conclusion that he should have relied on himself rather than trusted fate blindly after it had miraculously helped him. Jason's development is in the opposite direction. Placing complete dependence upon his own strength and wit, he wins through them; little wonder that he believes himself to be the tool of a higher power.

The final words of the Jason of *Die Argonauten* addressed to Aietes, expressing the warning "Dass sich der Frevel rächt auf dieser Erde" (1769), are fulfilled with dramatic irony in *Medea* at the expense of Jason.

The following factors, though not serving as an excuse for Jason's actions in the *Medea*, will at least help us to understand his human shortcomings. First, as was shown above, Jason did not love Medea. In view of the events that took place during the twenty-four hours he spent at Colchis, the impetuous youth could hardly be expected to consider the possible consequences of his step when he took the barbarian princess to his more highly civilized homeland. To Jason, Medea was merely a part of his adventure—a welcome diversion on his long trip home. Second, before he left for Colchis, Jason had been in love with Kreusa—as deeply, at least, as his nature permitted. Now it was not difficult for him to persuade himself that he had always loved her, especially in the face of the animosity he encountered on his witch-wife's account. His soul was plunged into a terrific conflict between his duty to his family, eternal persecution, and misery, on the one hand, and on the other, a serene life in his beloved Greece with the gentle daughter of the king of Corinth by his side. Moreover, Jason had learned to fear Medea: "Und nur mit Schaudern nenn' ich sie mein Weib." (475) Third, his brutal treatment of Medea is quite in keeping with the character of the Jason we know from *Die Argonauten*. The fact that he finally yields his consent to Kreon's plan, which sacrifices Medea alone, may be an indication of Jason's moral weakness; however, such weakness does not make him the "männlich-weiblich" type of man.

Medea is right when—in the second act—she describes her husband to the horrified Kreusa:

> Du kennst ihn nicht, ich aber kenn' ihn ganz.
> Nur Er ist da, Er in der weiten Welt
> Und alles andre nichts als Stoff zu Taten.
> Voll Selbstheit, nicht des Nutzens, doch des Sinns,
> Spielt er mit seinem und der andern Glück.
> Lockt's ihn nach Ruhm so schlagt er Einen tot,
> Will er ein Weib, so holt er Eine sich,
> Was auch darüber bricht, was kummert's ihn!

Later Medea sees to it that something does trouble ("kummern") Jason. Kreusa dead, his children dead, banished by Kreon, hungry, thirsty, and exhausted, Jason is refused a drink of water by a peasant. His old spirit flares up once more when he sees the murderess of his children; he wishes to kill her, but his weakness is such that he cannot even stand.

Johannes Volkelt[9] thinks it would have been better if Grillparzer had allowed Jason to die by his own hand. We have here an example of the kind of criticism that judges a work of art by purely arbitrary criteria—

arbitrary, at least, as far as the criteria of the drama itself are concerned. Such criticism never can do justice to the artist. The author has made it very clear—through the mouth of Medea, who says to herself: "Ein Dolchstoss wäre Labsal, doch nicht so!" (2350)—why he did not let Jason die:

> Ein kummervolles Dasein bricht dir an,
> Doch was auch kommen mag: Halt aus!
> Und sei im Tragen stärker als im Handeln.
> Willst du im Schmerz vergehn, so denk' an mich
> Und tröste dich an meinem grossern Jammer,
> Die ich getan, wo du nur unterlassen.

To die would be too easy a solution for Jason; he must live and bear his grief, his disgrace, and his pangs of conscience.

Aietes

Aietes, the barbarian king of Colchis, is a distrustful, cunning, greedy coward to whom the sacred rules of hospitality mean nothing. As he notices with apprehension that Phryxus, who has just arrived, is praying to his barbarian god, Aietes—in the truly childlike manner of primitive men—hurries on his part to appeal to the deity of the Colchians:

> Denk' der Opfer, die ich dir gebracht,
> Hör ihn nicht. Peronto,
> Höre den Fremden nicht!

As has been explained above under Phryxus, Aietes succeeded in his dastardly plan; but the last words of the murdered guest, "Rache! Rache!" (495) fill him with horror. Driven by superstitious fear, he tries to force the fleece on the slain Greek to evade the curse; but Aietes knows that the dead cannot take back curses. The last words of his daughter as she flees from him, "Weh uber dich, über uns!" (518-519) give Aietes a foreboding of the coming disaster.

In *Die Argonauten*, Aietes receives the first buffet when Medea turns against him. Absyrtus' death, the next blow, does not yet dishearten him; with the cry: "Mein Sohn!—Nun Rache! Rache! Stirb! (1757) Aietes hurls himself upon Jason. Only the realization that the bold Greek is in possession of the fleece—through Medea's disloyalty—unnerves the barbarian king; he collapses:

> Verschling mich Erde! Gräber tut euch auf.

As in the case of Jason, Grillparzer does not choose to let Aietes die:

> Zu spät, sie [die Gräber] decken deinen Frevel nicht.
> . . . ja stirb erst spat,
> Damit noch fernen Enkeln kund es werde,
> Dass sich der Frevel racht auf dieser Erde.

In the *Medea* we learn from Jason (748) that Aietes is dead, and from Gora (1202) that he died by his own hand.

Absyrtus

A careful analysis of Grillparzer's Absyrtus will show that he is not a "heiter-klare, in sich ruhende Natur."[10] Nor should we do Absyrtus justice if we saw in him nothing more than a younger edition of his cunning father.

Absyrtus had shown his courage repeatedly (34, 478, 942, 1136). He had shown himself capable of pity (1049). Then, after having pleaded with his father to take his curse back and to forgive Medea, he had come to persuade his sister to stay at Colchis rather than follow the stranger. However, a fatal change comes over Absyrtus as soon as he learns that the fleece is in the hands of Jason:

> So hast du uns denn doch verraten
> Geh hin in Unheil denn und in Verderben!

he says to Medea, forgetful of all gentler feelings toward his sister; and to Jason the enraged Colchian says:

> Behalt sie, doch das Vliess gib mir heraus!

The greed for gold has also taken possession of Absyrtus. For this reason he is not a "heiter-klare, in sich ruhende Natur." And through this greed—quite in conformity with the motive of the trilogy—death becomes Absyrtus' lot. Jason tries to avoid a combat with Medea's impetuous brother, but in vain; Absyrtus is dazed by Jason's blow and then captured. His pride and his thirst for revenge do not allow Absyrtus to bear the disgrace of captivity and of being used as a hostage to secure an unmolested departure for the hated Greeks. He chooses death:

> Ich komme Vater!
> Frei bis zum Tod! Im Tode rache mich!

Grillparzer's Absyrtus is a young barbarian whose main characteristics are courage, pride, loyalty to his country and to his father and king, love and understanding for his sister. His tragic guilt consists of his love for gold which leads him to sacrifice his sister unhesitatingly and which becomes the cause of his ruin. It need hardly be pointed out that Absyrtus—like Phaon, Phryxus, and the Jason of *Die Argonauten*—is a real man.[11]

Kreon

The figure of the king of Corinth suggests a comparison with another king of the trilogy, namely Aietes, the king of the barbarians. There are, on the surface, many differences which can be determined without difficulty: differences in clothing, in manner, in language and manner of expression. The primitive man makes no secret of his villainous plans; the more highly civilized Greek, on the other hand, is more subtle concerning his. Or did he himself believe in the righteousness of his course of action? Ilse Munch speaks of Kreon's "massvolle Gerechtigkeit . . . die doch im Grunde entspringt aus der Unfähigkeit, das Leben in seiner ganzen schweren Problematik zu erfassen."[12] Kreon, according to Münch, "hat—freilich ohne klares Bewusstsein—schweres Unrecht verübt an einer Verzweifelnden."[13] Judging him by his actions, it is impossible to detect any sense of justice in Kreon—at least, not in the manner of treatment to which he subjects Medea. The temptation is strong, however, to apply the term "massvolle Gerechtigkeit" in an ironic sense.

There is one main motive which directs Kreon's actions: his love for his daughter Kreusa. He had heard the rumors about Jason's crimes. Without the gates of the city, the king of Corinth meets the man whom he knows to be the object of Kreusa's affection. Cautiously Kreon listens to Jason's defense, and cautiously he dismisses the subject for the time being: "So lang ich kann, glaub' ich an deinen Wert." (316) He is ready enough to open his house to Jason; but Medea he admits very hesitatingly, and with the reservation that she forswear her magic.

News of the ban placed upon Jason and Medea by the Amphictyonic League having reached Kreon's ears, he determines to save Jason for Kreusa; to this end Medea, who has really lived up to her promise, must be sacrificed. Where is Kreon's sense of justice? If he had any, it should have told him that he could do only one of two things: either follow the dictate of the League and banish both Medea and Jason, or defy the League for the sake of both. However, "der falsche König mit der Gleisnermiene" (2244), as Gora rightly calls him later, now comes into the open with his scheme:

> Wer wagt es meinen Eidam anzutasten?
> Ja Herold, meinen Eidam, meiner Tochter Gatten!

Kreon, who—as we have seen—took in the married Jason with the greatest reluctance, now shows a remarkable determination. He is ready to defend Jason before the court of the Amphictyonic League (1350ff). If that should not avail, he incites Jason:

> Dann stehst du auf in deiner vollen Kraft,
> Schwingst hoch das goldne Banner in die Luft,
> Das du geholt vom Aeussersten der Lander,
> Und stromweis wird die Jugend Griechenlands
> Um dich sich scharen gegen Jedermann
> Um den Gereinigten, den Neuerhobnen,
> Den starken Hort, des Vliesses macht'gen Held.

What Kreon expects of Jason is nothing short of open rebellion against the existing form of government. It is obvious that Kreon is not a "vertreter des Lebensideals der Harmonie und des Masses."[14]

Returning to our comparison of the two kings: Aietes covets the fleece and gains possession of it through treachery and murder; however, he frankly discloses his plans to those near him. Kreon wants Jason and the fleece for himself; his procedure, as we have seen, is more subtle than that of the barbarian. It is possible that his sophistry led him to believe in his own hypocritical righteousness. A good example of Kreon's sophistry—of which the more primitive Aietes would be incapable—is the following statement:

> Des reifen Mannes Fehltritt ist Verbrechen,
> Des Jünglings Fehltritt ein verfehlter Tritt.

In other words, according to Kreon's "sense of justice" a young man may wed a woman who is really not congenial and later discard her and their children with impunity; however, if a mature man does the same, it is a crime.

Thus the differences between the two kings are merely surface distinctions of form, manner, and degree of civilization. In their guilt, how-

ever, Kreon and Aietes are alike: both covet that to which they have no
right. Their punishments, too, show a striking similarity. Aietes loses
not only the much-coveted fleece, but also his children. Kreon suffers the
loss of his only daughter around whom all his interests had been centred.

Although, as stated at the beginning of this chapter, Grillparzer was
mainly interested in Medea, the protagonist of *Der Gastfreund* is Phryxus;
that of *Die Argonauten*, Jason. Phryxus lives and dies like a man. He fails
because of his lack of prudence and the treachery of his opponent. Jason
wins in his adventurous enterprises on foreign soil through his heroic courage, determination, and quick-wittedness, but fails in the end—in *Medea*
—because he is morally incapable of coping with the forces of his own
civilization. Absyrtus, a minor character with a number of admirable characteristics, among them bravery, determination, and love of freedom, comes
to grief because he allows his greed for gold to suppress his gentler human
feelings. The two other minor characters, Aietes and Kreon, are cowardly
and cunning, the one from greed, the other, from a misguided love for his
only child.

CHAPTER FOUR

KOENIG OTTOKARS GLÜCK UND ENDE

Konig Ottokars Gluck und Ende is Grillparzer's first historical tragedy and probably his best drama. Long after its composition, in the year of his death, the author himself called it his best.[1] It excels in dramatic structure, diction, presentation of the background, and—which is of importance to our investigation—in character portrayal. Every figure is completely individualized—*i.e.*, language, thought, and action are entirely in harmony. The change that has taken place in the critical estimate of the characters in *Konig Ottokars Gluck und Ende* from the decade of its appearance to our time serves to illustrate the fact that it often takes years, decades, or even an entire century for the really great artist to be fully appreciated and valued. In 1829 Thomas Carlyle[2] has this to say:

> There is even some attempt at delineating character in this play: certain of the *dramatis personae* are evidently meant to differ from certain others, not in dress and name only, but in nature and mode of being; so much indeed they repeatedly assert, or hint, and do their best to make good,—unfortunately, however, with very indifferent success. In fact, these *dramatis personae* are rubrics and titles rather than persons; for the most part mere theatrical automata, with only a mechancial existence.

Of course, ludicrous as this statement of the erratic critic sounds, it reflects to some degree the opinion held in Norh Germany at that time concerning Grillparzer's talent. The next criticism of which mention will be made here dates from the year 1874 and comes from Wilhelm Scherer,[3] who falls far short of doing justice to Grillparzer's masterpiece, as indicated below in the discussion of Ottokar. Only with the turn of the century does our dramatist come into his own in the eyes of his critics.

König Ottokar is based chiefly upon the *Oesterreichische Reimchronik,*[4] which Grillparzer followed fairly closely.[5]

Aside from his intention of writing an Austrian national drama, Grillparzer's leading motive was the conflict between justice and arrogance.

The cast of characters in this historical drama includes the principal figures of Primislaus Ottokar, king of Bohemia, Margaret of Austria, Kunigunde of Massovia, Rudolf von Habsburg, the first German emperor of the Habsburg dynasty, and Zawisch von Rosenberg. Other characters of less importance are: the elder Merenberg, a Styrian knight, his son Seyfried Merenberg, Milota von Rosenberg, his brother Benesch von Diedicz Rosenberg, Berta von Diedicz Rosenberg, Bishop Braun von Olmütz, the chancellor of King Ottokar, Bela, the king of Hungary, and a number of other knights. The characters that have been selected for analysis are Ottokar, Rudolf von Habsburg, Zawisch, Milota, and Benesch von Rosenberg, the elder Merenberg, and the latter's son Seyfried.

Primislaus Ottokar, King of Bohemia

"Er ist der sich gegen Zeus, den Wächter der ewigen Gesetze, empörende Titane"; with these pithy words Ehrhard[6] characterizes Ottokar. The powerful Bohemian king had reached the zenith of his career not only through various fortunate circumstances, but also as a result of his bravery and the wisdom of his policies. He possessed many true friends who admired him not only for the liberality that his wealth made possible, but also for numerous praiseworthy qualities. That Grillparzer did not wish to minimize Ottokar's merits is borne out by Seyfried's words at the beginning of the tragedy:

> Hab ich nicht Knabenweis bei ihm gedient,
> Und war er mir ein Muster, Vorbild nicht
> Von jedem hohen Tun?

The dramatist is not portraying Ottokar's "hohes Tun," which belongs to a period prior to the beginning of the drama; therefore Scherer's[7] remarks seem unwarranted: "Warum ihm alle diese Kronen zufallen, weiss man nicht. Dass es sein Verdienst sei, kann man sich nicht denken."

It is not Ottokar's divorcing of Margaret which marks the beginning of his downfall. Margaret had never been his wife in the real sense of the word (259); moreover, he had been urged to this step by many of his subjects who desired an heir to the throne. Margaret's argument that Ottokar had known she would never have any children (260-261) does not appear sound, for Ottokar wished this union just as little as did Margaret; he was obeying his father.

We see the turning point of Ottokar's career in his tactless and arrogant treatment of Margaret and his retention of her lands. This usurpation is more than just a private sin.[8] It is his immense ambition coupled with arrogance and pride which causes—at least in part—his downfall. We can understand his enormous pride—the pride of a man fully aware of the power he has attained through the many victories which have brought almost all of Central Europe under his sway:

> Vom Belt bis fern zum adriatschen Golf,
> Vom Inn bis zu der Weichsel kaltem Strand
> Ist Niemand, der nicht Ottokarn gehorcht;
> Es hat die Welt, seit Karol Magnus Zeiten
> Kein Reich noch, wie das meinige gesehn.
> Ja Karol Magnus' Krone selbst,
> Sie dunkt mich nicht für dieses Haupt zu hoch.

We can also understand his failure to heed Margaret's warning (622ff.); Ottokar firmly believes in his good fortune and in his ability. Like Phryxus, he finally perishes by reason of this boundless assurance:

> Ich halte sie, seht Ihr? mit dieser Hand;
> Sie sollen sich nur regen, wenn sies wagen!

Ottokar's audacious over-confidence reaches its climax in the second act when he is pressed for an answer to the Electors concerning his acceptance or refusal of the crown of the German Empire:

> Doch soll man mir die Kron erst selber bringen
> Und legen auf dem Kissen dort vor mir,
> Bevor ich mich entscheide, was geschieht.

and

> Die Kron ist mein! das heisst: wenn ich sie mag.
> Doch lasst sie hier erst sein, dann will ich sprechen.

Scherer says:[9] "Ottokar ist ein ubermütiger Prahlhans, kindisch in seinem Hochmut, toricht in seiner eitlen Verblendung, ein Despot von rohen Formen ohne alle Grósse." The facts of the drama do not substantiate the severe criticism that is here leveled at Grillparzer's Ottokar. Volkelt[10] recognizes that Scherer's assertion is unfounded, but he agrees with Scherer that "das Tragische seiner Gestalt einigermassen darunter leidet, dass seine Herrschgier und Tyrannei nicht stärker auf ein inneres Recht gegrundet ist." We are in accord with Scherer when he maintains that Ottokar does not rely on any lucky star or the like; on the other hand, Grillparzer has sufficiently shown that Ottokar firmly believes—and thus stands on an inner right—that he could bring considerable benefits to the territories under his control. Ottokar is a progressive ruler; he has an open mind for anything that is practical and useful for the mass of his subjects. A reformer always encounters opposition, and the way in which the Bohemian ruler criticizes the impractical equipment of the Tartars (389-394) and orders the reforms in the city of Prague (455-505) is quite in keeping with his character. It shows also that he is convinced of his own mission as a progressive reformer. For the success of his innovations we have Olmutz's testimony (1561-1564).

Shortly after uttering the arrogant words quoted above, Ottokar learns of Rudolf's election (1220) through his chancellor, Braun von Olmutz, who returns from Frankfurt where the election had taken place. This scene marks the beginning of Ottokar's ruin. In his blind rage over this first terrific blow to his pride he defies the Empire by refusing to surrender the territory he has taken by force and to receive with proper ceremony the fiefs of Bohemia and Moravia which are due him. Does he perchance rely on his sword? Little does Ottokar realize how many enemies he has made by his inconsiderate treatment of his spouse, the popularly beloved Margaret. Nor does he know with what infinite cunning Zawisch von Rosenberg has plunged him, despite his otherwise trusting nature, into an "ocean of suspicion" (839), causing him to arrest many innocent knights and thereby in turn add to the number of his enemies. In short, Ottokar is no longer the same person. Even more manifest does this become in the third act. The man who utters his horrible threat against the "deserting" Austrians and Styrians (1440-1444) is not the same as the man who fought at Kroissenbrunn and was regarded by young Merenberg as "ein Vorbild von jedem hohen Tun" (20). Though he does not believe in the desperate condition of his army, Ottokar finally consents to accept the Emperor's invitation, not in order to yield, but to impress his opponent. With his wealth and pomp Ottokar naively expects to intimidate the simple emperor.

This momentous meeting of the two rulers is characterized by a change
in tone on the part of the Bohemian. "Gott grüss Euch, Habsburg!" (1726)
he says upon arriving. After it has become clear to him that Rudolf
holds all the trumps in his hand, we hear him say: "Ja, Herr Kaiser!
(1943).

After his initial boisterousness, Ottokar's genuflection may seem strange.
Yet he had always known how to take advantage of his opportunities.
Moreover, the genuflection will not compromise his dignity, he reflects, since
Rudolf assures him that there will be no witnesses. The proud king of
Bohemia had not expected Zawisch's perfidy.

In the fourth act Ottokar has our full sympathy. It is difficult to follow
Scherer who says in this connection: "Der Held ist mit einer gewissen
Antipathie gezeichnet und erweckt sie daher auch beim Zuschauer."[11]
In his great humiliation Ottokar has to listen to the scorn of his own
subjects. Kunigunde's and Zawisch's biting raillery finally shakes him
out of his lethargy—at least temporarily.

> Ein unbezwungner Führer der Kumanen
> Wiegt einen dienstbarn Bohmenkonig auf!

are the words of Kunigunde who is shameless enough to hint at her own
infidelity (2125-2126). He realizes that he is no longer the man he once
was:

> Ist das mein Schatten?—Nun, zwei Konige!

Ottokar's fierceness when he finally regains his memory is in no inconsiderable degree due to the biting scorn of his wife who would rather see
him dead than in disgrace (2401-2402). At the same time he knows that
she is driving him to his foolhardy defiance of the Emperor: "So stark?
Ein Tröpflein Milde tàte wohl," (2403) and further:

> Ich sehe Blut an deinen weissen Fingern,
> Zukünftges Blut! Ich sag: berühr mich nicht.

Ottokar is too trusting toward those who have good reason to hate
him:

> Kein Böhme hat noch seinen Herrn verraten.

Nor does he heed the warning words of Merenberg, the doomed victim of
Ottokar's resentment and hurt pride, who says to him: "Zu spät wirst du
bereun!" (2437)

Toward the end of the fourth act we note the softer and more conciliatory traits in Ottokar's nature; he desires Kunigunde to be with him,
but she does not appear; also, he thinks of Merenberg's comfort in prison.
If Grillparzer had portrayed his tragic hero with antipathy, he could
have omitted these little human touches. The fifth act which—outwardly—
brings Ottokar's fall also represents his rise—from the standpoint of
ethics. Only once more does his wrath flare up. Believing that Kunigunde is the "Queen of Bohemia" (2612) who is staying in the chapel at
the cemetery of Götzendorf, Ottokar hopes to find Zawisch:

Ha Schurk!—und Zawisch auch?
Es soll mir wohl tun meinen Zorn zu kühlen!

Before anyone can stop him, Ottokar has forced his way into the house and finds—the corpse of Margaret. Her memory brings about a complete change in him. Again we differ with Scherer who says: "Ottokar erwirbt sich durch nichts Anrecht auf unser Mitgefühl: das bisschen Gewissens-bisse im funften Akt zahlt kaum."[12] We quote Ottokar directly:

Wer war ich, Wurm? dass ich mich unterwand,
Den Herrn der Welten frevelnd nachzuspielen,
Durchs Böse suchend einen Weg zum Guten!

And furthermore, he is willing to suffer due punishment in his own person:

Hast du beschlossen
Zu gehen ins Gericht mit Ottokar,
So triff mich, aber schone meines Volks!

Ottokar is honest with himself:

O Gott,
Ich hab mit Willen Unrecht auch getan!

And what Ottokar feels is more than "ein bisschen Gewissensbisse;" it is complete abondonment of his egotistical self:

Es ist nicht Todesfurcht, was so .mich reden lässt.
Der du die Herzen aller kennst,
Du weisst, ob dieses Herz die Furcht bewegt?
Doch wenn dich eines *Mannes* Reu erfreut,
Den nicht die Strafe, den sein Unrecht schreckt;
So sieh mich hier vor deinem Antlitz knien, . . .

These last words are not needed to disprove Williamson's contention that Ottokar belongs to the "männlich-weiblich" type of man.[13] There is not a single act or word in the entire drama which could be used to substantiate this assertion. Ottokar, despite his wounds, fights heroically (2925 ff.) and dies like a man (2931).

Grillparzer had set himself a difficult task in the field of character por-trayal: he aspired to present disconnected and contradictory elements on the stage without offending against the unity of the characters. Therefore he turned to historical rather than fictitious figures in order to be spared the motivation needed to convince us of the necessity of. their actions. And he succeeded. In Ottokar the author has portrayed an ostentatious, ve-hement, overweening, egotistical, despotic ruler whose remarkable successes have not only brought him wealth and power, but have incited him to ar-rogance, pride, violence, and disregard of all laws. His unjust acts and arrogant manner overshadow his better characteristics of straightforward-ness, a keen eye and an energetic hand for constructive and progressive reforms, and a bluff frankness which causes him to forego hypocritical mourning over the death of an uncle whose domain he inherits ("Betrauern mag ihn wer sein Land nicht erbt!" 672). With the greatest sympathy Grillparzer pictures Ottokar as a victim blinded by dazzling fortune and

thus led to his ruin. Through his misfortune Ottokar is moved to renounce his egotistical philosophy of life and to regret his sins in a spirit
of genuine contrition. Ottokar's tragedy is more than individually human—
it is typically human. The world is full of characters like Ottokar. Volkelt[14]
as well as Münch[15] class the tragic elements in Ottokar as individually
human, but O. E. Lessing[16] rejects Volkelt's view. We quote Lessing:
"Welcher temperamentvolle, vorwärtsstrebende Mensch hätte nicht die
Keime des extremsten Egoismus in sich und könnte nicht fuhlen, dass er
unter entsprechenden Verhältnissen ähnlich handeln, dass er ein Ottokar
im kleinen sein müsste." In the field of literature we see many analogies;
to name a few: Schiller's Wallenstein, Fiesco, Karl Moor; Ibsen's Skule in
The Pretenders; Shakespeare's Richard III, Macbeth, Claudius, King Lear,
and others. Jason, too, has much is common with Ottokar.

Rudolf von Habsburg

As stated above, Grillparzer wished to write a national drama, which
would perforce involve—to some extent—a glorification of the ruling
dynasty in the Austria of his day—that of the Habsburgs. Moreover, the
historical Rudolf was an outstanding representative of justice and law
and order within the German Empire after the chaotic time of the Inter-
regnum. These considerations, together with the fact that the rulers of
Austria in Grillparzer's time were devout Catholics, undoubtedly exercised
some influence upon his emphasis of the good qualities in Rudolf. From
Ottokar himself we hear of Rudolf's decisive part in the Battle of Kroissenbrunn:

> Wo ist der Habsburg? Hei! beim reichen Gott,
> Er hielt sich wohl! Sonst ein gar stiller Mann,
> Doch wenn er angreift, wie der bose Teufel.

It is Rudolf who chivalrously becomes the protector of Margaret: "Stets
war bei Habsburg der Gekränkten Schirm." (734) It is Rudolf alone who
dares disobey Ottokar's orders:

> Als freier Krieger focht ich Eure Schlachten,
> Um Lohn nicht, und den Dank selbst schenk ich Euch!
> Ich bin nicht Euer Mann [*i.e.*, vassal].

Grillparzer also makes mention of noble deeds done by Rudolf before the
time at which this scene takes place (747-758).

In the third act—Rudolf has been Emperor for some time—we learn that
he has restored peace in Germany by settling old feuds, and that the Pope
and the princes are not only his friends, but also at peace with one another. During the memorable meeting with Ottokar, Emperor Rudolf is
complete master of the situation; in him wisdom, dignity, and firmness
are coupled with considerateness and a steadfast faith in God and in his
cause.

> Ich habs geschworen,
> Geschworen meinem grossen, gnadgen Gott,
> Dass Recht soll herrschen und Gerechtigkeit
> Im deutschen Land; und so solls sein und bleiben!

Rudolf would seem all too angelic to us, did we not learn from his own lips that in his younger days he also had lived to follow his selfish impulses. "Mich hat, wie Euch," he says to Ottokar, "der eitle Drang der Ehre mit sich geführt in meiner ersten Zeit." (1893-1894) He goes on to tell Ottokar how he picked quarrels with friends and relatives, how he was exiled by the Empire and subsequently fought at Ottokar's side against the heathen Prussians and later against the Hungarians. When God placed him on the imperial throne:

> So fiels wie Schuppen ab von meinen Augen
> Und all mein Ehrgeiz war mit eins geheilt.

Rudolf von Habsburg has attained an inner balance and self-control, a peace of soul, that knows no earthly ambition except that of serving his state and his God. This peace of soul lends him a greatness and dignity which play no inconsiderable part in determining Ottokar's willingness to pay him due homage as emperor.

Grillparzer's Rudolf, then, is the ideal prince who through his modesty, chivalry, diplomacy, forcefulness, and sense of justice is able to secure the proper respect for the office and function of emperor. He is a man of strength combined with superior, mature circumspection. Upon Rudolf's manliness all critics are agreed. Scherer[17] declares that Rudolf is

> zu sehr ein providentieller Held. Der Heiligenschein von dem er umgeben, trägt nicht bei, seine Physiognomie zu verschärfen, sondern zu verblassen. Der Dichter ist parteiisch gegen seinen Helden und für dessen Widersacher. Ja, es konnte mit Recht gesagt werden: das Stück hat zwei Helden.

C. E. Eggert[18] follows Scherer closely in this view:

> Rudolf receives almost too great prominence from the time he champions Margaret in the first act until he invests his sons with the fief of Austria. He is not quite enough the impersonal majesty of the empire but a little too much the successful rival of Ottokar, who wins by superior force of character.

Both Scherer and Eggert concede that Rudolf is morally superior to Ottokar. However, they both overlook the fact that Rudolf is no tragic hero and for this reason does not hold our interest to the same degree as Ottokar.[19] Nor does Rudolf receive too much prominence although he is not a secondary figure. The very nature of the play called for Rudolf's prominence in the third act; otherwise he remains in the background. We can only agree with Reich[20] when he says: "In dieser Tragödie ist er [Rudolf] technisch ebenso wichtig wie Elisabeth in *Maria Stuart*."

Zawisch von Rosenberg

"Arger liste was er vol:"[21] these five words were sufficient to inspire Grillparzer to create a character that seldom finds its equal on the stage.

Our first impression of Zawisch (91 ff.), his laughter and his sarcasm toward everyone in the face of his family's disgrace, makes us sense that this diabolical gaiety hides sinister plans, and we are reminded of Hamlet's words "that one may smile, and smile, and be a villain."[22] We also learn that Zawisch is by far the cleverest and shrewdest of all the Rosenbergs. Severely reproached by both Benesch and Milota, his two uncles, for his raillery and apparent disloyalty to the family, Zawisch becomes serious for a moment:

> Wer seid ihr denn, ihr beide, dass ihr schmàht?
> Die ihr auf offner Strasse Rachepläne
> Zu tauben Wänden schreit und—offnen Ohren!

For the benefit of young Merenberg he adds:

> Der König ist mein Herr, und damit holla!

Even the clumsy Milota takes notice:

> Fast glaub ich, Freund, du denkst mehr als du sprichst.

Indeed, Zawisch does think more than he speaks. He speaks little, but when he does, his innuendos and suggestions increase our admiration from act to act for Austria's greatest dramatist who is a master at adapting his language to his characters. To the puzzled Benesch and Milota he has Zawisch say:

> Was man verschweigt, erratet ihr auch nicht;
> Errietet ihrs, ihr könntets nicht verschweigen!

In his speech to the envoy of the Electors—at the end of the first act (also 1330-1331, and 1518 ff.)—Zawisch cleverly chooses his words in order to augment Ottokar's pride and arrogance and to call attention to the Slavic blood in his veins:

> Raubt ihr uns unsern König, unsern Herrn?
> Ist er nicht machtig? was bedarf er euer?
> Wie Gott im Himmel herrschet er auf Erden;
> Nur Sorgen, und nicht Nutzen schafft das Reich,
> Lasst ihn, und bietet Deutschen eure Gaben!
> Ihr gebt nur, weil ihr braucht! Lasst unsern Herrn!

The second act begins with Zawisch's soliloquy, a soliloquy of only fourteen lines (785-798) and yet how revealing! What an abundance of suggestion! he begins:

> Ich bin verliebt! O weh, mein Herz ist fort!
> Ihr Leute, kommt zu Hilfe! Ha, ha, ha!

A less subtle person, Milota, perhaps, if he were younger and if he possessed Zawisch's dash, would say: "I am in love! Ha, ha, here is my opportunity to retaliate! I shall pay the king in kind; he seduced my niece and then left her to marry another woman. Now I shall take his wife and make him the laughing stock of his people."—Zawisch goes on:

> Wie sie mich ansah mit dem schwarzen Blick,
> Die stolze Ungarin! Hilft alles nichts!
> Und schön ist sie, beim wunderbaren Gott!
> Ein adlich, wildes, reuterscheues Füllen,
> Den Zaum anschnaubend, der es bändgen soll.

Is he not rather over-confident in thinking that he will win Kunigunde?

He has seen her only once and hardly spoken to her; however, what little he had said had shown his courage, nay impudence. Standing very near King Bela's granddaughter when she had ridded herself of her disguise, he had exclaimed: "O schöner Krieger!" (720). Seeing the irritation of both Ottokar and Kunigunde about this uncalled-for remark, Zawisch had quickwittedly joined in the quest for the pert admirer. Turning around, he had said: "Von dorther schiens, vom Winkel her zu tonen!" (721) Kunigunde's answer, however, served to make the experienced Don Juan quite certain of himself:

> Ihr warts—
> > wohl nicht. Ihr würdet nicht so frech,
> Da ich so nahe stand, mir sonst es leugnen!

We hardly need the testimony of the queen's chambermaid (937-938) to convince us that Zawisch has been successful with women. At the same time, his opinion of women does not seem to be any too high; to the tortured young Merenberg he says concerning his own cousin, the unfortunate Berta:

> Weiss Gott! ich glaub, einmal zu Nacht, bei Wein,
> Gefiel mir selbst ihr rot und weiss Gesicht!
> Nu, gebt mir Eure Hand, Herr Bundesbruder!

The second part of Zawisch's soliloquy commences:

> Auch sonst geht alles, wie es Gott gefallt!

He reflects with satisfaction on the fact that the Austrians have been leaving Ottokar's court since Margaret's departure. They are probably going to Frankfurt where the election of the emperor is to take place. Again we are struck by the sarcasm of Ottokar's nemesis:

> Sie [the Austrians] legen dort wohl die Gesuche nieder,
> Dass man doch ja Herrn Ottokar erwähle!

Zawisch's affairs go even better than he thought. Again he puzzles his relative Milota when he lets Seyfried Merenberg escape with the letter the old follower of Margaret had sent to the Archbishop of Mayence:

> Der Brief kann viel enthalten—oder wenig.
> Ein Tröpflein Gift vielleicht—
> (Die Hand mit dem Briefe schnell auf den Rücken gelegt.)
> > Ein Meer von Argwohn!

How subtle, and yet how expressive is even this gesture! A drop of poison, perhaps, i.e., if Ottokar will know the name of this one traitor. However, if he never receives the letter—which Zawisch symbolizes by holding the letter behind his back—Ottokar will be plunged into an ocean of suspicion and will thereby be led to more violence and injustice.[23] Zawisch does not even deign to take his uncle into his confidence:

> Ich weiss am besten was sich fügt, was nicht,
> Zu seiner Zeit wird sichs dir offenbaren.

He has just won the tournament and is preparing for a more pleasant

campaign, this time against the resistance of the most recent object of
his affection. How could the puzzled Milota understand:?

> Und dann—das junge Blut, mein gutes Herz!
> Ha, ha!—Sprich nicht und geh! es kommen Dinge,
> Bei denen ich nach Zeugen nicht verlange.

The scene between Zawisch and the queen in front of the statue of
love and the awarding scene call to mind the spirit of so many comedies
of Lope de Vega, comedies filled with intrigues of that kind. Everything
is there, the beautiful young wife of a much older husband, the maid who
serves as an intermediary, the bold young lover, and the spouse who is
duped before his very eyes. We recognize the danger of introducing such
an episode into a drama which treats historical events of such high significance; a lesser talent than Grillparzer would have impaired the harmony
between the inner and outer form of the tragedy.[24] This interlude is so
well executed that the effect of the tragedy is in no wise impaired while
poetic justice of a subtle kind is displayed.

The first of these two scenes begins with Zawisch's ironic appeal to
Aphrodite, who, according to the tradition, was not any too faithful to
her ugly spouse Hephaistos:

> Du keusche Liebesgöttin,
> Getreue Gattin deines holden Gatten,
> Dich fleh ich an: verleih mir deinen Schutz!

Later when Zawisch—by his foolhardy display of the ribbon which
he had snatched from Kunigunde's arm—has called even Ottokar's attention to himself, the unabashed Don Juan again extricates himself by his
presence of mind:

> Herr, es gibt Dinge,
> Die man mit Recht dem König selbst verbirgt!

which remark is taken by the king as referring to an affair with the
chambermaid who is standing near Zawisch.

It is Zawisch who exposes the kneeling Ottokar to the crowd; and we
find it a foregone conclusion that no one but a villain with the cleverness
and alertness of a Zawisch could deal this death-blow to Ottokar's pride.
However, Rosenberg's perfidy is also mixed with honest contempt for the
boisterous potentate of a short time ago.

Messages in black and white, or even rumors of the existence of such,
can turn into dangerous evidence against the intriguer; the arch-rogue
Zawisch does not need the example of the Merenbergs to know this. After
his flight into Rudolf's camp the avenger of the Rosenberg family sends
a servant to his kinsman Milota to remind him of a little song:

> Der Winter kehrt zurück, die Rosen welken.

After some pondering the slow-witted Milota understands:

> Sag ihm, die Rosen mogen immer blühn,
> Der Schnee zergeht, der Winter kehrt nicht wieder!

With Milota's desertion in the decisive moment of Ottokar's last battle the fate of the unfortunate Bohemian king is sealed (2915-2920).

Grillparzer proved himself a master dramatist in constructing the figure of Zawisch, this perfidious rascal with the agility of a snake, the appearance and manner of a Don Juan, and the smiling cynicism of a Mephistopheles, who combines boldness with quick-wittedness. Zawisch's objective is revenge upon Ottokar. The means to this revenge he discovers in the course of the plot; and then his procedure is swift and adapted to his opponent's nature. To make Ottokar's downfall more certain and complete, Rosenberg strives to increase the king's arrogance, pride, and trust in his power. Zawisch contrives to make Ottokar suspicious of all his followers and to lead him—through his suspicions—to deeds that will create more enemies for him. And, last but not least, the cleverest of the Rosenbergs designs to destroy the conjugal happiness of the Bohemian king by seducing the latter's wife. Without exposing himself a single time, Zawisch carries out all these plans with such courage and expedition that he succeeds in all of them.

Milota von Rosenberg

Regst du dich auch, vierschrötger Milota?
Ei ja, da muss der König nun wohl zittern!

Thus Zawisch sneers at his uncle after the latter—intent on revenge—has said:

Ich sann soeben, und gedenk zu handeln!

These two lines characterize Milota perfectly, and his subsequent actions confirm our impression. He is always slow to comprehend; and opposite his cunning, quick-witted nephew he cuts a poor figure: in the antechamber of the queen in the first act when he cannot see that one can laugh and still be loyal to the disgraced house of Rosenberg (172-173); in the second act when he considers Zawisch insane because he lets young Merenberg go free (846-847); and again in the scene mentioned above when he receives the mysterious message from the brain of the family (2697-2700). Milota is a courageous fighter. However, we could not imagine him taking the initiative in his thirst for revenge. Nevertheless, he is equipped with enough common sense to follow the younger man whom he recognizes as intellectually superior to himself. Thus he also becomes instrumental in Ottokar's downfall.

Benesch von Rosenberg

Benesch had had soaring plans for his daughter Berta. In the hope of seeing her as the queen of Bohemia some day he had encouraged an affair with the husband of Margaret. "Pfui, des Kupplers!" (33) Seyfried Merenberg says about the father of the girl whom he had once wished to marry. And Margaret speaks of him as the "Geifrer Benesch." (201) Indeed, he is venomous in speech: "Gift und Pest" (132) and "Rache" (161) he cries when he learns that Ottokar will divorce Margaret, not to wed Berta, but Kunigunde. Benesch's revenge, however, unlike Zawisch's and Milota's, is only a verbal one (2076-2090). His well-deserved misfortune has broken his spirit and he dies insane, as we learn from Milota (2918).

Der alte Merenberg

Merenberg the elder, a Styrian knight, is characterized by his loyalty to his queen, Margaret of Austria. His sense of justice in the face of the wrong done her does not allow him to remain inactive, especially since the queen herself refuses to turn to the Empire for help. He sends a letter to the Archbishop of Mayence through his son Seyfred. This letter draws upon him the bitter hatred of Ottokar into whose hands he falls through his own too trusting nature and through the bold coup of two of Ottokar's knights. Merenberg is held along with a number of hostages who are finally released in accordance with the treaty between Ottokar and Rudolf. The former, however, refuses to free Merenberg on the grounds that he is a traitor. Merenberg clears himself in our eyes of that charge by warning the king against the Rosenbergs. As Ottokar at this time still believes that no Bohemian ever could betray his king (2435, 2439), the well-meant warning of the Styrian serves only to stir the unseeing Bohemian to even greater anger.

Seyfried Merenberg

Merenberg the younger had been in love with Berta von Rosenberg before she had become the mistress of the king. He had served Ottokar from childhood and idealized him as a brave warrior and king. This devotion, however, was not greater than that which he had for Margaret. And now—at the beginning of the drama—his faith in Ottokar is being shaken. At every turn we are struck by Seyfried's ingenuousness—most of all when he finds himself in the hands of Zawisch. What a contrast between the genuine youth and the Mephistophelian rascal who toys with all who come into contact with him!

> Herr Zawisch, seht, ich hab Euch nie geliebt!
> Für doppelsinnig hielt ich Euch und falsch,
> Doch sagt mein Vater, Menschen kennt ich nicht:
> O zeigt mir, Herr, dass ich Euch nicht gekannt!
> Gebt mir den Brief, lasst ihn uns hier vernichten,
> Mit mir konnt Ihr beginnen, was Ihr wollt.

At this one point these two have a common interest. Yet little does Seyfried know what are Zawisch's real motives for allowing him to escape.

It is Seyfried who kills Ottokar:

> Gib das Vertrauen mir auf Menschen wieder;
> Den Vater wieder, den ich selbst geliefert,
> Ich selbst in deine Hand.

Seyfried von Merenberg has our full sympathy, not only because he has to become the avenger of his father and because he is exiled by the Emperor, but also on account of his great disillusionment.

With Ehrhard[25] we sum up the figure of Seyfried as "der mit viel Glück fortgebildete Typus des Max Piccolomini."[26]

The three principal figures in Konig Ottokar, namely Rudolf von Habsburg, Ottokar von Böhmen, and the latter's vassal Zawisch von Rosenberg, were shown to have many definitely manly characteristics. Rudolf combines all the traits one could wish for in an ideal ruler. Ottokar has attained wealth and power through energy, courage, and resourcefulness. Success and exuberance lead to pride, arrogance, and violence, a not uncommon change among heroes of tragedies. After his downfall, Ottokar sees and regrets the error of his ways in genuine contrition. He dies like a man. While Zawisch must be considered morally weak, his bold actions could not be classed as unmanly or cowardly. Among the minor characters, the two Merenbergs are "manly men," whatever their failings, Milota is a courageous fighter, though lacking in brains and initiative. Benesch is a weakling and procurer who ends in insanity.

CHAPTER FIVE

EIN TREUER DIENER SEINES HERRN

In September 1825 the Empress Carolina Augusta was to be crowned queen of Hungary at Pressburg. As might have been expected, the author of *Konig Ottokar* was called upon to write a play based on Hungary's history. Mindful of his experience with the censorship which had pigeonholed his first national drama for two years for no apparent reason, Grillparzer's main objective in the choice of his material was to avoid difficulties from that side. A second motive was the dramatization of Kant's "categorical imperative," the great philosopher's epitome of all morality which was in accord with the author's devotion to the imperial house. The third motive—overlooked by so many critics—was the expression of Grillparzer's resentment to the treatment he had received at the hands of his government to which he had been, and still was, so devoted. That this manifestation of resentment had to be very subtle is apparent under the circumstances.

Grillparzer's choice finally fell on the story of the Palatine Bancbanus whose wife had been ravished by a German prince, the brother of the queen of Hungary (year: 1213). As the historic accounts differ concerning the ensuing revolt and Bancbanus' actions, Grillparzer had free range for expressing his own ideas which may be summed up briefly: it is imperative that a man should keep his word, especially if not keeping it would endanger the lives and the peace of the whole nation; honor consists in doing one's duty faithfully and honestly, regardless of the cost to the individual concerned and regardless of what people may think about it.

Of the literary models the most important are undoubtedly Lord Byron's *Marino Faliero* and *The Two Foscari*, which has been shown by Wyplel[1] who compares the related traits of character of Bancbanus and Foscari as well as the similarities in the motives. Wyplel proves that Foscari is the model for Bancbanus although he lacks the humorous traits of the latter.[2]

We are here concerned with the following characters: Graf Bancbanus, Herzog Otto von Meran, King Andreas of Hungary, Graf Simon, and Graf Peter.

Graf Bancbanus[3]

Perhaps no character has been more under dispute, more misunderstood and misinterpreted than Grillparzer's Bancbanus. Before proceeding to our analysis of this figure, we shall give some of the unfavorable criticisms: Scherer[4] says:

> In Bancbanus merken wir keinen Konflikt. Und recht betrachtet ist auch keiner vorhanden. . . . Ich glaube nur, dass (dieses Stück) einen ästhetisch verwerflichen Helden hat. . . . Die Gesinnung des Bancbanus ist gewiss sehr brav und ehrenwert. Aber—man mag sagen was man will—seine Handlungsweise entspringt aus dem treuen, redlichen Wollen einer engen, beschränkten, kleinlichen, nur das Nächste ins Auge fassenden Natur. Es ist—wir müssen an eine ähnliche Bemerkung beim Ottokar erinnern—es ist leider eine Treue ohne Grösse.

Volkelt[5] speaks of the "Mangel an selbstbewusster Männlichkeit" in Bancbanus' character. G. Witkowski[6] has this to say: "There is after all something painful and whimsical in it [the drama] because the servant's faithfulness gains the victory over more worthy human characteristics and
because one can only with difficulty put himself in the place of Bancbanus."
Arturo Farinelli[7] says: "Uns Modernen erscheint eine solche masslose
Aufopferung, ein solcher Heroismus im Drama wie im Leben unvernünftig."
L. Beriger[8] expresses his criticism as follows:

> Er, der sich seiner Schwäche bewusst ist und sich zu ihr bekennt—
> "ich bin ein schwacher Mann" (384)—soll als Vertreter des
> Herrschers eine Stellung versehen, die
> 　　Rasch persönliches, selbsteignes Walten
> 　　Zutun und Fassen fordert und bedingt.　(236-237)
> Von dieser instinktiven Sicherheit und Tatkraft, dem Grunder-
> fordernis des Herrschens, besitzt Bancbanus nichts.

It must be pointed out that Bancbanus used the first quoted statement in
his objection to his appointment by the king; it shows his modesty; moreover, the aged man was not strong physically. Beriger neglects to say
that the second quotation is taken from Gertrude's lines who was trying
frantically to persuade the king to appoint her brother Otto vicegerent.
We shudder at the thought of the possible results of the "rasch persönliches,
selbsteignes Walten, Zutun und Fassen" of a man of the calibre of Otto von
Meran, a person dissolute and unable to control himself. E. J. Williamson[9]
has Bancbanus in his list of figures whom he calls "männlich-weiblich."
Max Speier[10] writes:

> Ihm gilt als einziger Gradmesser für sein und anderer Verhalten
> und Handlungen nicht der göttlich entstammte, in uns wirkende
> Moralbegriff, sondern die Art der Stellungnahme jener zum, die
> Art ihrer Auffassung vom Königspaare.　Dadurch wird in erster
> Linie eine bedenkliche Abgestumpftheit, ja sagen wir es nur
> gerade heraus, Abgestorbenheit des Rechtsgefuhls hervorgeru-
> fen. . . . Kein Wunder also, dass er die Selbstrache für Ernys Tod
> verschmaht und verpont.　Nicht aber wie er in selbsttauscherischer
> Bemantelung meint, weil die Sicherung der staatlichen Ruhe ihm
> allein massgebend ist, sondern eben weil ihm der Glanz und die
> Wurde der Persönlichkeit fehlt, die von dem Granitfelsen des
> Rechts getragen wird.

R. M. Meyer expresses his opinion in these words:[11]

> Ich kann mir nicht helfen—wir nennen das heute servil. . . . Wir
> sagen uns: in dem alten, kleinen, dürren Mannchen ist alles
> ausgestorben, ausser der eingewohnten Unterwürfigkeit. . . .
> Uns, die wir denn doch das Recht moderner Empfindung so gut
> haben wie der Dichter das der seinen, bleibt das Stück fremd wie
> ein Thesenstück voller Paradoxie.

Emil Reich[12] says: "Ein von allen Schrecknissen unbewegter, unverrückt sich gleich bleibender Charakter mag bewundernswürdig sein, dramatisch ist er nicht." Heinrich Bulthaupt:[13]

> Das Nächstliegende wäre doch, dass der edle Bancbanus, wenn es die Ehre und das Leben seines Weibes gilt, den Mann und den Gatten in seiner Brust fühlte, und niemand würde es bedenklich gefunden haben, wenn er das ihm zugefügte Leid gerächt hatte.

In brief Bancbanus is charged with lack of foresight, of dramatic force (Scherer, Reich), of a sense of justice (Speier), of manliness (Volkelt, Beriger, Williamson), of energy (Beriger). The count's devotion and loyalty to his king is called void of reason (Farinelli, Bulthaupt), less worthy than blind vengeance (Witkowski), and servile (R. M. Meyer). As will be shown, our dramatist is by far a greater psychologist than these critics. The motives in the portrayal of the loyal servant were stated above. The intended personification of the categorical imperative, which means an absolute law that has to be obeyed without consideration of conditions and consequences, makes this drama, of course, an "Ideendrama" in Hebbel's[14] sense. Nevertheless, Bancbanus is a perfectly viable figure, although individually human rather than generally human.

From the very beginning Bancbanus' manner shows self-assurance, insight, and judgment based on the experience of a long life. He knows that Count Otto is the leader of the noisy serenading crowd outside of his castle. He knows that the best thing to do is to ignore the childish activity of the youngster:

> [to a servant]
> Was kummert dich die Strasse? Sieh du hier!
> Ein jeder treibe, was ihm selber obliegt,
> Die andern mogen nur ein Gleiches tun.

How effective this attitude is can be seen by Otto's reaction when Bancbanus passes the boisterous crowd without even showing that he knows that they are there:

> Er ist nicht aufzubringen, nicht zu ärgern,
> Was ich beginn, er spottet meiner Wut!

Bancbanus' words:

> Der Ungar trägt im Frieden auch den Stahl,
> Zückt er ihn gleich nicht ohne herbe Wahl; . . .

make us realize why the king's choice falls on him for the office of vicegerent rather than on the irresponsible brother of the queen. Modestly the Count objects to his appointment; as a reason he advances the fact that he is not strong physically[15] and that he is old; and he objects again when the queen shows her hateful attitude (411). The king entrusts his wife and child to his loyal servant; he, furthermore, expects of Bancbanus that he keep peace in Hungary during the king's absence. We shall see that Bancbanus lives up to the expectations of Andreas (425-427): that he is able to control himself, that he does not forget his faithfulness, that he keeps his word like a man.

We observe Bancbanus' high sense of duty at every turn. It was also, to some extent, from a sense of duty that he had married Erny, the daughter of his life-long friend Nemaret whose wish it had been to know his daughter in the safe hands of a tried and worthy friend. Although he loved Erny, Bancbanus had married her only after he had made certain that she loved him and that she really wished to be his wife. Nevertheless, he feels a sort of guilt at having married a young girl. Unlike many old men with young wives Bancbanus does not torture Erny with vain jealousy:

> Was gibt ein Recht mir, also dich zu qualen?
> Weil dus versprachst? Ei, was verspricht der Mensch?

Bancbanus is the modern husband who wants a "free" wife whom he trusts rather than a husband who considers his wife a chattel:

> Doch Unwill gluht in ihrem Angesicht.
> Das sagst du [Graf Simon] selbst, und willst: ich soll sie hüten?
> Tanz zu! tanz, Erny, zu! Du wahrst dein selbst!

Through this very attitude Erny becomes so much more certain again of her love for her husband (834[2] and, above all 882). This attitude of the wise old man is by no means an "unrealistic sentiment" nor a "conventional idealism." As in many other cases, Grillparzer shows himself as a much better psychologist than many of his critics: Bancbanus knows that love cannot be forced. He knows that, should he lose Erny's love, he could do nothing about it. Some critics make the understandable mistake of judging this scene in terms of what happened later.[16] It never occurred to Bancbanus—and even the queen's actions would have been quite different, had she foreseen—that the maddened prince would resort to physical violence. If Bancbanus had foreseen the events leading to Erny's suicide, he would, indeed, have guarded his wife, though for quite a different reason, in the manner (812-819) which he described so ironically.[17]

In the second act, to be sure, Bancbanus is the object of mirth and raillery for some of the empty-headed courtiers. However, his conscientiousness concerning the unfinished items among the affairs of state is quite in keeping with his high sense of duty, the same sense of duty which—at the end of the fifth act—leads him to have his own brother and brother-in-law chained and led before the king. Bancbanus is too great a man to be ruffled by the mockery of the scoffers. One of the noblemen entering the castle for young Bela's birthday party asks the vicegerent jokingly if he is the gatekeeper and what has to be paid as an entrance fee. Bancbanus' answer

> Klugheit nicht;
> Ihr bleibt sonst haussen wohl!

shows his alertness. In his business transactions with the queen, his co-regent, Bancbanus not only shows his efficiency, but he also belies the charge of servility brought against him:

> [Queen] Sprach ich denn nicht schon: gewährt?

> [Bancbanus] Gewährt! gewährt! Lag diese Schrift nicht vor,
> So war nichts zu gewähren!

The queen has no more time to spare, for she wishes to attend the festivities; Bancbanus, however, insists, disregarding her unkind "Das nenn ich lästig!" (454). He suggests that Otto be placed at the head of a detachment of soldiers. Since both the queen ("Das ist zu viel!" 463) and the duke object, Bancbanus is unable to force the latter inasmuch as he shares his authority with the queen. However, there is no trace of servility in Bancbanus. Later—toward the end of the drama—when asked by the king: "Wo ist mein Weib?" (1974), Bancbanus does not deign to make any explanation. His answer sounds more like scorn and defiance, than servility:

> Dass Gott! die kehrte heim.
> Sie wollte sehn, wie's meinem Weib erging!

R. M. Meyer—who believes that everything has died within the "little withered man except his accustomed servility"—seems to overlook some of the scenes in the fourth act. Also Bulthaupt[18] does not notice that Bancbanus' taciturnity prevents him from showing the conflict in his soul: "Wir verlangen zum mindesten Zeugen seiner Seelenkämpfe, seines Wehs seines Grimmes, und des endlichen Sieges seiner Geduld zu werden." And Emil Reich[19] joins Bulthaupt in this demand. Bancbanus, who had been crushed by the grief over Erny's death and, therefore, had been unable to prevent the uprising instigated by his incensed relatives, had made his way into the castle in order to save the queen and the child. When the former insists that he take Otto also, Bancbanus retorts:

> Dankt Gott, dass, als ich kam, ich seiner nicht gedacht!
> Nehmt Euer Kind und folgt!

We are accustomed to Bancbanus' laconicism; therefore, these few words are sufficient to reveal to us the terrific struggle in the heart of the man whose pledge to the king forces him to save the murderer of his wife: Gertrude insists that he save either all three or none. Bancbanus (there is no time to be lost as the rebels are breaking into the castle) replies:

> Ich will nicht sehn, wer Euren Schritten folgt,
> Doch hüt er sich, wenn draussen wir im Freien.

Bancbanus has no choice. Convinced that Otto is guilty although the queen had taken the blame for Erny's death, he had rightly looked forward to the king's judgement:

> Der nun wird sitzen mit dem Schwert des Rechts,
> Wer rein, wer schuldig, wird sein Wort entscheiden.

And now the duke was to escape aided by Bancbanus himself! The conflict within Bancbanus is apparent enough in this scene. Bancbanus' feelings toward Otto, however, finally find their verbal expression at the beginning of the fifth act:

> Ich dachte längst, sie hätten dich gefunden,
> Geschlachtet, abgetan, wie dus verdienst.
> Rühr mich nicht an, sonst brauch ich meinen Stock!
> Du Wolf, du Hund, du blutger Mörder du!

Indeed, not everything has died in Bancbanus except his loyalty to the king. The first two lines reveal the loyal servant's train of thought which may have been: my pledge kept me from forsaking you when I had to save the queen, but I had hoped that you had fallen into the hands of the men who had revolted on your account.

All the scenes just described have also made manifest Bancbanus' manliness. We quote a man with unusual insight into Grillparzer's psychological motivation, O. E. Lessing-Dilg:[20]

> Freilich im Bulthauptschen [we would add: Im Volkeltschen, Berigerschen, Williamsonschen] Sinn ist Bancbanus kein tragischer Held. Er haut nicht, was ihm entgegentritt, in Stücke; auch erdolcht er sich zum guten Schluss nicht selbst, um im tragischen Pathos seine eigene Leichenrede halten zu konnen. Trotzdem hat er Eigenschaften genug, die ihn zur Fuhrung eines Dramas sehr wohl geeignet machen. Bancban ist nicht die Fratze eines Mannes, sondern ein ganzer Mann.

Max Speier[21] compares Bancbanus with Kleist's Michael Kohlhaas:

> Wie ganz anders pulst da die in ihm [Bancbanus] bis zum Verschwinden gedampfte Kraft in seinem literarischen Gegenstuck, der wie aus Erz gegossenen Gestalt von Kleists Michael Kohlhaas! Auch ihm ist, obzwar nur mittelbar, durch die Vorenthaltung seines Rechtes die heissgeliebte Gattin gemordet, aber zu welch' ruhiger und imposanter Unbeugsamkeit wächst er vor unseren Augen dadurch empor, dass er das Hohere: die Beleidigung und Verteidigung desselben, nicht vergisst, sondern auf seinen Schein besteht.

The only similarity between the two heroes is the fact that they lose their wives. Kohlhaas is not a high state official bound by pledges; he does not have a superior who will mete out just punishment to the person who wronged him. Moreover, even Kohlhaas—who had as keen a sense of justice as Bancbanus—reaches for the sword only after long hesitation. The "auz Erz gegossene" figure of Heinrich von Kleist, would, most likely, have acted in the same way in the major situations in Grillparzer's drama, had he been in the place of Bancbanus. In Bancbanus' actions in the fifth act—his ability to persuade the rebels to submit and thereby to prevent an attack by Andreas on his own capital, which would have caused a great deal of bloodshed—may be seen the most courageous and manly procedure of the entire drama when one considers the terror and bloodshed caused by the fact that two horses were unjustly taken from the horsedealer Kohlhaas.

Bancbanus, then, is a dramatic hero; to be sure, not strictly in the classical sense, but one who exemplifies the ideals of the modern drama. The strongest impulse within him is his sense of honor and of duty. Such a man can, indeed, be expected to be a man of his word, especially if it was pledged to a king in whom he not only sees the embodiment of the only valid rulership, but on whose sense of justice he relies. Bancbanus is wronged, not by his king—as is Kent by King Lear—, but by the relatives of the king. The wrong suffered by Bancbanus is the severest which could be done to a man in his position, his beloved wife is murdered; moreover, there remains the suspicion of a stain on her character, at least in the eyes of the public. The shock which almost breaks the aged man prevents him from preserving the peace, as he had promised the king for the time of the latter's absence. Suppressing his impulse for vengeance, Bancbanus does everything in his power to live up to his promise. However, the events are stronger than he; the queen loses her life because she wishes to save her brother. With foresight, wisdom, and courage Bancbanus manages to save Bela, King Andreas' only child, and—at the risk of his life—to bring the rebels under his control. That he is free from servility is made manifest by his actions throughout the drama, especially in the admonition to the king [addressed to the child, but meant for Andreas]:

> Sei mild, du Furstenkind, und sei gerecht!
> Auf dem Gerechten ruht des Herren Segen.
> Bezähm dich selbst, nur wer sich selbst bezähmt,
> Mag des Gesetzes scharfe Zügel lenken.
> Lass dir den Menschen Mensch sein, und den Diener
> Acht als ein Spargut fur die Zeit der Not.[22]

Herzog Otto von Meran

King Andreas has no illusions (252) about the morals of his young brother-in-law. To Gertrude's question: "Was fehlt ihm also" the king answers "Sitte." (279). The ruffian-like street scene at the beginning of the drama has convinced the spectator of Andreas' charge. The queen's blind partiality for her brother, however, causes her to extol his virtues in the highest tones. After praising his splendid appearance, his flashing eyes, his hero's chest, his strong physique which "verkündet ihn als Herrn und als Gebieter" (267), she goes as far as to say in her desperate attempt to secure Otto's appointment as vicegerent of Hungary by the king:

> Sagt selbst, ist nicht mein Bruder tapfer, klug,
> Entschlossen und verschwiegen, listig, kühn,
> Kein Zaudrer?

The dramatic irony in this statement becomes apparent at the end of the second act when we see the young duke act like a spoiled child because he meets with resistance on the part of Erny:

> Und bin ich toll, so wahrt euch vor dem Tollen.
> Du hasts gesagt, und so beruhr mich nicht!
> Hin auf den Boden werf ich meinen Leib,
> (Er wirft zur Erde.)
> Und mit den Händen greif ich in den Grund.
> Nicht horen und nicht reden! Rase, stirb!

Max Speier[23] says: "Man darf wohl getrost Otto als den eigentlichen Herrscher ansehen, da er die Königin und diesen ihren Gemahl am Gängelband führt." This statement is only a half-truth, for, while Gertrude is controlled by Otto to be sure, Andreas is not ruled by his wife. He does not yield to the kneeling "Mannweib"—who ultimately perishes through her one and only weakness, her foolish love for her brother—when as vital an issue as the appointment of a vicegerent must be settled. Emil Reich holds that:[24]

> Er [Otto] ist eine kräftige Natur von Mark und Kern, aus
> dem ein tüchtiger, auf jedem Platz brauchbarer Mann
> hätte werden konnen; weniger ihm als den Verhältnissen
> fällt es zur Last, dass es anders kam.

Considering that Otto himself realizes that he is the product of his surroundings (1220 ff.), it would appear that he would change after the public rebuff he receives from the virtuous Erny (898) if he had any force of character whatsoever. He would shake off his adolescent cynicism that had led him to believe that all women are alike. Instead he persists in his role of a stubborn child, refuses to eat, and goes so far as to throw a knife (982) at his servant. With the cleverness of a spoiled child he knows how to obtain what he wishes from Gertrude. He threatens to leave her in order to return to his sisters and brothers who will do his bidding (1053 ff.). In the manner of a foolish mother who by yielding to the child's whims becomes its slave, the queen succumbs to the ruse and lures Erny into Otto's room and thus prepares the way for the occurrences leading to the catastrophe.

The figure of Otto is one of the most complicated and has no equal on the stage, for Otto is neither a Prinz Gonzaga nor a Zawisch. Fortunately we have some information concerning the role of the Duke of Meran from Grillparzer himself which will be helpful in our analysis of this character. In a letter to the sister of the actor Ludwig Lowe, who was to take the role of Otto,[25] Grillparzer explains:

> Der Grundzug dieses Charakters ist Übermut, aus zweifacher Quelle: als Prinz und als Liebhaber der Frauen. Von Kindheit an gewohnt, allen seinen Neigungen gehuldigt zu sehen, bringt ihn jeder Widerstand ausser sich... Er schatzt Ernyn gering, wie alle Bewohner Ungarns, wie alle Weiber. Als er statt Liebe Verachtung findet, bricht das Ungestum seines Wesens übermächtig hervor und Wut, Trotz, Rachedurst, ja die Spuren einer durch den Widerstand erst mehr zum Bewusstsein gekommenen Neigung fur die Widerstrebende versetzen ihn in jenen Zustand, in welchem wir ihn am Schluss des zweiten, vornehmlich aber zu Anfang des dritten Aufzuges erblicken. In der darauf folgenden Szene mit Erny durchlauft er alle Tasten der Empfindung, durch die er Eindruck auf die Eingeschüchterte zu machen hofft. Trotz seines alle seine Reden begleitenden schadenfrohen Lauerns ist er in dieser Szene doch nur halb ein Heuchler.

Grillparzer goes on to say that if Erny had succumbed to Otto's pleading, he would sooner or later have returned to his dissolute life. As she resists, however, his wrath is augmented to the utmost by the humiliating feeling that he has compromised his dignity.

Grillparzer is right when he says that the fourth act would be the most difficult for the actor inasmuch as Otto is not meant to be insane:

> Unter zehn Schauspielern würden neune uns den Prinzen als einen eigentlich Wahnsinnigen geben, das ist er nicht. Fast würde vorübergehender Blödsinn eher seinen Zustand bezeichnen. . . . Ein guter Mensch würde vielleicht wahnsinnig geworden sein. Otto wird stumpf, was jedoch einzelne Fieberanfälle von Schreck und Reue nicht ausschliesst. . . . Er weiss nicht, wie schuldig er ist, das Ereignis von Ernys Tod hat sein Leben in zwei ungleiche Hälften geteilt und die Erstere liegt ihm im Dunkeln.[26]

Whatever Otto's condition may be, one basic instinct remains in him, that of self-preservation, which apears as extreme cowardice:

> Dass sie mich fangen? toten?
> Pfui über allen Tod! Durch Schwert, durch Feuer,
> Durch Gift, durch Strick, durch Beil, pfui allem Tod!
> Ei, ich will leben, ich!

He seeks protection behind little Bela and behind the chambermaid (1482 ff., 1580, 1581); and when his sister insists that he be saved first, he says: "Ja, mich zuerst!" (1621).

In the fifth act—as Grillparzer himself points out—there is not a trace of the strange condition resembling insanity in Otto, or the careful Bancbanus would not have placed the crownprince into the hands of the "Mann des Unheils." (1702) Silent, in rags, crushed, in the deepest contrition, the duke is eager to help the man who saved his life. —After he has testified to Erny's innocence, he is deported by Andreas,—"Wo Sünde selber straft, brauchts da noch Strafe?" (2035)—left to his remorse.

In Otto von Meran the dramatist has created a figure who is entirely controlled by boundless passion, a representative of the egotistical philosophy of the ruling class. His early surroundings had been detrimental to his development. At the Hungarian court he displays an unheard of insolence. His disregard of all moral principles leads to the death of two persons and to armed revolt. When he sees the result of his stubborn wilfulness, he is unable to face the consequences like a man. Terror and fright confuse his mind temporarily. Only the instinct of self-preservation remains intact. Like Jason he does not atone for his crimes by death, but by a life of remorse and contrition. This masterfully drawn figure stands side by side with Zawisch von Rosenberg among Grillparzer's creations.

Konig Andreas von Ungarn

> Heisst Euer Konig der Gerechte
> Und hast du doch gezittert um dein Recht?

are the words addressed to Simon by one of Andreas' commanders after the king's return. To be sure, the King of Hungary has every intention of being just; he also is endeavoring to rule wisely: his choice of a vicegerent falls on the sage and wise Bancbanus. However, Andreas has one weakness: he yields, more than he should, to his wife Gertrude. He is unwise in endowing her with as much power as he gives her. Her arrogance toward Bancbanus—"Tolldreist und Tor." (398)—angers Andreas. He almost decides to limit her power:

> Ich will Euch Grenzen setzen, dass Ihrs wahrnehmt,
> Und wart Ihr blind vor Hochmut und vor Grimm!

Gertrude's haughty condescension in allowing Bancbanus to kiss her hand

> Hier meine Hand! ich will Euch gnädig sein,
> Wenn Ihrs verdient,

should convince the departing ruler of Hungary that his wife is unfit to control the destiny of a whole nation.

Andreas seems more than sufficiently punished by the outcome. He returns, called back by Bancbanus. The country is in disorder: the king cannot help comparing the sad homecoming with many a triumphal return in former days (1860-1869). And now! His wife dead, his son's fate uncertain:

> Hier war der Ort, da kam sie mir entgegen,
> Mit ihrem Sohn, mein Weib, mein teures Weib!
> Nun ist sie tot, und ungewisses Bangen
> Wird mir als Antwort, frag ich um den Sohn.

Andreas is rash in his opinion concerning Bancbanus; although he does not know all the facts that led up to the queen's death, he continues:

> Bancban, Bancban, wie hast du mich getäuscht
> Um mein Vertraun, das ich auf dich gewendet!

While he cannot believe that Bancbanus could have become a traitor when that possibility is mentioned:

> Doch er Verräter? Nun, dann bin ichs auch,
> Dann sind wirs alle. Nein, Bancbanus nicht!

yet he greets the loyal servant who has just succeeded in avoiding civil war:

> Bancban, Bancban! Du ungetreuer Knecht!
> Wie hast du deines Herren Haus verwaltet!

Does he feel the reproach in Bancbanus' reply?

> Herr, gut und schlimm, wies eben moglich war.

Does Andreas realize that he himself bears part of the blame for the disaster because he entrusted his wife with too much power, which bound the loyal servant's hand?

The King of Hungary is fully aware of his failings concerning his libertine brother-in-law:

> Wie gräbt Erinnerung mit blutgen Zügen,
> Und zeigt, was ich versehn, wie ich gefehlt.
> Unsittlichkeit! Du allgefrassger Krebs,
> Du Wurm an alles Wohlseins tiefsten Wurzeln,
> Du Raupe an des Staates Lebensmark!
> Warum liess ich beim Scheiden dich zurück?
> Warum zertrat ich nicht, verwies dich?
> Wie schlecht verwahrtes Feuer gingst du auf
> Und frassest all mein Haus, mein Heil, mein Glück!

That Andreas pardons the murderers of the queen[27] only half-heartedly and after Bancbanus' pleading is understandable. King Andreas, however, does not dignify Otto with a trial; contemptuously he accords the Duke of Meran safe conduct to the border.

Only after Otto's confession does Andreas realize what Count Bancbanus has done for him:

> Wie aber soll ich dir die Treue lohnen,
> Zum Teile nur vergelten, was du tatst,
> Was du erlittst im Dienste deines Herrn?
> Der Erste sei nach mir in meinem Reich,
> Dein Wort dem Worte deines Konigs gleich.

Although Andreas—like Bancbanus—loses his wife, we feel greater sympathy for his faithful vassal. The ruler of Hungary is not a bad king; in fact, his ruling has brought him the surname "the just." He endeavors to rule wisely; and when he has made mistakes, he is ready to admit them and to draw his lessons from them. He is generous and appreciative of loyal services and sacrifices made for him and his people. —However, in dramatic effect he remains far behind the great figure of Bancbanus, who is, of course, the central character of the drama.

Graf Simon, der Bruder des Bancbanus

Of the two leaders of the revolt, Peter and Simon, the latter is by far the more passionate, by far more jealous of the family's honor in the eyes of the world. While Bancbanus persists in clinging to the intrinsic values in the conception of honor which prompts him to keep his solemn promise under the most trying conditions, his younger brother Simon lays stress on the outward appearance of honor. Brave, determined, and impetuous, he is all action and therefore dramatically very effective on the stage. He is one of the first to break into the room in which Erny has just ended her own life. Realizing that his sister-in-law is dead, Simon at once goes on to the next thing:

> Nichts mehr fur sie zu tun, als sie zu rachen!
> Dort ist der Morder! Dieser hats getan.
> (Auf Otto zeigend.)
> Heraus mein Schwert und freu dich auf ein Fest!

and

> Auf ihn! Haut ihn in Stücke! Stosst ihn nieder!

It is Simon who incites the Hungarians:

> Ein Ungar bin ich, rufend um Gericht.

And he clashes with his more circumspect brother. In his indignation Simon cannot agree with Bancbanus who wishes to postpone the trial until the king's return, and is thus led to his most unjust outburst against the man who is most deeply affected by Erny's death.

Fearful that Otto might escape, it is Simon who storms the castle with his followers; it is he who orders Peter to hurl the fateful dagger which kills Gertrude instead of Otto. The accident, while it strikes terror into the heart of Peter, incites Simon even more:

> Um desto heisser nach dem Doppelmörder!
> Ich schlacht ihn allen Beiden.

The mere sight of some of the duke's followers changes him into a raging lion; he kills one of the foreigners:

> Zahl deines Herren Zeche, Sündenknecht!

In the fifth act—the king is returning and matters look rather unfavorable for the rebels—it is Simon again who is conspicuous for his
courage and his undaunted spirit:

> Ich liebe, dass man vor der Tat erwäge,
> Nachher ertrage, was die Folge beut.
> Wen reut, was er getan, fehlt zweimal:
> Weil ers getan, und dann, weils ihn gereut.

He is willing to surrender on condition that justice be done and pardon
granted to all who fought in his cause. He prefers death to cowardly surrender (1824-1830). However, the odds are against him; Bancbanus has
brought the city to peaceful surrender. When we see Simon again, he appears before the king in chains. As a vassal of the king—so Bancbanus
tells his brother—he will not compromise his dignity if he kneels with the
rest of the rebels. It is Bancbanus who secures him a pardon from Andreas.
Simon then forces Erny's exoneration from the lips of the Duke of Meran.

Count Simon is a dramatic hero in the classical sense. Bold, determined,
a fighter, quick to act when his knightly honor is at stake, and ready to
take the consequences of his actions, without remorse or regret. Such a
figure is always a success on the stage. It is not difficult to see why many
critics prefer a man with Simon's philosophy of life to Bancbanus, whose
complex character is drawn more in accord with the theories underlying
the modern drama.

Graf Peter, der Bruder Ernys.

Peter is gentler and less independent than Simon. Although he is much
closer to Erny than Simon, Count Peter never takes the lead, he always
follows the former. The rebels who demand the surrender of Otto, send
Peter to the queen as a spokesman; and we are made to feel that he is
not a man of steel like Simon:

> (Queen)
> Ich seh in Euren Augen, Graf, ein Etwas,
> Das eine mildre Meinung mir verbürgt.
> (Peter)
> Hier ist von meiner Meinung nicht die Rede,
> Von meinem Auftrag nur.

Later it is Peter's dagger that kills the queen; again he had followed
Simon's order:

> O all ihr Engel, die ihr Böses abwehrt,
> Steht bei! Ich hab die Königin erschlagen!

As Ehrhard[28] points out, the terror of the murder is greatly toned down
by the fact that it is the result of an error. Grillparzer thus avoided putting
on the stage an intentional murder of a royal person.

From this moment on a change takes place within Peter; he doubts whether the course they have taken is the right one. In the fifth act he meets Bancban who is on his way to the city:

> (Bancban)
> Das ist wohl gar eines Verraters Stimme.
>   (Hinauf blickend.)
> Lauf, Peter, lauf! Du kommst wohl noch ans Ziel.
> Pfui, über alle Schelmen!
> (Hauptmann)   Soll ich, Herr!
> Zurück ihn [*i.e.*, Bancbanus] halten?
> (Peter, der herangekommen ist.)
>   Lass ihn; Dass er Recht hat!
> Dass ich mirs selbst in meinem Innern sage!
> Ein Schurk und ein Verräter! Grosser Gott!
> Ein Mörder noch dazu.—O meine Hände.

We know that Peter will not execute Simon's instructions when—later—the latter sends Peter to hold Bancbanus at any cost to prevent him from entering the city with the injunction:

>   Und eh Bancban du losgibst,
> Hab ihn das Grab, dich, mich, uns alle!

Count Peter is pardoned with the other rebels by the king.

Peter has courage and a keen sense of knightly honor in common with his sister's brother-in-law, but lacks the latter's determination and initiative. However, he is a more profound character than Simon; a thinker. Thus his unfortunate murder leads him to the realization that he had chosen the wrong way to defend his honor since the taking of the law into one's own hands may lead to deeds which can never be repaired, and thus to life-long remorse.

Our minute analysis has demonstrated that the faithful palatine Bancbanus passes the test of manliness. Also three of the four figures of lesser importance were found to be men of courage: King Andreas, Count Peter, and Count Simon, the latter representing the type of dashing stage hero of the classical drama. Otto von Meran is a dissolute libertine and weakling.

CHAPTER SIX

DES MEERES UND DER LIEBE WELLEN

The plan for a drama based on the classical Hero and Leander theme was conceived in the year 1819, but not until ten years later, early in 1829, did Grillparzer begin his work on *Des Meeres und der Liebe Wellen*. It was finished in 1831 and first produced on April 3, 1831. The dramatist's chief source was an elegy by the late Greek grammarian Musaeus, written around 500 A.D. Of the many other adaptations of the legend Grillparzer knew Ovid's treatment in the *Heroides*, the "Volkslied" of the "zwei Königskindern," and Schiller's ballad, *Hero und Leander*. As the dramatist relates in his diaries,[1] he was constantly reading the Greeks and the Spaniards—Homer, Euripides, Aristotle, and Lope de Vega—during the time of the creation of this excellent and unique tragedy of love. It is of special importance here that at this time the reading of Lope de Vega had become a daily necessity for Grillparzer. Without losing his German individuality he tried to combine the Greek ideal of form with Lope's perceptual presentation, fervor, compactness, and terseness of dramatic expression. He succeeded in avoiding all false pathos and sentimentality. For the minute psychological exploration of the various stages of the passion developing in Hero, however, Grillparzer needed no teacher. Thus was created the best tragedy of love which exists in German literature. Many critics have rightly said that *Des Meeres und der Liebe Wellen* may well be compared to Shakespeare.[2]

Of the small cast of characters we shall consider Leander, the Highpriest, and Naukleros.

Leander

While Schiller's ballad glorifies Leander, his daring and sacrifice for his all-consuming love, the main interest in Grillparzer's drama centers around Hero. Nevertheless, Leander is not an unimportant figure.

Several similarities between Hero and Leander become apparent at once. The first similarity presents itself in their unfortunate early environment. Hero's early youth had been most unhappy. Between a harsh, unreasonable, fault-finding father, a silent, maltreated, and intimidated mother, and a brother who vented his wantonness on the younger and weaker sister, Hero had conceived distorted ideas about men and about woman's lot in the world. Untouched by human passions, the immature girl had found in the temple of Aphrodite a veritable haven. Her self-sufficiency is not egotistical presumption,[3] but the logical outgrowth of her immaturity and the melancholy outlook on life which her childhood experiences had given her. Leander's lonely childhood had been spent on an isolated shore with a morose mother, for whom he cared devotedly (518). With her death, he felt, the world had come to an end for him. As we learn from Naukleros, Leander had not been able to shake off his melancholy. Timidity and ignorance of the ways of the world in addition to his despondency had contributed to his inability to overcome his gloom. His friend, the jovial gallant, had discovered that only a woman could stir the melancholy dreamer out of his self-centered existence (656, 660 ff.).

The second point of resemblance in the two leading figures is the fact that love had never come to either; the word love had no meaning for them. And now (499) at the statue of Hymenaeus, the god of marriage, in the very moment when Hero takes her vow of chastity as a full-fledged priestess of Aphrodite—Cupid's arrow strikes them unexpectedly: on first sigh both fall in love. However, neither of them knows at once what has happened. Leander, who is still being teased by Naukleros for his gloom, believes that he is ill (533). Yet he who had been so reluctant to join the festive crowd at the temple, now does not wish to leave. The alert Naukleros guesses the reason for his younger friend's lingering. In a light-hearted way the former describes the beauty of the priestess only to find Leander in tears: "Und sprich nicht ohne Achtung von ihrem Hals und Wuchs.—O ich bin dreifach elend!" (654-655).

When during the ensuing night Hero asks why Leander had made his bold entrance into her room, the ingenuous youth replies:

> Ich sah dein Licht
> Mit hellem Glanze strahlen durch die Nacht.
> Auch hier wars Nacht und sehnte sich nach Licht.
> Da klomm ich denn herauf.

He could do nothing else; he had not reflected about the reasons for his actions or the consequences they might have. We are at once struck by a similar situation in *Romeo and Juliet*.[4] Shakespeare's heroine asks the bold intruder: "By whose direction found'st thou out this place?" and Romeo replies:

> By love that first did prompt me to inquire;
> He lent me counsel, and I lent him eyes.
> I am no pilot; yet wert thou as far
> As that vast shore wash'd with the farthest sea,
> I would adventure for such merchandise.

Yet there is a difference between the two lovers. Romeo—on a higher social level than the fisherman of Abydos—is by far the more worldly-wise, to whom, moreover, love has not come for the first time. Leander, unsophisticated child of nature, follows this powerful new impulse and—when asked for reasons—says with the same direct simplicity: "Auch hier wars Nacht und sehnte sich nach Licht."

Simplicity is the keynote and the singular charm of the ensuing scene between Hero and Leander which culminates in the former's complete surrender. We quote one instance. Leander is to leave and begs for a "Zeichen deiner Huld" (1238) and—as Hero does not understand what he wants—he goes on with his pleading explanation which also shows the tenderness of his wooing:

> Nicht mindestens die Hand?—
> Und dann!—Sie legen Lipp an Lippe,
> Ich sah es wohl, und flüstern so sich zu,
> Was zu geheim für die geschwätz'ge Luft.
> Mein Mund sei Mund, der deine sei dein Ohr!
> Leih mir dein Ohr für meine stumme Sprache!

Although Naukleros knows his companion very well, he is mistaken about him in one respect. He reasons that now—since sensuality has been awakened in Leander—he will be joined by him in his amorous pursuits:

> Nun, Gotter, Dank, dass ihr ihn heimgesucht!
> Nun schont ihn nicht mit euren heissen Pfeilen, . . .

Mindful of the penalties which are placed on pursuing a priestess, the lighthearted philanderer believes that he can direct Leander's passion on some other beauty:

> Komm mit zurück zur Stadt! dort sind die Mädchen,
> Die wir beim Fest gesehn, noch all versammelt.

Only later does the loyal friend learn that Leander is the type to whom love comes only once and in such an all-consuming, self-forgetful fashion that all reasoning seems to be set aside. Naukleros finds not only that Leander has accomplished a feat—which for centuries seemed a myth until Lord Byron and others after him proved that it could readily be accomplished—and that he has visited his lady-love, but also that the melancholy youth has overnight become a man, exuberant and almost wanton. Naukleros tries in vain to convince his younger friend of the dangers that a renewed crossing of the Hellespont will entail:

> Nun ja, ich, seh' es wohl, wir haben,
> Die Platze haben wir getauscht. Ich furchtsam,
> Du kuhn; Leander frohen Muts, Naukleros—
> Ich werde doch nicht gar noch weinen sollen?
> Wohlan, geh in den Tod! Nur eines,
> Ein Einziges versprich mir: Dieses Mal,
> Diesmal such mir ihn nicht. Bleib fern von Sestos.

Having failed in his pleading, Naukleros attempts to use force in order to prevent Leander from crossing the sea during the storm; but he discovers that Leander is no longer a timid, helpless lad. He finds himself outwitted by strategy. Leander rushes toward the sea, shouting:

> Amor und Hymen, ziehet ihr voran,
> Ich komm', ich folg', und wäre Tod der Dritte!

In the morning his lifeless body is found on the rocks of Sestos below Hero's tower.

Brunet, small, but muscular, a bold rower, and an untiring swimmer, the melancholy dreamer Leander has attracted the yearning looks of many a girl, much to the regret of the taller and blond Naukleros. However, the world in general and woman in particular do not seem to exist for the diffident youth until—he sees Hero. His love for the priestess of Aphrodite changes him to a hero of gigantic proportions. Since astounding feats done under the influence of a powerful passion are not unusual, even for persons who would be unable to perform the same exploits under ordinary circumstances, it seems quite plausible that a lover so passionate as Leander would swim the Hellespont and thereby win Hero so readily.[5] Leander's tragic death must be attributed to his disregard of the dangers of the crossing during a storm and of the Highpriest's hostile precautions.

The atmosphere of this great German drama of love is built up largely by means of Hero's "monodrama," but the dramatist by no means fails to show the poetic spiritual quality of Leander's love.[6] We shall let Leander make his own plea for a just evaluation of the nature of his love:

> Als diese Nacht ich schlaflos stieg vom Lager,
> Und, offnend meiner Hutte niedre Tur,
> Aus jenem Dunkel trat in neues Dunkel,
> Da lag das Meer vor mir mit seinen Küsten,
> Ein schwarzer Teppich, ungeteilt, zu schaun,
> Wie eingehullt in Trauer und in Gram.
> Schon gab ich mich dem wilden Zuge hin!
> Da, am Gesichtskreis flackert hell empor
> Ein kleiner Stern, wie eine letzte Hoffnung
> Zu goldnen Faden tausendfach gesponnen,
> Umzog der Schein, ein Netz, die trübe Welt:
> Das war dein Licht, war dieses Turmes Lampe.
> In macht'gen Schlagen schwoll empor mein Herz,
> Nicht halten wollt' es mehr in seinen Banden;
> Ans Ufer eilt' ich, stürzte mich ins Meer,
> Als Leitstern jenen Schimmer stets im Auge.
> So kam ich her, erreichte diese Kuste.
> Ich will nicht wiederkommen, wenn du zürnst,
> Doch raube nicht den Stern mir meiner Hoffnung,
> Verhülle nicht den Trost mir dieses Lichts.

The Highpriest

However much our modern feeling may lead us to revolt against the attitude of Hero's uncle, we must try to understand his conception of life and the motives for his actions. Above all, we must learn whether or not he is sincere.

The Highpriest serves the goddess of spiritual love:

> Nicht ehrt man hier die ird'sche Aphrodite.

and

> Kein Vogel baut beim Tempel hier sein Nest,
> Nicht girren ungestraft im Hain die Tauben,
> Die Rebe kriecht um Ulmen nicht hinan,
> All was sich paart bleibt ferne diesem Hause, . . .

This scion of a privileged family which prides itself on having furnished many a celibate to the temple, does not deny the existence of the natural instincts in man. However, to follow them is folly for him. The life of a priest or priestess for him is independence, is walking on a luminous path, is being

> Ein Selbst . . . , ein Wesen, eine Welt.

Composure is the essence of happiness, he believes:

> Du hast genannt den mächt'gen Weltenhebel
> Der alles Grosse tausendfach erhöht,
> Und selbst das Kleine näher rückt den Sternen.

Before this composure

> Des Staubes Wünsche weichen scheu zurück.

The Highpriest is fair to his neophite niece: *she* must know what she wishes, and *she* must decide before she takes the decisive vow:

> Was lange dauern soll sei lang erwogen,
> Wusst' ich sie schwach, noch jetzt entliess' ich sie.

For the priest, a vow such as Hero has taken is irrevocable; he knows enough about the world to realize the dangers that lie in waiting for a young woman in Hero's position. He is honestly endeavoring to help:

> Den ersten Anlass meid! . . .
> . . . .
> Doch wessen Streben auf das Innre fuhrt,
> Wo Ganzheit nur, des Wirkens Fulle fordert,
> Der halte fern vom Streite seinen Sinn,
> Denn ohne Wunde kehrt man nicht zurück,
> Die noch als Narbe mahnt in trüben Tagen.

His great sense of duty becomes apparent when he says to Hero:

> Und so schlaf wohl! Bedarfst du irgend Rat,
> Such ihn bei mir, bei deinem zweiten Vater.
> Doch stiessest du des Freundes Rat zuruck,
> Du fandest auch in mir den Mann, der willig,
> Das eigne Blut aus diesen Adern gösse,
> (Mit ausgestrecktem Arm.)
> Wüsst' er nur einen Tropfen in der Mischung,
> Der Unrecht birgt und Unerlaubtes hegt.

In other words: he would shed his own blood, should he find himself guilty of any violation of his cult, and—by implication—he certainly would not stop at meting out punishment to Hero in the event that she should become guilty of a false step.

The hand of the master dramatist is evident in the fourth act when Grillparzer skillfully leads the Highpriest from suspicion to the conviction that Hero has broken her sacred vows:

> In meinem Innern reget sich ein Gott,
> Und warnt mich, zu verhuten, ehs zu spät!

and finally:

> Was dort? Die Lampe strahlt. Unselig Mädchen!
> Sie leuchtet deiner Strafe, deiner Schuld.

The Highpriest is convinced that his cunning scheme through which he contrives to drive Leander to his death is inspired by the deity and that he is doing only his duty. Yet is he, perhaps, not also thinking of the family's honor when he tries to keep the whole incident secret instead of investigating whether or not Hero is still worthy of the office of a priestess of Aphrodite, and whether or not she has kept her vow of chastity? It is made difficult for us to believe that he is entirely sincere as her "second father."

The merciless removal of Leander's body is part of the Highpriest's

attempted cure of Hero's wound (984), but the fate of this ardent lover
is that suggested by Lovell Beddoes':

> But would'st thou cure thine heart
> Of love and all its smart,
> Then die, dear, die!

When he has convinced himself of Hero's death, the stern servant of the
gods leaves the stage silently, hiding his face. He has just said:

> Und galts ihr Leben! Gab ich doch auch meins,
> Um Unrecht abzuhalten.

This covering of his face seems to indicate more than grief over the loss
of his niece. Is he beginning to realize that his interpretation of the wishes
of the gods was wrong? Or does he feel now that his stern sense of duty,
which would drive him to suicide if he should do wrong, was mixed with
some selfish interest, namely the protection of the reputation of his family,
which had led him to disregard the intrinsic significance of the doctrines
of his cult?

The Highpriest, then, is a serious, dignified man, the typical church
official who has made the doctrines of his institution his own. He has a
high opinion of his office, and is fully aware of the duties which are part
of it. That his purely human feelings, if he has any, will not be allowed
to interfere with his duties, seems a foregone conclusion. As the drama
shows, he remains consistent to the end. He believes that his cunning
scheme to bring the intruder to ruin is inspired by the gods; the author
has portrayed this so convincingly that we cannot doubt the priest's sincerity in this matter. However, his selfish interests induce him to carry
his zeal to extremes. His attitude at the end appears to make manifest
that his self-assurance is shaken by the destructive results of his ruthless
procedure.

Naukleros

In the vivacious Naukleros Grillparzer has created an admirable foil
to the sensitive, reserved character of Leander. Naukleros is in every
respect the opposite of Leander. The latter is brunet and small, while
the former is tall and blond. Naukleros is talkative, witty, ever
active; Leander, on the other hand, is melancholy, depressed, ignorant
of the ways of the world, and timid. It is Naukleros' self-assigned duty to
cheer up the gloomy Leander. By constant encouragement and mockery,
the experienced and spirited philanderer endeavors to combat his friend's
melancholy:

> Wer wagt gewinnt.
> . . . .
>   Allein, sieh dort!
> Die beiden Mädchen. Schau! es sind dieselben
> Die heute fruh wir sahn am Gittertor.
> Sie blinzeln her. Gefallt dir eine? Sprich!

Naukleros lacks the depth of feeling which Leander shows when, in his
great passion, he disregards all common-sense consideration. Naukleros,
however, does not lose sight of reality; he does his best—as we mentioned

above—to dissuade Leander from his perilous undertaking. Having failed in this, he is no less devoted to his friend. Far from abandoning Leander, he induces friends to join him in an attempt to rescue the impassioned boy. Despite the hostile attitude of the Highpriest at Sestos, Naukleros ventures to the other shore only to find his friend's corpse: "O Schmerz!" (1944) Leander, o, mein mildgesinnter Freund!" (1974)

In Naukleros Grillparzer presents a well-rounded character. A lively, facetious, loquacious man of the world, this young Greek has an optimistic outlook on life and takes his pleasures where he finds them. He has offered his friendship to Leander and has made it his task to convert the despondent youth to his own philosophy of life. When the latter is in need of sound advice and help, Naukleros shows that he knows the meaning of real friendship.—Naukleros displays manly courage in his argument with the Highpriest. Referring to the constant quarrels between the people of Abydos and Sestos (840 ff.), the priest says insults suffered from Abydos would be avenged doubly; to which Naukleros, honest and straightforward, replies:

> Ich aber denke: Mann, Herr, gegen Mann!
> So hielt ichs gegen Sestos' frommes Volk.

Naukleros is on the side of life, and, likewise, his gods—in contrast to the Highpriest's—are on the side of life:

> Seit wann sind Gotter neidisch missgesinnt?
> Daheim auch ehrt man Himmlische, bei uns;
> Doch heiter tritt Zeus' Priester unters Volk,
> Umgeben von der Seinen frohen Scharen,
> Und segnet Andre, ein Gesegneter.

In *Des Meeres und der Liebe Wellen* Grillparzer has added two dramatic creations to his long line of manly men: Leander and Naukleros. While the Highpriest seems to be a man of strong principles, his actions in the drama do not enable the spectator or the reader to attribute manliness to the zealous official.

CHAPTER SEVEN

DER TRAUM EIN LEBEN

In 1815 Schreyvogel translated Calderon's *La vida es sueño*. Its stage success in Vienna when it was produced in June, 1816, is probably due to the masterful translation. From this day on *La vida es sueño* enjoyed great popularity in Vienna. Grillparzer began *Der Traum ein Leben* in 1817 and completed the first act in the same year. Then, on April 6, 1818, the drama *Schlummre, traume und erkenne* by C. von der Velde was produced. As its thought seemed to be practically the same as that of Grillparzer's dream play, he lost all interest in it. After various new attempts later *Der Traum ein Leben* was completed in 1831 and produced in 1834. It was Grillparzer's most popular drama, for it experienced more productions on the Vienna stage than any of his other plays.

Although the title is almost identical with that of Calderon's play, the influence of the latter on Grillparzer's "dramatic fairytale" as he called it, is, indeed, very small. Friedrich Kummer[1] says: "Mit Calderons einen ähnlichen Titel tragendem Stück: *Das Leben ein Traum* hat Grillparzers Märchendrama allein den Gedanken der Nichtigkeit des irdischen Glucks und Ruhms gemeinsam." Calderon denies the creative spirit in man and sees in the dream the symbol of destruction which dominates all. Grillparzer's philosophy, which is not pessimistic, does not go to such extremes. As we shall see, he merely condemns ambition for power and fame in persons whose capacities are limited.

As in *Des Meeres und der Liebe Wellen* the influence of Grillparzer's constant reading of Lope de Vega is evident in *Der Traum ein Leben*: in the terseness and precision of the dialogue, in the strict economy of the language in general; in the quickly progressing action, in the colorfulness and sudden transition of the events; and in the clear perceptual presentation despite the fact that most of the action occurs in a dream. Vivid action is always in the foreground; psychological motivation is intentionally neglected. The spectator is interested in the fate of the characters, not in their psychology. However, the plot and, above all, the transitions from dream to reality are masterfully executed and psychologically true. As for the dream itself, every figure and every situation is derived from persons Rustan knows and from the sphere of experiences and thoughts he has had in the first act before the dream begins. Zanga is his companion throughout the dream. The king, good-natured and devoted to his daughter, resembles Massud as well as the real king of Zanga's accounts. Gülnare shows some of the traits of Mirza. The "Mann vom Felsen" is the personification of all that to Rustan appears abominable. Now and then it seems to the dream-Rustan that the man on the rock resembles the only enemy he has. The old Kaleb—the father of the man slain by Rustan—seems to bear a certain resemblence to the old dervish.

The influences on *Der Traum ein Leben* are numerous: the main source is probably Voltaire's *Le blanc et le noir;* furthermore *Zadig* and *Candide* by the same author; Lope's *Con su pan se lo coma* and *Los Donayres de Matica*; Klinger's *Geschichte Giafars des Barmeciden*.[2]

The present study includes Rustan, Zanga, and Massud. The characters of the dream: the king, Gülnare, the "Mann vom Felsen," are dream-like and indistinct, *i.e.*, little individualized.

Rustan

While Massud and his men spend their days in toil (94-95), Rustan prefers to go hunting. Before his appearance on the scene we learn a great deal about him from his uncle Massud:

> Ja, fürwahr, ein wilder Geist
> Wohnt in seinem düstern Busen,
> Herrscht in seinem ganzen Tun
> Und lasst nimmerdar ihn ruhn.
> Nur von Kampfen und von Schlachten,
> Nur von Kronen und Triumphen,
> Von des Kriegs, der Herrschaft Zeichen
> Hòrt man sein Gesprach ertònen;
> Ja, des Nachts, entschlummert kaum,
> Spricht von Kämpfen selbst sein Traum.

Our first impression of Rustan is that of an adolescent boy (216 ff.). He has had a quarrel with Osmin, the son of the Emir, and now is afraid to face his uncle. Rustan has been hiding like a school boy, and causes Mirza and her father considerable worry. To Zanga, who rails at him, Rustan explains that he is not afraid of his uncle but that he regrets that they do not seem to understand one another. The reason for this misunderstanding, as Zanga explains, is Massud's philosophy of life:

> Bleibt im Land und nàhrt euch redlich!

while Rustan's ambition goes beyond being a farmer although he is evidently made to be just that. Rustan is filled with envy and wrath toward Osmin, a man higher in station who is employed at the court and who had mockingly told Rustan:

> Guter Freund, bleibt fein zu Hause,
> Hinterm Pfluge zeigt die Kraft!

Rustan believes:

> Bin ich nichts, ich kann noch werden,
> Rasch und hoch ist Helden-Brauch;
> Was ein Andrer kann auf Erden,
> Ei, bei Gott! das kann ich auch.

However, when it comes to making decisions, his soft heart (344) is in his way. It takes Zanga's constant goading to determine Rustan to ask to leave his uncle's home. "Was man weiss, befriedigt nur" (559), says Rustan brushing aside all of Massud's warnings. However, the young man is persuaded to delay his departure till morning.

The text of the tune played by the dervish in front of the window and

repeated by Rustan before he falls asleep, represents the only direct relation to Calderon's play:

> Schatten sind des Lebens Güter,
> Schatten seiner Freuden Schar,
> Schatten, Worte, Wunsche, Taten;
> Die Gedanken nur sind wahr.
>
> Und die Liebe, die du fühlest,
> Und das Gute, das du tust,
> Und kein Wachen als im Schlafe,
> Wenn du einst im Grabe ruhst.

The dream-Rustan is elated over his newly won freedom. However, his
rapture is not to last long. Life with its grim realities, its demands for
quick decisions does not linger. Only after Zanga's encouragement does
Rustan throw his spear at the snake which is pursuing the King of Samarkand and . . . misses. The mysterious stranger saves the king, and the
spectator is made to feel that Rustan is not cut out to be a hero. "Wirst du,
Glück, mir nimmer hold?" (789) he complains.—It is Zanga, Rustan's
Mephistopheles, who tells the king that his life was saved by Rustan. The
latter shows his moral scruples by his whole attitude; however, his ambition
is stronger.

The first step on the wrong path has been taken; and Rustan's subsequent actions seem to bear out Schiller's: "Das eben ist der Fluch der
bosen Tat, dass sie fortzeugend Boses muss gebaren." —All scruples vanish
when Rustan sees Gulnare who seems to resemble Mirza, and yet is so
different. Having been placed at the head of the army, Rustan is eager
to hide his humble origin:

> Nichts lass unsern Stand verraten,
> Wir sind Kinder unsrer Taten,
> Und nach aufwärts strebt der Fuss.

Misfortune seems to pursue Rustan when the man of the rock appears
again who, moreover, resembles his greatest enemy, Osmin. Rustan tries
to bribe the man, then he threatens him, and when that does not avail,
begs on his knees for mercy. But the inexorable one replies:

> Willst mit Andrer Taten prahlen,
> Willst mit fremdem Golde zahlen?
> Glück und Unrecht? Luftger Wahn!
> Ruhm dich des, was *du* getan!

For a moment Rustan wavers, wishing to return home; but since he cannot
bear the thought of it, he rushes after the man and struggles with him on
a bridge. However, the other proves stronger and Rustan is pushed to the
edge of the bridge. At this point it is his evil spirit, Zanga, who urges him
to use his dagger. Thus Rustan becomes a murderer:

> O, wär ich nie geboren!

But there is little time for reflection or despair; the king needs his new general and sends for him.

> Nun gilts fallen, oder siegen!
> Ausgedauert und—geschwiegen!

says Rustan at the end of the second act.

He has been victorious—at the beginning of the third act—and his Mephistophelian servant characterizes Rustan's development:

> Da kommt Rustan mit dem König,
> Tut schon vornehm, blickt schon stolz.
> Ei, umguldets nur ein wenig,
> Dünkt sich Edelstein das Holz.

However, the crime is discovered when the body of the murdered man is washed ashore and in his breast is found the jewelled dagger which the king had given to Rustan. The dream hero is again in the depth of despair and wishes he had never left home. He thinks of flight for a moment but finally decides to stay. Zanga comes with an old woman who "sent herself" (1538). She is the thought of murder personified. She leaves a cup containing a potion which she praises very highly:

> Was dir kommt, das musst du tragen,
> Eine Leiche, auf dem Thron.
> Bist nun deines Schicksals Meister,
> Sprichst ein Wort im Rat der Geister,
> Trägst dein eigen Los davon.

The king is convinced of Rustan's guilt and—in the kindness of his heart—wishes to give him an opportunity to escape. The ruler reaches for the cup the old woman had brought. Rustan tries to stop him by means of a subterfuge which the king recognizes at once as a lie. Nevertheless, he gives Rustan another chance to confess and to repent. Rustan allows the king to drink; he has taken another step on the path of crime. He experiences a number of terrifying visions, first of Massud and Mirza, and then of the murdered man. The old woman reappears with the king's own cup which Rustan tries in vain to hide. When the dying ruler shouts for help and vengeance, Rustan is again near despair. Since flight is impossible. he orders Zanga to stab him in the back in case the king's men should attempt to arrest him. However, Rustan is saved in the last minute through the intervention of Gülnare. She believes that the king has been murdered by the mute Kaleb who had come to demand requital for the crime of which his son had been the victim. The king's last word had been "Rustan." Misinterpreting it, Gülnare begs Rustan to be the ruler and to protect her. Thus, through another murder, Rustan gains the woman he desires. Unlike Libussa, Gulnare keeps the crown, however. While Rustan presses his forehead on the ground in wild despair and the people hail Gülnare as their ruler first and then Rustan, the curtain falls on the third act.

What a contrast between the day-dreaming Rustan of the first act who had been revelling:
> Starker, nimm dich an der Schwachen!
> Kühner, wage! Wagen siegt!

and the tyrant of the fourth act who says to some of his victims:

> O, ich kenne euer Treiben!
> In dem Innern eurer Häuser
> Lauern meine wachen Späher,
> Was ihr noch so leis gesprochen,
> Reicht von fern bis an mein Ohr.
> Fort mit ihnen, ohne Zaudern!

He has kept the mute Kaleb in prison without giving him a trial although he knows that the man is innocent. Kaleb's friends and relatives, however, have not been inactive but are organizing a revolt. Even Gülnare demands a trial for Kaleb. Zanga has not been able to execute Rustan's order to kill the mute witness. Despite the cruel attempts to prevent his writing down what he knows, the truth is learned by all: Kaleb, who has never spoken before, names Rustan as the murderer. The accused dream-ruler gains consciousness for a moment and hears the clock in Massud's hut strike three. But Rustan's nightmare is not over as yet and the harrowing end is still to come. Gülnare turns against him and he is deserted by most of his followers. Rustan challenges any one to fight with him in single combat; but he shrinks back when Gulnare presents herself. He has to retreat fighting until he finds himself near the fatal bridge again, defeated, surrounded by his enemies, and wounded. Zanga had intended to set the town on fire which would have saved them, but Rustan had not allowed it. He must hear the bitter truth about himself from his servant.

> Nicht weils Frevel, weils gefährlich,
> Machts der frommen Seele bang.
> Und mit also schwankem Gang,
> Mit so armlich halbem Mute
> Wolltest du der Herrschaft Sprossen,
> Du den steilen Weg zum Grossen,
> Du erklimmen Macht und Rang?
> . . . .
> Doch du konntest nicht ertragen,
> Eng der Sinn, das Aug nur weit,
> Willst du siegen, musst du wagen;
> Kehre denn zur Niedrigkeit!

Rustan quarrels with Zanga only to find himself disarmed by the wary adventurer and at the latter's mercy. The enemies approach and surround Rustan who throws himself into the river after Zanga's urging:

> Stürz hinab dich in die Fluten,
> Stirb als Krieger, fall als Held!

Massud's nephew wakes up; the dream has been so vivid that he wishes to murder the real Zanga when he appears at his bedside. He takes Massud and Mirza for the king and Gülnare, but gradually becomes aware of his error. Deep contrition takes hold of his entire being:

> Hasse euch nicht! Hasse niemand!
> Mochte aller Welt vergeben,
> Und mit Tränen, so wie ehmals
> In der Unschuld frommen Tagen,
> Fühl ich neu mein Aug sich tragen.

His gratitute for the warning dream is boundless. The new insight he has gained is generally considered the theme of this, dramatic fairytale:

Breit es aus mit deinen Strahlen,
Senk es tief in jede Brust:
Eines nur ist Glück hienieden,
Eins, des Innern stiller Frieden,
Und die schuldbefreite Brust.
Und die Grösse ist gefährlich,
Und der Ruhm ein leeres Spiel;
Was er gibt sind nichtge Schatten,
Was er nimmt, es ist so viel.

He has three requests to make of Massud; first he begs his pardon, second he asks him to set the slave Zanga free, and third he desires Mirza's hand in marriage.

In Rustan Grillparzer portrays a youth with a kind, feeling heart who is consumed by a boundless ambition for adventure, fame, and splendor. Rustan is too young and inexperienced to know himself and his capacities. He is saved much suffering and many disappointments by a dream which makes him see his limitations: lack of initiative, of courage, and of persistence. Without these traits of character fame and power can only be attained by crime which will breed more crime at the expense of peace of the soul. Rustan is made to realize that peace of the soul is the greatest thing on earth, and that it can be found only in the sphere of activity for which one is suited. Rustan's life work will be farming, and he will be happy at the side of a devoted wife. In this connection Joachim Müller[3] says: "Der Mensch gibt die Tat auf." This critic then quotes the two lines:

Und die Grösse ist gefährlich,
Und der Ruhm ein leeres Spiel.

However, if a person gives up all desire for greatness and fame, it does not mean that he ceases all action. It has been shown that it was not Grillparzer's intention to show the futility of all activity, but that he believes man should restrict his endeavors to that field for which nature has equipped him. Generalizing on the basis of Rustan's character, Joachim Müller[4] states: "Der Grillparzersche Mensch hat zur Verwirklichung seiner nach Welt verlangenden Kräfte nicht genügend Substanz." Grillparzer has created another farmer: Primislaus in *Libussa*. As will be shown later, Primislaus is a born ruler, though a farmer, and he certainly has enough "substance" to attain what he desires.

Rustan has much in common with Jaromir. Emil Reich[5] compares the two as follows: "Jaromir und Rustan sind Vertreter der Ich-Sucht, wie Jason, Ottokar, Otto von Meran, beide jedoch keine konsequenten Selbstsüchtigen, sondern Frevler ebenso sehr durch den Gang der Umstände als durch eigene Schuld."

Zanga, Negro Slave

For Zanga, the colored slave of Rustan, the quiet life of a farmer is unbearable. He is a soldier of fortune who knows the world and sees in

young imaginative Rustan his opportunity of escaping his present surroundings. The slave excites his master's imagination:

> Zanga kam. Sein Hauch, verstohlen,
> Blies die Asche von den Kohlen
> Und entflammte hoch die Glut.

Mirza speaks thus about Zanga whose eloquence is evident in the description of his first battle (344ff.).

> Klar ward's, dass im Tun und Handeln,
> Nicht im Grubeln 's Leben liegt.
> . . . .
> Herr, das heisst leben! Es lebe der Krieg!

he says. Naturally, his views are diametrically opposed to those of Massud
of whom he says mockingly to Rustan:

> Nun, so lernt denn seine Sprache,
> Er wird eure nimmer lernen!
> Und wer weiss? An Lektionen
> Lassts der alte Herr nicht fehlen.
> Bleibt im Land und nahrt euch redlich!
> Auch die Ruhe hat ihr Schones.

Zanga sees in Mirza another opponent, as can be seen from his views on
the effect of love on the two sexes:

> Deut mir eins der Liebe Werke,
> Ob Verlust sie, ob Gewinn?
> Gibt dem Weibe Männerstärke
> Und dem Manne—Weibersinn!

The Zanga of the dream is not exactly the same as the real Zanga; yet
what we learn about the slave in the first act makes us realize that he
would, indeed, be capable of the actions he performs in the dream. Zanga's
role in Rustan's dream life was repeatedly referred to. The slave shows
himself not only equipped with common sense, but also with a capacity to
make use of his opportunities at the right moment. A contempt for Rustan
gradually develops in the servant whose knowledge of human nature is
remarkable:

> Herr, um selig einst zu sterben,
> Denkt bei Allem mir ans Ende;
> Doch wollt ihr, ein Tüchtger, leben,
> So erwägt und prüft den Anfang,
> Denn das Ende kommt von selber.

When he is accused by Rustan of having led him astray (1432 ff.), Zanga
tells his master that if he followed an honorable course he would, at best,
become a captain some day and have his bones shot to pieces, but:

> Ich stellt euch mit Einem Ruck,
> Seis im Guten, seis im Schlimmen,
> Auf des Berges höchsten Hang,
> Dessen Mitte zu erklimmen
> Ihr gebraucht ein Leben lang.

In the fourth act, as was mentioned above, Zanga has failed to kill the bothersome witness Kaleb; when he is reproached by Rustan, Zanga says:

> Herr, gar alt
> Ist der Spruch: vor Recht Gewalt,

i.e., it was too late, he could not get near the prisoner while he was alone. However, this fiend, in the eyes of all the bystanders, cuts off the hand of Kaleb as he is writing down his accusation of Rustan, only to find himself forsaken by his master (2230 ff.). But, as we should expect, Zanga shows himself quite equal to this naive act of Rustan which was prompted by the latter's fear: "Stumm der Alte, doch nicht ich!" (2240) Thus fear again causes Rustan to say:

> Bleib bei mir, ich will dich schützen,
> Ewig sei der Treue Band!

Circumstances had made a servant of Zanga, though not intended by nature to be one, least of all Rustan's servant. To Zanga's speech of contempt, quoted above, Rustan replies:

> Das zu hören von dem Diener,
> Von der Frevel Stifter, Helfer!

only to call forth Zanga scorn:

> Helfer? Stifter? Das vielleicht!
> Aber Diener? Lass mich lachen!
> Wessen Diener? wo der Herr?
> Bist du nicht herabgestiegen,
> Nicht gefallen von der Hohe,
> Die mein Finger dir gewiesen,
> Weil dem mächtgen Willens-Riesen
> Fehlte Mut zur kühnen Tat?
> Gleich umfangt uns Schuld und Strafe,
> Gleich an Anspruch, Rang und Macht;
> Und wie gleich im Mutterschosse,
> Schaut als Gleiche uns die Nacht.

However great a villain this adventurer may be, we are forced to admire the unflinching courage with which he faces the consequences of his acts. —And Zanga is prepared for emergencies; he holds his drawn sword under his cloak and is thus enabled to intercept Rustan's blow and to disarm him by knocking the sword out of his hand.

The spectator is reminded that all is a dream when Rustan notices snakes in Zanga's hair and black wings on his back (2514-2517). Grillparzer wants to make manifest that Zanga represents the evil side in Rustan's own nature to which he—much to his regret—has yielded too much.—

—As a result of Rustan's dream, Zanga is given his freedom. He plays a flute, accompanying the old dervish playing the tune that describes life's goods and joys as shadows while thoughts appear as the only reality. Does Grillparzer mean that also Zanga has been converted to this view? Or is he merely trying to show Zanga's joy over his regained freedom?

Zanga is a soldier of fortunate whom the author presents in a situation into which any soldier of fortune is apt to get. Determined to regain his freedom, Zanga, equipped with intelligence, initiative, courage, and common sense, succeeds in persuading his young master to leave the secluded life in the valley. —The dream-Zanga leads Rustan on a dishonorable path to fame and power. It is only through the servant's initiative and courage that his master reaches the doubtful height. Both of them are unable to maintain themselves there because they have violated every law of justice and ethics. —In a sense Zanga might be called Rustan's Mephistopheles, for he represents and reflects the dark side in Rustan's own character.

Massud

The list of the *dramatis personae* gives Massud as a "rich farmer." His outlook on life is conservative as might be expected of a man in his circumstances and of his age. He is as fond of Rustan as he is of his own daughter Mirza. If the old farmer lectures his restless nephew, he does so because he knows him and also knows the world which attracts the ambitious youth:

> Rauh und dornicht ist der Pfad.
> . . . .
> Und das Ziel, es ist verderblich.

Massud is doubly concerned, for his daughter is in love with Rustan. As no pleading avails, Massud brings himself to tell Rustan of Mirza's love for him. When Rustan still insists on leaving and Mirza in her deep love which knows no pride joins in her father's pleading, the old man exclaims in indignation:

> Halt, So meint ichs nicht!
> Kann er deiner, Kind, entraten,
> Massuds Tochter bettelt nicht.
> Zieh denn hin, Verblendeter,
> Ziehe hin! und mögest du
> Nie der jetzgen Stunde fluchen.

He realizes that:

> Jedem Sprecher fehlt die Sprache,
> Fehlt dem Hörenden das Ohr.

However, Massud is glad that Rustan is willing to spend another night with his relatives.

Massud shows devoutness when he expresses his belief that the dream was the warning of an unknown power. He is glad to grant Rustan's wishes since they are also his.

Massud is an old farmer whose main concern in life is the happiness of his daughter. In this respect he resembles Count Borotin in *Die Ahnfrau*, the drama which was written only a year before *Der Traum ein Leben* was begun. —Massud is conservative in his outlook on life. He has a normal amount of pride and a deep respect for all which is beyond the knowledge of humans.

In *Der Traum ein Leben*, which might be called a "symbolical fairy story," the question of manliness itself is dramatically treated as part of the main theme which deals with a common-sense truth in regard to fame, greatness, and overweening ambition. Rustan lacks, in addition to a number of other characteristics, the manliness needed to realize his boundless ambition. The world is full of Rustans who, in contrast to Grillparzer's creation, come to grief or lead unhappy lives because they do not realize their limitations or realize them too late. Zanga, the dare-devil adventurer with many traits usually considered manly, served the dramatist as a foil to his protagonist. Massud, the kind old farmer, displays a number of manly characteristics. Although Zanga and Massud play subordinate roles, Grillparzer has demonstrated once again that he is capable of creating "manly men."

CHAPTER EIGHT

WEH DEM, DER LÜGT!

That Grillparzer was capable of writing a good comedy is shown in *Weh dem, der lügt!*[1] Although he did not begin to write it until 1836—after his trip to London and Paris—, he had been acquainted with the theme since 1818. The topic is taken from the history of the time of the Merowingians as reported by Gregory of Tours in his *Historia Francorum*. Grillparzer completed his "comedy in five acts" on May 30, 1837. The first stage production took place on March 6, 1838. For several reasons did it prove to be a complete failure as far as the appreciation of the public was concerned: the aristocrats objected to the union of a cook and a countess and to the weak and egotistical character of the comic young nobleman Atalus; the Puritans to the scene in the barn in which Edrita and Atalus are seen sleeping side by side; a number of the actors were not equal to the roles assigned to them; and, last but not least, the members of the contemporary literary movement, of "Das junge Deutschland," who clamored for "Tendenzdramen," ridiculed the romantic comedy. *Weh dem, der lügt!* is, indeed, a "Tendenzdrama;" however, not with a political, but with an ethical trend, *i.e.*, it deals with the inner moral development of a man rather than with social problems.

Only in our days has *Weh dem, der lügt!* been fully appreciated and acclaimed one of the few great German comedies. Grillparzer leads us into the fabulous quaint world which we know from Shakespeare's and Lope de Vega's comedies, and places it into the service of a great ethical idea: inner veracity stands higher than literal truth. Attempting to explain why the stage production fell through, Scherer[2] states (in 1874) that the main question in *Weh dem, der lügt!* is whether or not the escape will be successful. He goes on to say that the flight alone was not sufficient to arouse dramatic suspense. Scherer's discussion of the play shows that he did not see the fine psychological motivation of Grillparzer, who shows once again how far in advance of his time he was.[3]

All the characters are splendidly individualized and reveal the dramatist's careful work and artistic skill. The spectator learns to know them not only through their speech and their views, but also through their actions; they are consistent throughout. We shall consider Leon, Gregor, Atalus, Kattwald, and Galomir.

Leon

It seems that we would not quite do Leon justice if we should simply say that he is a "cook by profession."[4] It is true, he happened to be a cook. He had seen the Bishop Gregor of Châlons in the street and—struck by the "noble and sublime" in his appearance—had decided to seek employment in his household, be it even as a stablehand. He had been taken in as a kitchen boy and, after the cook had been discharged, had himself been entrusted with these most important duties in the household of the bishop.

Leon's ideal was marred somewhat when he learned of Gregor's extreme avarice. Like many of Grillparzer's servant characters Leon is extremely outspoken and does not hesitate to call the bishop to account for this defect in his character. The very first scene with Sigrid, Gregor's majordomo, exhibits Leon as a bold, playful, wanton, humorous boy who is quick at repartee. As it were in jest he threatens Sigrid with a kitchen knife should he persist in refusing to allow him to see the bishop.

Gregor, the stern lover of truth, detects the young scallawag in a lie when he asserts that the roast he was ordered to sell again because it seemed too expensive to the bishop had returned to his kitchen as a gift from pious people. He doesn't believe in lying, Leon says, but he despises avarice. Then he learns the reason for Gregor's frugal way of living. At once the devoted Franconian is ready to come to his master's aid by freeing Atalus: "War ich nur dort, ich log ihn schon heraus," he says only to hear Gregor's "Weh dem, der lügt!" (329). Leon is very disappointed at the idea of having to outwit the heathen without telling a lie. Gregor, however, remains stern; God will help, he believes. Convinced that he saw lightning at this very moment, Leon believes in a divine call. He is admonished by Gregor to do what seems right to him, but to remain loyal to himself and to God.

The problem for Grillparzer was to show how Leon could be led from his superficial belief in literal truth to the higher truth, to a sincere inner veracity, and how he could with this handicap carry out his daring plan which seemed to call for deception as well as adroitness.

The second act opens with Leon's arrival at the house of Kattwald, Count of the Rhine district. The pilgrim who had served as his guide reminds Leon of the reward promised him; and Leon conceives the ingenious idea of having himself sold to Kattwald by the pilgrim. The bishop's cook plans to kill two birds with one stone: to get into the household of the man who holds Atalus prisoner and, by the same transaction, to pay his guide. "Weh dem, der lügt! So mindstens wills der Herr. (Achselzuckend) Man wird ja sehn," (425-426) he says. When Kattwald appears, Leon shows his rather unique salesmanship, whose object is his own person, while at the same time he expresses frank scorn of Kattwald's dwelling:

> Ein schmucker Bursch aus fränkischem Geblüt,
> Am Hof erzogen, von den feinsten Sitten,
> Und den in ein Barbarennest verkauft,
> Halb Stall, halb Gottes freier Himmel. Pah!

Leon has told his first lie. It is the pilgrim, however, who says: "Er ist ein Koch, berühmt in seinem Fach" (481) of the kitchen hand of two months' standing, who—as ready-witted as ever—manages to sell himself for thirty pounds by making the gourmand's mouth water.

Leon wishes to be considered an equal by his new master and gains his end through his humor and wittiness. However, he is far from being veracious:

> Ihr fallt schon wieder
> In euern alten Ton. He, Knechte, ho!
> Kommt her und bindet mich! Bringt Stricke, Pflöcke!
> Sonst geh ich fort, fast eh ich da gewesen.
> He, holla, ho!

Then he takes over his new duties while giving orders and railing at the poor equipment; the kitchen appears a mere doghouse to him. In the first meeting with Kattwald's daughter Edrita, the spectator is reminded of Till Eulenspiegel. At first Leon pretends not to see her. When she asks him what he is doing—he is cutting meat—he says: "Ihr seht, ich spalte Holz." (638) However, the two become friends very quickly. Through Edrita Leon meets the obstinate Atalus whom he manages to obtain as a helper in his kitchen despite the young nobleman's empty pride.

In the third act Leon is made to realize that he must act at once since Atalus is to be taken to the interior of the country after Edrita's wedding on the next day. The deft Franconian has peppered the food excessively and thereby caused Kattwald and his guests to indulge in too much wine. The general intoxication offers Leon his chance:

> Auch ist Gelegenheit ein launisch buhlend Weib,
> Die nicht zum zweitenmale wiederkehrt,
> Fand sie beim erstenmal die Tür verschlossen.

Kattwald has gone to sleep; Leon steals into the count's room in order to take the key of the gate which hangs over the count's bed. If Kattwald should wake up, Leon says to himself, he can lie himself out of it; then he thinks of the bishop's demand and calls it foolish, silly and ridiculous. When the count actually does wake up, Leon throws the key on the floor. He answers Kattwald's angry questions truthfully: he took the key but he no longer has it. However, he looks for it at the opposite side of the room. Meanwhile Edrita has exchanged the key on the floor with another one.

The failure to obtain the key serves to show Leon his over-confidence in his ability. Atalus has done his share, i.e., he has undermined a pillar of the bridge, while Leon has failed in what he ventured to do. Much to his surprise he finds the gate open and concludes that an angel must have helped him. It is Edrita who has unlocked the gate for him. From now on Leon finds an advocate of veracity in this lively, unspoiled child of nature.

> Du irrst, kein Engel hilft, da wo der Mensch
> Mit Trug und Falsch an seine Werke geht.

When he says that he has never tried to hide the fact that he wishes to escape, she points out to him that one can tell the truth and still be false, for she feels in her heart that he has deceived her. Leon is impressed by the veracity and the unselfishness of the girl who divulges the password to him after he refuses to yield to her plea that he stay and let Atalus escape alone.

Leon seems to be converted to the bishop's view on truth, for—in the fourth act—he refuses to take Edrita who has helped again by doing what he and Atalus had failed to do: she has locked the gate from the outside.

> Ich habe meinem frommen Herrn versprochen:
> Nichts Unerlaubtes, Greulichs soll geschehn
> Bei diesem Schritt, den nur die Not entschuldigt.
> Hab ich den Sklaven seinem Herrn entführt,
> Will ich dem Vater nicht die Tochter rauben,
> Und mehren so den Fluch auf unserm Haupt.

But he cannot prevent Edrita's flight from her father when Atalus is ready to take her.

With Edrita's help the three safely reach the river where Kattwald's daughter tells the ferryman that Leon and Atalus are her father's servants. This time Leon tells the truth although there is no need of it. They are saved because it happens that the ferryman has turned against Kattwald. Leon is no longer the man who takes the truth very lightly when he says to Edrita: "Siehst du, man ist nicht klug, wenn man nur klügelt." \(1542)

In the fifth act Leon comes to believe that God will help him who is honestly veracious. While Atalus and Edrita are still asleep in the barn near the gates of Metz, and Kattwald's men appear again in order to capture the trio, Leon prays ardently for a miracle to happen. The city gates open; Metz had been taken from the heathens the day before. Atalus sinks into the arms of his uncle.

Asked concerning the methods he employed in bringing about the escape, the loyal servant, conscious of his guilt, says:

> Nun, gar so rein gings freilich denn nicht ab.
> Wir haben uns gehütet wie wir konnten.

Jealousy, however, leads him to another insincerity which the bishop discovers at once. Leon asks for leave, giving as his reason that he wishes to join the army. But he is made to tell the truth: he does not wish to see Edrita married to someone else. Thereupon he learns that Kattwald's daughter has always cared for him although during their escape she seemed to prefer Atalus:

> Ei, gehen musst ich,
> Du aber stiessest grausam mich zuruck.
> . . . .
> Du aber stahlst mein Inneres und hasts.

Leon is fundamentally generous, for he lends his services so unselfishly to a man who impresses him by his noble appearance. However, Leon is not "naive"[5]. Joachim Müller contradicts himself when he says: "Denn seine aufgeweckte und köstlich frische Klugheit hat langst erkannt, dass die Welt betrogen sein will,"[6] a statement which is in itself an unwarranted generalization. A man who has arrived at such a conviction is far from being naive. Leon is an amiable, clever, ingenious, ready-witted wag who is able to cope with the world. In the beginning he takes the bishop's demand very lightly and tries rather to dodge it than to fulfill it honestly. However, Gregor's maxim—which, incidentally, is Kantian, pure and simple—controls Leon more and more, especially after his self-confidence and presumption have been shaken by his own failure, by Edrita's unselfish assistance, and by the conviction that God, after all, has a hand in human fate.

The figure of Leon is unique in dramatic literature despite its possible Spanish models. In one or the other of his traits he reminds of some of Grillparzer's previous creations. Like Jason, Leon is helped by a woman who loves him; however, Leon's quest is free from selfish motives and purer than that of the "Argonauten." Leon reminds of Zawisch—in the first half of the play at least—in the ease with which he seems to deal, in fact almost to toy, with every one with whom he comes in contact. In his unselfishness and in his moral strength, shown in his self-control, Leon resembles Bancbanus. —Like Rustan, Leon is poor and fond of adventures and travel.

Gregor

When asked by the king whether he could do something for him, Gregor had proudly answered in the negative, adding that the king might bestow gifts on his flatterers who were robbing the country. Yet he ought to have asked for the liberation of his nephew who is still held as a hostage by the heathens. Gregor later regrets this false pride (160). His maxim is stated in the very first line the spectator hears him say—part of a sermon he is writing: "Dein Wort soll aber sein: Ja, ja; nein, nein." (117)

Accused by his kitchen boy of hoarding his money and even kissing it, Gregor explains that he is economizing in order to pay the ransom of a hundred pounds which will free Atalus. The bishop cannot take anything from the huge church funds he handles, but—and the dramatist makes us see Gregor's scrupulous, self-tormenting endeavor to be honest—he can save from that which he uses for his own needs, perhaps, perhaps not; so, at least, he has dared to interpret his own practice.

Kant's categorical imperative is evident in the bishop's statement that he would rather see Atalus die or die himself than see his nephew saved through lying.

Although he never gives up this principle which seems perfect in the theory of a churchman, Gregor has come to realize—in the fifth act after Atalus' return—that it is difficult to maintain the maxim of absolute truthfulness in a chaotic world:

> Wer deutet mir die buntverworrne Welt!
> Sie reden alle Wahrheit, sind drauf stolz
> Und sie belügt sich selbst und ihn, Er mich
> Und wieder sie; Der lügt weil man ihm log—
> Und reden Alle Wahrheit, Alle. Alle.
> Das Unkraut, merk ich, rottet man nicht aus,
> Glück auf, wächst nur der Weizen etwa drüber.
>
> . . . .
> Ich weiss ein Land das aller Wahrheit Thron;
> Wo selbst die Lüge nur ein buntes Kleid,
> Das schaffend Er genannt: Vergänglichkeit,
> Und das er umhing dem Geschlecht der Sunden,
> Dass ihre Augen nicht am Strahl erblinden.

Gregor is a sincere, scrupulously honest churchman who realizes that he himself is not above human failings. He is an idealist and believes in the uncompromising application of the categorical imperative. In the course of the drama, however, he learns that the earth is full of error and deception and that absolute truth is found only in heaven. Thus the stern demands of the first act are modified: one cannot condemn lying at all times and under all circumstances.

Atalus

While Leon is consciously comical, Atalus represents unintentional comicality. He serves constantly as a butt for jokes on the part of other characters. As Kattwald's prisoner the young nobleman has to herd horses. He rails at the crude farmers as well as at his own uncle whom he accuses of having forgotten him and of refusing to help him. Atalus complains about the coarse shirt which irritates his skin and about the food. He is distrustful of every one; and when he is approached by Leon, Atalus does not believe him and, from false pride, refuses to serve as a kitchen hand until he is forced to do so by Kattwald.

When Atalus complains about Leon's impudence, the heathen count replies:

> Zu frech? Und du zu albern, leerer Bursch!
> Wer etwas kann, dem sieht man etwa nach,
> Das Ungeschick an sich ist schon ein Ungemach.

Atalus, although very shy in her presence, believes Edrita loves him and tells her he might deign to marry her some day provided that her rank is sufficient to obtain the king's sanction for their union.

In the third act Atalus shows himself stubborn, malicious, and contrary when he is to take part in the preparations for the escape. However, Leon finally manages to wheedle the conceited young nobleman into undermining the pillar of the bridge.

Atalus' refusal to fight for Leon displays his extreme selfishness; he will look out only for himself, the ungrateful egotist tells Edrita. During the escape Atalus is a handicap rather than a help. He shows himself mean and ungrateful to Leon ("Du bist mir widrig," 1250), who has done so much for him.

After their safe return Bishop Gregor says to his nephew: "Du bist nicht, wie du sollst" (1711). However, Atalus does acknowledge Leon's services. Learning that Edrita loves Leon, Atalus says:

> Ich denke, Herr, das Mädchen dem zu gönnen,
> Der mich gerettet, ach, und den sie liebt.

He then enters the profession for which he had been chosen, the church.

Atalus is a degenerated, empty-headed nobleman. Pride, narrowness, distrust of every one, extreme selfishness, and hate of all physical work are his main characteristics. He is shy in the presence of women and yet certain that he has made an impression. Thus he finds himself laughed at and teased. However, like Leon, he develops in the course of the play. He recognizes that Leon has done him a great service. He overcomes his pride and conceit when he resigns his love for Edrita and no longer begrudges Leon his happiness.

Kattwald

Another comical figure is Kattwald, Count of the Rhine district, a representative of the heathen barbarians. Of huge stature and capable of great violence, the count has a sense of humor. His weakness is his

palate; and through this weakness Leon succeeds in outwitting him. After
the scene with the key in his bedroom, Kattwald says about Leon:

> Im Grunde kann man dem Burschen gram nicht sein.
> Er sagt grad alles 'raus und ist gar lustig.
> Wàr ich an seiner Statt, ich machts nicht anders.

Kattwald's rage is enormous when he finds himself outwitted by Leon
and Edrita:

> Schiesst immer, schiesst! Und, tràft ihr auch mein Kind,
> Weit lieber tot—verwundet wollt ich sagen—
> Als dass entkommen sie; mein Kind mit ihnen.

Kattwald has much in common with Aietes, who lacks, of course, the
count's sense of humor, which is shown in the second act where he permits
Leon to use his bold and humorous tone. The scene at the bank of the
river—Kattwald wishes to throw himself into the stream in order to die
if he cannot reach the fugitives—calls to mind the final scene of "Die
Argonauten" in which Aietes is left behind in despair while Jason and
Medea sail away.

Galomir

Galomir, another unintentionally comical figure, is the man whom
Edrita is expected to marry because he is her nearest relative and to whom
the bright young girl always refers as the "dumme Galomir." Galomir
hardly speaks, simply because he does not think.

Galomir is the first to step on the undermined bridge which collapses
under his weight, throwing him into the moat, much to the joy of Edrita.
Later during the pursuit he happens to get nearest the fugitives, but is
outwitted and disarmed by Edrita and tied to a tree by Leon. Through
Edrita's cleverness he is made to indicate the wrong direction to the
pursuers.

In the fateful first performance of *Weh dem, der lugt!* the actor (Lucas)
portrayed Galomir as an idiot. To this circumstance we owe Grillparzer's
statement which leaves us no doubt as to Galomir's nature: "Galomir ist
so wenig dumm, als die Tiere dumm sind; sie denken nur nicht. Galomir
kann darum nicht sprechen, weil er auch nicht denkt; das würde ihn aber
nicht hindern, z. B. in der Schlacht den rechten Angriffspunkt instinkt-
massig recht gut herauszufinden. Er ist tierisch, aber nicht blödsinnig."[7]
Galomir is Grillparzer's Caliban.

Both Leon and Bishop Gregor, as far apart as they may be in age,
background, and philosophy of life, were shown to be men. We see them
develop in the course of the plot, each influenced by the other in his outlook
on life. The bishop, like the Highpriest of *Des Meeres und der Liebe
Wellen,* a churchman with stern principles, is more human and ready to
learn from life's lessons than his dramatic predecessor. Kattwald, an
erratic man of enormous physical strength, loses on account of his one
weakness, his gluttony. His sense of humor earns him some sympathy
from the spectator. Atalus is a degenerate weakling; Galomir, a physically
strong creature who can't think.

CHAPTER NINE

LIBUSSA

Friedrich Hebbel's idea of the drama was that it should be at once historical, social, and philosophic, that it should be universal, and, though picturing the past, represent the problems and struggles of the day. At the same time it should illuminate the inner nature of the times. Hebbel further demanded that dialectics should be placed into the idea itself. It is evident that the customary idea of guilt and punishment in the drama (Schiller) was put aside. Grillparzer's *Libussa* is a drama much more in Hebbel's sense than the latter's own dramas! *Libussa*—like many of Hebbel's dramas—depicts the turning point from one epoch to another: the change of the early Bohemia from an agricultural to an industrial state is here symbolized by the foundation of the city of Prague. Grillparzer used the traditional Libussa legend to symbolize many of his highest problems in the development of man that had occupied his thoughts during his mature years: the contrast between the peaceful unity with nature and industrious activity in a progressive civilization, the struggle between the two sexes, the contrast between the emotions and the intellect, between poetry and prose, between the divine and the human, between vocation and avocation. Grillparzer does not take sides; he stands above the problems for which he finds the most beautiful dramatic expression. With its abundance of verse and profound pronouncements *Libussa* constantly reminds the reader of Goethe's *Faust*.

Grillparzer's interest in the Libussa legend began with the year 1819 when his source studies for *Ottokar* acquainted him with the early history of Bohemia. It is known that he worked on *Libussa* late in 1831; but most of the work on this drama was done between 1837 and 1849. The first act was produced at the *Burgtheater* on November 23, 1841. However, the completed drama was not taken from the author's desk until after his death in 1872. It was first produced on January 1, 1874.[1]

The cast of characters include the three sisters Kascha, Tetka, and Libussa; Primislaus; the three "wladyky" or noblemen Domaslav, Lapak, and Biwoy; and the servants of the princesses: Wlasta, Dobromila, Swartha, Slawa, and Dobra. This study includes Primislaus, Domaslav, Lapak, and Biwoy.

Primislaus

The marriage of Queen Victoria and Prince Albert in 1840 had aroused Grillparzer's interest in the inner relationship between two such persons and the difficulties that might arise. What sort of a man could take the position of a prince-consort without compromising his dignity and his pride? the dramatist asked himself. He answered his question most satisfactorily in the character of his Primislaus.

Although his ancestors had been wealthy and high in rank, Primislaus (Przemysl—the thoughtful one) of Grillparzer's play earns his bread by farming; but even should he be one of the noblemen, he would not come to

ask for Libussa's hand in marriage, for he has very decided ideas about
the husband-wife relationship in general and among rulers in particular:

> Der Furst verklart die Gattin die er wählt,
> Die Konigin erniedrigt den als Mann,
> Den wählend sie als Untertan erhoht,
> Denn es sei nicht der Mann des *Weibes* Mann,
> Das Weib des *Mannes* Weib, so stehts zu Recht.
> Drum wie die Frau ist aller Wesen Krone,
> Also der Mann das Haupt, das sich die Krone aufsetzt,
> Und selbst der Knecht ist Herr in seinem Haus.

All his actions up to the beginning of the third act had been determined
by this proud attitude, and, as will be seen, also his subsequent actions are
determined by it. Yet he is pining for the woman Libussa. He goes on,
railing at himself:

> So sprichst du, prahlst, und trägst im Busen doch
> Was dich an jene Hoffnung jetzt noch kettet.

Is he toying with the thought of compromise?

> Man sage nicht das Schwerste sei die Tat,
> Da hilft der Mut, der Augenblick, die Regung;
> Das Schwerste dieser Welt ist der Entschluss.

After having been summoned to appear before Libussa, Primislaus approaches his queen with the proper reverence of a subject. Yet his pride
is apparent in his speech. Handing his gifts, a basket filled with fruit
and flowers, to the proud sovereign, he says:

> Ich biet' es dir als ärmliches Geschenk,
> Wie es dem Höhern wohl der Niedre beut,
> Der sich als niedrig weiss, obleich nicht fühlt.
> Und so aus meinem Haus, das meine Burg,
> Komm ich zu Hof und, neigend dir mein Knie,
> Frag' ich, o Fürstin: was ist dein Gebot?

Primislaus had no intention of keeping the chain which he had obtained
so cleverly from the three noblemen in exchange for the jewel. He has
hidden the chain under the flowers and the fruit. He pays Libussa in kind
by telling her so in the form of a riddle:

> Unter Blumen liegt das Rätsel
> Und die Lösung unter Früchten.
> Wer in Fesseln legte trägt sie,
> Der sie trägt ist ohne Kette.

Libussa, however, does not understand the simple riddle; she shows
her vexation by letting him feel her superior rank. She wishes to force
Primislaus to admit that he saw her before; but he cleverly evades her
questions by saying that many saw her when she was crowned Queen
of Bohemia. When he is asked whether he ever possessed the white horse
(Libussa had ridden it home from his house and never returned it), the
proud farmer answers that what he once gave is no longer his. His con-
cluding remark reveals his firmness and determination: "Ein Mann geht
zögernd vorwärts, rückwärts nie." (1310) The word "Mann" reminds Li-

bussa that she is looking for a judge for her people. A judge, she says, must, first of all, not be a thief himself. Again she tries to bring Primislaus to admit that he has her chain:

> Drum sag nur an: ist nichts in deinen Händen
> Was mir gehört und du mir vorenthältst?

And again Primislaus shows that he is equal to the situation:

> Dein bin ich selbst und all was ich besitze,
> Was ich *besass* ist nicht in meiner Hand.

Angered the second time by the double meaning of his words which she does not understand, King Krokus' daughter is almost led to ask Primislaus directly concerning the chain. However, checked by her pride, Libussa haughtily asks him in the guise of a parable; she even includes a veiled threat of death should he refuse to return what is hers. But she learns that Primislaus cannot be intimidated; he is familiar with the parable and continues:

> Unschuldig, sprach er (the man in Libussa's parable),
>   soll mich Unschuld schützen,
> Wenn schuldig, sei die Strafe mir die Schuld.
> Auf alle gleich der Fürst den Zorn entlade,
> *Dem Zufall dank' ich nichts, noch eines Menschen Gnade.*

Ostensibly disappointed, Libussa refuses to make the "stubborn" farmer judge of her people. Naively she believes that he might be impressed by the splendor and the riches of a royal castle; she assigns him a room in the castle for the night.

In the fourth act Libussa delegates her servants Wlasta, who can wield a sword like a man, and Dobromila, who excels in book-learning, to question Primislaus further. Although they learn that he can neither fence nor read, they find him to be wise, noble, brave, strong, and equipped with a keen sense of justice. The splendors of Libussa's castle have created no desires in him:

> In meiner Hütte isst und schläft sichs wohl;
> Der Überfluss ist schlecht verhullter Mangel.

When the necessity of knowing history is pointed out to him by Dobromila, he replies:

> Wer klar das Heut erfasst,
> Erkennt die Gestern alle und die Morgen.

Concerning truth he has this to say:

> Die Wahrheit lebt und wandelt wie du selbst,
> Dein Buch ist nur ein Sarg für ihre Leiche.

The most difficult thing to Primislaus seems justice:

> Den Anspruch bändigen der eignen Brust,
> Nicht mild, nicht gütig, selbst grossmütig nicht,
> Gerecht sein gegen sich und gegen Andre,
> Das ist das Schwerste auf der weiten Erde,
> Und wer es ist, sei König dieser Welt.

As for his inability to use the sword, he can well defend himself if necessary, against four or five men at a time, with his father's axe and with his courage.

The next test is also designed to obtain a compromising statement from Primislaus. Slawa, another servant, rushes in calling for protection from the impertinence of men whom she despises:

> Mein Kind, was dich die Männer heisst verachten,
> Birgt etwa wohl Verachtung für dich selbst.
> . . . .
> Mir ist das Weib ein Ernst, wie all mein Zielen,
> Ich will mit ihr,—sie soll mit mir nicht spielen.

thus Primislaus states his stand concerning women.

When asked by Libussa as to the result of their tests, Dobromila characterizes the proud farmer by the four words: "Er ist von Stahl." (1498) Libussa wishes to see how far his "obstinacy" will go and—veiled in the disguise of a torch bearer—she enters the room where Wlasta is questioning Primislaus concerning the chain. He senses Libussa's presence and takes the offensive in his turn. He can reveal his heart to Wlasta without compromising his pride. In the most eloquent language he describes their (*i.e.* his and Libussa's) first meeting in the woods:

> . . . aller Unterscheidung bar,
> Sie mir erschien als Königin der Weiber,
> Nicht als das Weib, das selber Königin.
> . . . .
> Doch ist auch Primislav nicht niedern Stamms,
> Ein Enkelsohn von Helden, ob nur Pflüger.

New hope had come to his heart when Libussa had summoned him:

> Doch kalter Spott und rücksichtsloser Hohn
> Kam mir entgegen auf des Hauses Schwelle.

As Wlasta says, he expected to find a woman and found a princess.—He goes on to describe his ideal of woman:

> So ist das Weib, der Schönheit holde Tochter,
> Das Mittelding von Macht und Schutzbedürfnis,
> Das Höchste was sie sein kann nur als Weib,
> In ihrer Schwäche siegender Gewalt.

Pride in woman is most distasteful to him. He drives Libussa to the end of her patience and even arouses her jealousy by feigning to make love to Wlasta; what he says to her reveals a delightful sense of humor and the spectator is pleased at his roguish wit:

> Du bist nicht stolz, wie jene Freundin scheint,
> Die mit unwill'gem Fusse tritt den Boden;
> So bist du schön, dein Auge, nicht mehr starr,
> Es haftet milden Glanzes an dem Boden
> Die Wange färbt ein mädchenhaft Erröten.

He does not leave Libussa in doubt as to his idea of a perfect union:

> Bregreifst du dass ein Innres schmelzen muss
> Um Eins zu sein mit einem andern Innern?

If Wlasta should be willing to give up all unwomanly characteristics and retain only "Demut, Milde, Schwache" (1683), he would, indeed, place her above Libussa. At these words Libussa drops her torch and rushes out. Through his cleverness and quickwittedness Primislaus contrives to place himself into the possession of the jewel Wlasta had left on the table. In the next moment he falls through a trap door, a trick by means of which Libussa intends to upset Primislaus' composure; she succeeds, but only for a moment. Though he finds himself opposite three black figures who threaten his life, there is no trace of fear in him: "Der Willkür fugt kein Freier sich, kein Mann" (1732). He refuses to hand over the jewel, even though he should be killed:

> Mein Leben setz' ich ein für meinen Willen.
> Stoss, Mörder, zu! ich bin in eurer Macht,
> Der Gotter Schutz vertrau' ich meine Seele.

The black figures disappear, and Libussa stands before him. It is at this point that, as Primislaus observes, she is speaking to him as a woman, no longer as a princess. His tone changes to the solicitude of an ardent lover. Libussa's pride too is forgotten, she is no longer giving orders: "Nun denn, ich bitte" (1774).

> Wir waren wie die Kinder, wenn sie schmollen,
> Wegweisend was der Wunsch zumeist begehrt,

Primislaus says and returns the jewel voluntarily. As he wishes to leave, Libussa requests him to stay as her regent. But he will not serve under another man, Primislaus says, should she ever marry. Another objection on his part is that he would have no power. At this point a mob outside the palace, fearing for his safety, is threatening to revolt should he be harmed. Primislaus' courageous words convince Libussa that he is a born ruler and her man:

> Ist hier kein Schwert? Wo sind die Waffenmänner,
> Die kurz vorher sich feindlich mir genaht?
> Ich will hinaus! Ich will den Aufruhr lehren,
> Dass rohe Macht nur Macht ist im Gehorsam
> Und Niedres sich vor Hoherm willig beugt.

Sure of Libussa's love, Primislaus is determined to overcome her last resistence, which is the resistence of a modest woman, not of a princess:

> Weil ohne Worte du versprichst, und sprechend
> Der Sprache deiner Anmut *wider*sprichst.

He argues that in reality he had possessed her before, not in fact but in thought:

> Als ich aufs Pferd dich hob, bei jedem Straucheln
> Dir Hilfe bot, da fühlt' ich deine Nahe.
> . . . .
> Und wer dich freit, wer dich von dannen führt,
> Ich werd' ihm sagen: du bist nur der Zweite,
> Den Vorschmack deines Glücks hab' ich gefühlt.

Libussa tells Primislaus indirectly that she is his:

> Bleib hier! Ob stolz, sollst du mir dienstbar sein.
> Leg an den Gurtel, hier an seinem Platz,
> Und weh dem, der ihn noch nach dir beruhrt!

The fifth act shows Primislaus not only as a firm ruler, but also as a wise one. He listens to advisers in most matters:

> Nicht nur den eignen Nutzen liebt der Mensch,
> Die eigne Meinung hat ihm gleichen Wert,
> Er hilft dir gern, sieht er im Werk das seine.

In contrast to Libussa who wishes to secure happiness for her people for her own satisfaction, Primislaus strives after the good of all; it is not his own satisfaction he desires, but the happiness of the people:

> Er liebt im fremden fast das fremde nur,
> Das Edle selbst, das wohltut höherm Sinn,
> Weist er zuruck und duldet das Gemeine
> Wenn allgemein der Nutzen und die Frucht.

Primislaus expresses most beautifully his view of the new order which he is initiating because it is forced on Bohemia by the competition of other states:

> Es ist der Staat die Ehe zwischen Bürgern,
> Der Gatte opfert gern den eignen Willen,
> Was ihn beschränkt ist ja ein zweites Selbst.

Grillparzer has equipped his Primislaus with deep psychological insight, or—as Scherer[2] expresses it—with tact; he has avoided becoming merely the husband of the queen. With fine consideration Primislaus says to his wife:

> Du bist die Frau in diesem weiten Land
> Und ich der erste deiner Untertanen.

Yet we realize constantly that *his* will prevails—and his will is making for progress:

> Wir wollen weiter, weiter in der Bahn,
> Ich und mein Volk, als Bürger und als Menschen.

Primislaus, then, is a born ruler though living in humble circumstances. He is proud, strong, fearless, honest, wise, just, and noble. He makes use of his opportunities with caution, shrewdness, and especially persistance, and thus he succeeds. He obtains the woman he loves and a throne. He proves himself to be a ruler equipped with vision and the ability to introduce the social order which is needed to secure the well-being of his subjects. His well-balanced soul, his wisdom, and his sense of justice are revealed in the loftiness and the easy flow of his speech. Indeed, he is a master of symbolic and enigmatic speech. A look at a literary relative of Grillparzer's Primislaus, namely Bamba in *Vida y muerte del Rey Bamba* by Lope de Vega, serves to increase our admiration for the creation of Austria's greatest dramatist. Lope's peasant Bamba is dry and taciturn; he—unlike Primislaus—accepts the crown only because he is forced to, and

—unlike Primislaus—he finds it only a burden. In the midst of his affairs of state Bamba expresses his concern about his beloved oxen. As Farinelli[3] says, Bamba has the soul of a farmer rather than the soul of a king.— As stated above: Grillparzer more than succeeded in showing to himself— for he wished his posthumous dramas to be burned—what sort of a man could be a prince-consort without becoming merely the husband of his queen. The figure of Primislaus is convincing; Scherer's statement concerning this master creation is not tenable:

> Wenn man den Begriff der Regententugend in seine Merkmale auflost, edel, klug, tapfer, stark, gerecht, vorsichtig, vor allem stolz, und diese nach der Reihe in Szene setzt an dem Verhalten eines einzelnen Menschen, so hat man Primislaus.[4]

This detailed analysis of Primislaus has shown, above all, that Libussa is not "infinitely greater"[5] than the man she chose to be her husband and the king of her people. While she may be considered the "leading spirit" in the drama that bears her name, if only by virtue of the fact that she is the tragic figure, not her husband, Primislaus equals her in dramatic force.

Domaslav, Lapak, and Biwoy.

In *Libussa* we miss the little accidentally characterizing traits which we observed in several of the other dramas. The three "wladyky" or regents, or noblemen, appear always together and their role is not a noble one. We learn that Domaslav is rich and powerful, Lapak, wise, and Biwoy, strong. After Krokus' death they approach the latter's three daughters with the request that they choose one from their midst to be their queen. They are eager to swear allegiance to Libussa. In the second act, however, after the latter has introduced her rather hazy communism, the trio is not any too well satisfied with the state of affairs, for their prestige has been greatly reduced. The three wladyky voice the wish of the people that Libussa marry, and each of the three hopes that he will be the chosen one. They agree to let her decide, and that the fortunate one shall gratefully remember the other two. Their ignoble role in the solving of the riddle which Libussa gave them has been touched upon above. Domaslav and Lapak follow Biwoy, the strong, who evidently is the most stupid of them when he suggests they give up the chain in exchange for the jewel although the riddle stipulated that the belt should be undivided. Returning to Libussa, they find her in a bad humor: "Noch mehr der Toren! Wollt ihr auch ein Recht?" (920) From them the Bohemian queen learns that Primislaus knows of the riddle and that he, nevertheless, does not come to the court of his own accord.

The noblemen are slow in comprehending that they have been duped both by Libussa and by Primislaus (Domaslav: "Wir sind betrogen," 957). In the third act the trio is used again to approach Primislaus. They find him at his plow. In Biwoy new hope is awakened as he notices the farmer's pride:

> Nun um so besser.
> Stolz gegen Stolz, wie Kiesel gegen Stahl,
> Erzeugt, was Beiden feind, den Feuerstrahl.

The objection to the building of the city (2288 ff.) is in keeping with the aims of Domaslav, Lapak, and Biwoy voiced by them in the second act (543 ff.). Domaslav gives his attitude in an undertone:

> Was ist auch diese schlauentworfne Stadt
> Als Schwächung unsers Ansehns, unsrer Macht?
> Wenn erst das Volk in grosser Zahl vereint,
> Ist von uns Jeder minder als er war,
> Der Mächt'ge kaum gewachsen so viel Kleinen.

Domaslav, Lapak, and Biwoy are members of the privileged class. They represent the old order, here the agricultural state which they wish to perpetuate, not from ideal motives as Libussa and her sisters, but from short-sighted practical motives, if not from mere egotism. Grillparzer lets Domaslav foresee what later actually took place toward the end of the Middle Ages when the growing power of the middle classes checked and curtailed the traditional "rights" of the nobility. Although the trio are discontented with the order introduced by Libussa and later with the order introduced by Primislaus, they do not feel confident to take over the reign, and, in consequence, have to look on while the one who is stronger, wiser, and more influential than they executes his more progressive plans.

In Primislaus Grillparzer has added another to his already considerable number of "manly men" among his dramatic creations. In the words of Dobromila, Primislaus is a man "of steel" in every respect, and, we might add, a well rounded personality. The three wladyky Domaslav, Lapak, and Biwoy are too little individualized to permit a definite classification.

CHAPTER TEN

EIN BRUDERZWIST IN HABSBURG

Ein Bruderwist in Habsburg is Grillparzer's third historical drama.
It was his idea to portray in his characters the rise of a new epoch, the
beginning of the Thirty Years' War. He did not at all observe the chrono-
logical sequence of the historic events. Inasmuch as he placed his emphasis
on the characters, he restricted himself to an inner psychological chronology
as it were. A careful study of the drama itself leads to the conviction that
Rudolf II is not its axis, but that it was the dramatist's intention to show
the flow and and change of time in the characters of the members of the
house of Habsburg: the imperial power passes from Rudolf to Mathias,
from Mathias to Ferdinand who hires the able war lord Wallenstein. As we
know from history, Wallenstein in the course of the war becomes Ferdinand's formidable enemy.[1]

The first outline of Grillparzer's third historical drama dates from the
same period in which he wrote his *Konig Ottokars Gluck und Ende* and
Ein treuer Diener seines Herrn. Ein Bruderzwist in Habsburg was begun
in 1824, but not finished until 1850. His discouraging experience with *Ein
treuer Diener seines Herrn* retarded Grillparzer's work *Ein Bruderzwist in Habsburg.* When in 1838 *Weh dem, der ligt!* was rejected by the
public and Grillparzer decided to discontinue writing for the stage, he
shifted his emphasis from the plot to the portraiture of the characters. As
in *Libussa,* he placed dialectics into the idea itself; the idea being the
ever-present question: action or non-interference? However, the development
never reaches the stage of synthetic harmony between thesis and antithesis.[2]

Ein Bruderzwist in Habsburg was first produced on the stage on September 24, 1872.[3]

The main characters are Rudolf II, Mathias, Ferdinand, Leopold, Don
Cäsar, Bishop Melchior Klesel. Figures of minor importance are Maxi-
milian, Duke Julius of Brunswick, Mathes Thurn, Count Schlick, Seyfried
Breuner, Colonel Wallenstein, Wolf Rumpf, Colonel Ramee, a captain, Field-
marshal Russworm; Prokop, Lukrezia. We are here concerned with Rudolf,
Mathias, Ferdinand, Leopold, Don Cásar, Bishop Melchior Klesel, and
Maximilian.

Rudolf the Second

Leopold von Ranke, the famous historian (1795-1886) sums up his
account of Rudolf II (1552-1612) as follows:[4]

> Es ist das seltsamste Hagestolzenleben, in welchem das Kaisertum
> gleichsam sich selber abhanden kam. Rudolf war mürrisch, eigen-
> sinnig, argwohnisch, empfindlich, man möchte sagen, für jede
> Zugluft der Welt; bittere Enttäuschungen, dunkle Einwirkungen
> religiösen Aberglaubens konnten denn doch nicht vermieden wer-
> den; zuweilen hatte er Momente einer mit Jähzorn gemischten
> Melancholie, in denen man an seinem gesunden Verstand zwei-
> felte.

The identity with Grillparzer's Rudolf is apparent; however, the dramatist portrayed with keen psychological penetration a character generally recognized as one of the most magnificent on the German stage. What history reports as Rudolf's weakness the author re-interprets in his three acts and sums it up in a note on the title page of the manuscript: "Das Tragische wäre denn doch, dass er das Hereinbrechen der neuen Weltepoche bemerkt, die andern aber nicht, und dass er fühlt, wie alles Handeln den Hereinbruch nur beschleunigt." What Friedrich Nietzsche says concerning Hamlet is equally true of Rudolf II:

> Die Erkenntnis tötet das Handeln, zum Handeln gehört das Umschleiertsein durch die Illusion—das ist die Hamletlehre, nicht jene wohlfeile Weisheit von Hans dem Träumer, der aus zu viel Reflexion, gleichsam aus einem Überschuss von Möglichkeiten, nicht zum Handeln kommt; nicht das Reflektieren, nein!—die wahre Erkenntnis, der Einblick in die grauenhafte Wahrheit überwiegt jedes zum Handeln antreibende Motiv, bei Hamlet, sowohl als bei dem dionysischen Menschen.[5]

In the first act Rudolf is characterized by a violent temper and distrustfulness toward his own relatives; by his reluctance to act on behalf of the empire which is in contrast with the sternness he displays toward Don Cäsar. Rudolf's inactivity has been called weakness; but he is convinced that the approach of the new times cannot be prevented:

> Die Zeit kann ich nicht bänd'gen, aber ihn,
> Ihn will ich bänd'gen, hilft der gnäd'ge Gott.

When he is reproached concerning his belief in predictions by the stars, Rudolf defends astrology in a most eloquent speech:

> Ich glaub' an Gott und nicht an jene Sterne,
> Doch jene Sterne auch sie sind von Gott.
> Die ersten Werke seiner Hand, in denen
> Er seiner Schöpfung Abriss niederlegte,
> Da sie und er nur in der wüsten Welt.
> Und hätt' es später nicht dem Herrn gefallen,
> Den Menschen hinzusetzen, das Geschöpf,
> Es wären keine Zeugen seines Waltens,
> Als jene hellen Boten in der Nacht.
> Der Mensch fiel ab von ihm, sie aber nicht,
> Wie eine Lammerherde ihrem Hirten,
> So folgen sie gelehrig seinem Ruf
> So heut als morgen wie am ersten Tag.
> Drum ist in Sternen Wahrheit, im Gestein,
> In Pflanze, Tier und Baum, im Menschen nicht.
> Und wers verstünde still zu sein wie sie,
> Gelehrig fromm, den eignen Willen meisternd,
> Ein aufgespanntes, demutvolles Ohr,
> Ihm würde leicht ein Wort der Wahrheit kund,
> Die durch die Welten geht aus Gottes Munde.

He regrets that he himself is not able to read in the stars:

> Ich bin ein schwacher, unbegabter Mann,
> Der Dinge tiefster Kern ist mir verschlossen.

He has great respect for those who possess this gift.

This word "respect" or "awe" has a high meaning for Rudolf; he uses it ("Ehrfurcht") again and again. In the third act, when the estates come to demand religious freedom for themselves and the people, he warns them of the danger to them once the respect for his high office is gone. The people will turn against their masters as the latter are now turning against their emperor:

> Und einmal Ehrfurcht in sich selbst gespalten,
> Lebt sie als Ehrsucht nur noch und als Furcht.
> Masst euch nicht an zu deuteln Gottes Wahrheit.

Told by Julius of Brunswick—also in the third act—that the Protestants have promised help to Mathias in return for freedom of worship, Rudolf says sarcastically that Mathias is more of a Catholic than he himself:

> Er ists aus *Furcht*, indes ichs nur aus *Ehrfurcht*.
> Die Glaubensfreiheit stünde gut mit ihm!

Another word which exerts a magic spell over Rudolf is "order;" order can be found only in the universe, among the stars, while the earth is chaos:

> Kennst du das Wortlein: Ordnung, junger Mann?
> Dort oben wohnt die Ordnung, dort ihr Haus,
> Hier unten eitle Willkür and Verwirrung.

He would prefer to study the stars and the thought of such happiness causes him to lose himself in a reverie.

His distrust of Mathias is not based on the threat of the stars, Rudolf says, but on the aspirations and the secrecy of his relatives. Yet he follows Ferdinand's suggestions and appoints Mathias commander of the Hungarian army.

Ferdinand is a welcome guest to Rudolf. He seems to find in his nephew a man after his own heart, for he speaks to him very confidentially. However, Rudolf is greatly disappointed in the ardent Catholic who accuses his uncle of speaking for the Protestants. The emperor's initially benevolent tone changes to sarcastic scorn, disgust, and horror mingled with pity for the victims of this inhuman monster:

> Nun, ich bewundre Euch.—Weis deine Hände!
> Ist das hier Fleisch? lebendig, wahres Fleisch?
> Und fliesst hier Blut in diesen weichen Adern?
> Freit eine Andre als er meint und liebt—
> Mit Weib und Kind, bei zwanzigtausend Mann,
> In kalten Herbstesnächten, frierend, darbend!
> Mir kommt ein Grauen an. Sind hier nicht Menschen?
> Ich will bei Menschen sein. Herbei! Herbei!

At the beginning of the third act Rudolf is deeply absorbed in his study of alchemy. Stubbornly he has rejected all affairs of state. His loyal friend, Duke Julius of Brunswick, a Protestant, has to resort to a ruse to get near the emperor in order to warn him against the approaching danger.

Again Rudolf shows how little his high office with its responsibilities and duties means to him:

> Damit ich lebe muss ich mich begraben,
> Ich wäre tot, lebt' ich mit dieser Welt.
> . . . .
> Mein Name herrscht, das ist zur Zeit genug.

Hereditary rulership was introduced only because a centre is needed around which all the good and just gathers, he believes. Rudolf, an idealist and humanitarian, has designed his own way of spreading his ideal: he has founded the secret order of the Knights of Peace which is symbolized in a golden medallion, cast by the Emperor himself in his own laboratory, to be worn by the initiates secretly on the heart. In a very impressive scene he presents one of these emblems to the Protestant Duke Julius of Brunswick whom he considers worthy of being a member:

> Die (the Knights of Peace) wähl' ich aus den Besten aller Länder,
> Aus Männern, die nicht dienstbar ihrem Selbst,
> Nein, ihrer Bruder Not und bitterm Leiden;
> Auf dass sie weithin durch die Welt zerstreut,
> Entgegentreten ferner jedem Zwist,
> Den Landergier und was sie nennen: Ehre,
> Durch alle Staaten sat der Christenheit,
> Ein heimliches Gericht des offnen Rechts.

As a rule, a man will adopt a philosophy which suits his nature; that is the case with Rulolf as his excuse for his inactivity reveals:

> Zudem gibts Lagen wo ein Schritt voraus
> Und einer ruckwärts gleicherweis verderblich.
> Da hält man sich denn ruhig und erwartet
> Bis frei der Weg, den Gott dem Rechten ebnet.

However, as Julius says, time marches on; and while Rudolf rests, the others do not. Rudolf's persistence in refusing to believe that rebellion has reached the doors of his castle bears witness to the fact that he knows little about human nature. When he finally realizes the danger, he is unable to decide what course of action he should take. He does not know whether he should grant to the estates what they demand, or whether he should defy them. He would like best to resign the crown if he only knew of an efficient person who could take it; only then he would feel like a human being. However, scruples again find their way into this train of thought:

> Doch wenn es wahr, dass Gott die Kronen gibt,
> Geziemt es Gott allein nur sie zu nehmen,
> Sie abzulegen, selbst, auch ziemt sich nicht.

When the scroll is brought on which the estates have stated their demands in return for their loyalty, Rudolf has a vision of the approaching disaster:

> Ists doch als ginge wild verzehrend Feuer
> Aus dieser Rolle, das die Welt entzündet
> Und jede Zukunft. bis des Himmels Quellen
> Mit neuer Sündflut bändigen die Glut,
> Und Pöbelherrschaft heisst die Überschwemmung.

He is ready to fight for the honor of the Empire; however, as soon as he hears the first cannon shot fired against Mathias' army about to attack Prague, Rudolf starts back:

> Was ist?—Mein Geist ist stark, mein Leib nur zittert.
> . . . .
> Man soll nicht schiessen! Soll nicht! sag' ich euch!
> . . . .
> Vertragt euch mit dem Feind! Und diese Handvest,
> Die ihr als Preis des Beistands abgetrotzt,
> Sei euch geschenkt.
> . . . .
> Ist es mein Bruder doch, bestimmt zu herrschen,
> Wenn mich der Tod, ich hoffe bald, hinweggrafft.
> Er übe sich vorlaufig in der Kunst,
> Der undankbaren, ewig unerreichten,
> In der verkehrt was sonst den Menschen adelt:
> Erst der Erfolg des Wollens Wert bestimmt,
> Der reinste Wille wertlos—wenn erfolglos.
> In Böhmen aber will ich ruhig weilen
> Und harren bis der Herr mich zu sich ruft.

What others call his weakness is really his kindness, Rudolf says. Yet:

> In diesen Adern sträubt sich noch der Herrscher
> Und Zorn und Rachsucht glüht in meiner Brust.
> Zu züchtigen die sich an mir vergessen,
> Die schwach mich nennen, schwächer weit als ich.

The impetuous Leopold succeeds in wheedling Rudolf into giving orders for the attack of the troops gathered at Passau; a decision which later throws the emperor into the deepest remorse.

In the fourth act Grillparzer's Rudolf demonstrates his capacity for firmness in the relentlessness toward his son Càsar. It must be remembered that the following scene is Grillparzer's invention and that it was introduced to show that Rudolf was capable of energetic action whenever he was convinced that he was right while the historical Rudolf II was known as a weakling. Julius pleads for Don Càsar's life, but in vain:

> Der Kaiser
> (der auf den Stufen des Brunnens stehend, den Schlüssel
> hinabgeworfen hat, mit starker Stimme).
>   Er ist gerichtet,
> Von mir, von seinem Kaiser, seinem—
> (Mit zitternder, von Weinen erstickter Stimme.)
>   Herrn!

He means to say "Vater" but instead he says "Herrn." Rudolf is not only firm, indeed too firm, with his son in whom he sees the child of the new times which he despises (325), but also with himself, for Don Cäsar, "Ein Zerrbild zwischen Niedrigkeit und Grosse" (1895) is his son and the evidence of the dissolute life of the emperor's own youth. In Rudolf's action we recognize his great sense of justice and his condemnation of all the abuses of the new epoch which he has not been able to halt in his empire. In discussing Rudolf's wavering nature, E. J. Williamson[6] states: "Even when Don Càsar is bleeding to death he (Rudolf) hesitates and refuses to interfere." However, the emperor did not have the key to Don Cäsar's cell; he demanded it from Julius (2179) when a servant requested it from the latter very urgently. Rudolf, uttering the few words quoted above *"mit starker Stimme,"* then walked straight to the well and dropped the key despite the eloquent plea of Julius. Then the stage direction reads (before line 2190) "Er wankt nach der linken Seite von Rumpf unterstützt, ab." By this attitude is expressed the grief of the father over his dying son. Rudolf, far from wavering on this occasion, makes a quick and irrevocable decision.

Whenever he is deeply vexed or moved, Rudolf is very taciturn as we saw at the occasion of his initial appearance in the first act. In the fourth act—after the dramatic execution of Don Cäsar's death sentence —when he learns that he is a prisoner in his own residence, the emperor makes one short reference to his grief over the loss of his son:

> *Drum fort von mir du menschlich naher Schmerz,*
> Gib Raum dem Ingrimm der verletzten Würde.

It is his hurt dignity which drives Rudolf to pronounce his curse (2267) over Prague, the city he had preferred to Vienna but which, nevertheless, had betrayed him. As we may expect, Rudolf retracts his curse and even blesses the city (2416). The unfortunate emperor realizes his shortcomings and sums them up; but the word "weakness" does not occur:

> Ich habe viel gefehlt, ich seh' es ein,
> Seitdem ich aus den Nebeln, die am Gipfel,
> Herabgestiegen in das tiefe Tal,
> In dem das Grab liegt als die letzte Stufe.
> Ich hielt die Welt für klug, sie ist es nicht.
> Gemartert vom Gedanken droh'nder Zukunft,
> Dacht' ich die Zeit von gleicher Furcht bewegt,
> Im weisen Zögern seh'nd die einz'ge Rettung.
> Allein der Mensch lebt nur im Augenblick,
> Was heut ist kümmert ihn, es gibt kein morgen.

Rudolf the Second is the most complex of Grillparzer's characters. Placed on the throne of a vast empire through no desire of his, the emperor would prefer to be a private citizen who devotes himself entirely to his studies. The keynote to his character is indecision based on the conviction that disaster is impending, and that no action can prevent it. Grillparzer has created a character full of contradictions, yet representing a perfectly viable individuality. This most dramatic figure is constantly vacillating between his spiritual world of dreams and religious superstition and the grim realities of the outer world, between thought and action. Thus his moods change quickly. Too great generosity changes with cruel severeness; distrust with blind confidence.—Culturally Rudolf finds himself far above his fellowmen. Though a devout Catholic, he believes in the predictions read in the stars by astrologers. He is tolerant in matters of religion. He is filled with a deep love of men, and has given much thought to social, political, and religious questions. He is not opposed to progress, but to any sudden and violent change of government. He has a high opinion of the imperial dignity which he represents even though it may temporarily be divorced from power.

That such a man should prefer solitude and seclusion to the hustle and bustle of the world seems logical. Also his distrust of his relatives is well motivated by the superstitious beliefs which he as a child of his time accepted. Emil Reich says: "Wer sich schwach fühlt, wird leicht geneigt, anderen üble Absichten gegen sich zuzutrauen."[7] But why look for a motivation not intended by the dramatist? It must be kept in mind that Rudolf believed implicitly in the predictions of the stars made to him by his astrologers (398-399). Against other attacks Grillparzer's Rudolf II has been very ably defended by O. E. Lessing.[8]

Franz Gillparzer has, in his figure of Rudolf II, re-interpreted a historical personality. Through minute attention to psychological motivation, the master dramatist has succeeded in bringing to life an unusual, yet plausible and convincing individuality that differs from its historical model, or rather from the generally accepted view of its historical model. Grillparzer's Rudolf, an idealist with high ethical principles, is not a weakling but a man whose inactivity grows out of the firmly rooted conviction that action will only hasten predestined disaster.

Archduke Mathias

Mathias has much in common with his brother Rudolf:

> Wir beide haben
> Von unserm Vater Tatkraft nicht geerbt,
> —Allein ich weiss es, und er weiss es nicht,

says the latter who possesses what Mathias lacks: intelligence, wisdom and insight. —Mathias had had ambitious plans: he had placed himself at the head of the rebels in the Netherlands without Rudolf's consent and brought on discord between the courts of Vienna and Madrid. His plan to obtain a throne had failed. At the beginning of the first act he is greatly depressed. As Rudolf has remained unmarried, Mathias is the successor to the throne; yet he wishes to resign all claims to it and humbly beg Rudolf for a small fief, the domain Styria. Klesel's answer throws a significant light on the characters of both Rudolf and Mathias:

> Nun allzu wenig, wie nur erst zu viel.
> So treibt ihr euch denn stets im Aeussersten
> O Maximilians unweise Söhne!

Klesel has great plans for his tool Mathias; and the fact that the latter subsequently becomes emperor is, indeed, achieved through the clever intrigues of the sly bishop. When Mathias finally understands what Klesel has in mind, he suddenly changes to the other extreme: his bearing shows great arrogance.

This changeability may be observed again in the second act. The archdukes have been called for the purpose of a counsel which is to decide on peace with the Turks. Since a battle and one third of the army have been lost, peace would, indeed, be the wisest thing for Mathias who has as yet

never won a battle. However, his pride has been hurt and he craves revenge
for his defeat. Nevertheless, this sudden opposition to the long contemplated
plan probably does not go very deep; for when Leopold declares that he is
on his uncle's side against peace, the latter, from a spirit of contradiction,
suddenly votes for peace himself.

In the fifth act—Mathias has been the ruler for some time— we learn
from Ferdinand that conditions are the same as formerly under Rudolf:

> . . . war er nicht heisser Tatendurst,
> Zu zügeln kaum und kaum zurückzuhalten,
> So lang die Krone lag im Reich der Hoffnung;
> Und nun, bedeckt mit ihr als einem Helm
> Den Szepter als ein Schwert in seiner Hand
> Schläft er auf trägen Purpurkissen ein
> Und bringt die Zeiten Kaiser Rudolf's wieder.

The spectator is made to realize that Klesel is the driving force behind the
throne. Ferdinand who objects to the tolerance toward the Protestants has
the ecclesiastic counselor removed. Reminded of his own disloyalty toward
Rudolf, Mathias eyes his nephew with apprehension. Since Klesel is gone,
Mathias is as helpless as a child: "Mein Bruder tot. Wär' ich es erst nur
auch." (2816)

While the people hail their new emperor—the news of Rudolf's death
has just arrived at Vienna—Mathias is crushed by contrition and remorse:

> Am Ziel ist nichts mir deutlich als der Weg,
> Der kein erlaubter war und kein gerechter.
> (Sein Blick trifft die Reichskleinodien, er wendet die Augen ab.)
> O Bruder, lebtest du und wär' ich tot!

Mathias is ambitious and vain. He has an enterprising spirit, but lacks
the talent, intelligence, and persistence to accomplish what he plans to do.
He becomes emperor merely by virtue of his birth and accomplishes nothing through his own initiative and strength. Even his victory over Leopold
at Prague he owes to chance. His own words characterize Mathias splendidly:

> Das ist der Fluch von unserm edeln Haus:
> Auf halben Wegen und zu halber Tat
> Mit halben Mitteln zauderhaft zu streben.

Archduke Ferdinand

The most interesting question in regard to Ferdinand is: was he stronger
and better than his two uncles Rudolf and Mathias, whom—in history—
he succeeds as German Emperor?

First and foremost Ferdinand is an ardent, in fact, fanatic, Catholic.
We mentioned above his harsh treatment of the twenty thousand Protestants
in his lands who refused to be converted by force, and we quoted Rudolf's
opinion of his ruthless nephew. —A strong man must, above all, stand on
firm ground. Ferdinand meets this requirement: his faith in his church
is unconditioned and uncompromising; there is evidence[9] of his firm Catholicism throughout the fifth act:

> Fluch jedem Wissen, das nicht aufwärts geht
> Zu aller Wesen Herrn und einz'gem Ursprung.

In fact, it is Ferdinand who declares void the charter given to the estates of Bohemia by Rudolf (2560), it is Ferdinand who begins the Thirty Years' War when he sends his troops to Prague in order to suppress the Protestants. He says: "Doch zeigt die Weisheit sich im Handeln meist." (2826)

It would, indeed, seem as if Ferdinand were a strong man. However, he shows himself energetic only when he is certain of the proper backing, not only by the church of Rome, but also by Spain and the Catholic part of Germany. —In the second act when the Habsburgs have to decide whether or not the war with Turkey should be continued, Ferdinand does not show any firmness or decision. He finally votes for termination of the war:

> In mir ringts wirren Zweifels.
> Was gäb' ich nicht war' mir der Schritt erspart.

However, the intelligent Klesel is making full use of this rare meeting of the Habsburgs who have just taken their first disloyal step against their senior and emperor. What are they to do, should Rudolf disapprove of their step? They will not remain assembled always. Therefore, one of them should be given full authority to act on their behalf if necessary. Klesel is, of course, scheming in the interest of Mathias and arrives at his goal most ingeniously. He says that the man for this office would—most logically —be Mathias, but—ironically enough, what he says is true—:

> Allein zu solchem Amt fehlt ihm die Festigkeit,
> Nicht Kraft, doch das Beharren im Entschluss.

Just as Klesel expected, Mathias is aroused to angry contradiction. Maximilian declines, naturally. It is Ferdinand's turn: here is his opportunity to show his ability and energy. Would Klesel take the chance of seeing Ferdinand accept unless he knew his Habsburgs very well? Turning to Ferdinand, the bishop says:

> Nun denn: ein Muster hier der Festigkeit,
> Der Herr der Steiermark, der, rascher Tat,
> Die Ketzerei getilgt in seinem Land.

However, Ferdinand declines, saying that the root of his "firmness" is his conscience:

> Mathias ist des Hauses Aeltester,
> Tut Not denn übertragene Gewalt,
> Wie es fast scheint, so sei sie ihm vertraut.

Ferdinand signs the document with a foreboding of disaster. He is filled with doubts and apprehension. Later—in the fourth act—he comes to Rudolf, begging the emperor's pardon on his knees.

In the fifth act it is Klesel again who—although in Ferdinand's power —predicts the fate of the latter, Ferdinand's fate at the hands of Wallenstein:

> Vollführt denn die Befehle eures Herrn,
> Der sich von Eisen fühlt, wie euer Harnisch
> So oft ihn Glaubenseifer vorwärts treibt,
> Doch kommts einmal zu menschlicher Zerwürfnis
> Vor Jedem zittern wird, der, starken Sinns
> Sich dienend aufgedrungen ihm zum Herrn.

Ferdinand, then, is neither stronger nor better than Rudolf. The servant of Rome displays great energy at times, but it is the convulsive energy of the religious fanatic. As Ehrhard[10] says: "Grillparzer zeigt uns in Ferdinand die Frucht der Jesuitenerziehung." The archduke acts as a tool of the church; and he has no idea concerning the duties of a ruler; nor does he know what will become of the empire, half of whose subjects are Protestants. He lacks the foresight and wisdom of Rudolf, which would have resulted in tolerance. However, unlike Mathias, Ferdinand acts less from selfish motives.

Archduke Leopold

> Ein verzogner Fant,
> Hubsch wild und rasch, bei Wein und Spiel und Schmaus.
> Wohl selbst bei Weibern auch; man spricht davon.
> Allein er ist ein Mensch,

says Rudolf about the younger brother of Archduke Ferdinand. Indeed, what a contrast between the two brothers!

Leopold is devoted to his uncle and emperor, Rudolf II, with an absolute loyalty. He is the only one at the meeting of the archdukes who insists on knowing whether or not it takes place upon the desire of the emperor. And all his impetuous youthful energy Leopold places in the service of this loyalty. Of all the Habsburgs whom Grillparzer brings to life in this drama Leopold is probably the most manly:

> Ich aber will nur was ich selber will,
> Und Herrscher heisst wer herrscht nach eignen Willen.

For some time Leopold had been anticipating difficulties for the inactive emperor and—taking the initiative—had gathered troops at Passau:

> Voraussicht ist ja Vorsicht, oder nicht?
> Die Klugheit gibt nur Rat, die Tat entscheidet.
> Es soll sich alles noch zum Guten wenden.

His attempt to relieve Prague which has just fallen into Mathias' hands is unsuccessful through a misunderstood order. However, he has not given up his effort to aid and liberate Rudolf: he has gone to Germany to unite the estates of the empire and to induce them to protect their emperor.

Young Leopold is impetuous, a lover of gambling, wine, and women. It is, indeed, refreshing to find a character among the Habsburgs presented in this play who knows his own mind, is straight forward, candid, and ready to act for a good cause from his own initiative.

Don Casar

Rudolf's natural son has much in common with Leopold, to wit: love of gambling, wine, and women, as well as candor. However, while the nephew embraces the cause of love of country and emperor, the son represents license, skepticism, arbitrariness, want of discipline and respect for the moral code. In these latter characteristics he resembles Otto von Meran with whom he also shares pride and disdain of hypocrisy. Like Otto von Meran, Don Casar has been scorned by a woman. As we mentioned above in the discussion of Rudolf II, Don Cäsar attempts to kidnap Lukrezia, fails, is captured, and then jailed. Leopold's revolt frees him. Despondently he broods on the uselessness of his life:

> Den der mich tótet nenn' ich meinen Freund.
> Doch vorher noch ein Wortchen oder zwei
> Mit ihr, die mich verdarb.

He makes his way into Lukrezia's house:

> Was soll ich auch in dieser wüsten Welt,
> Ein Zerrbild zwischen Niedrigkeit und Grosse;
> Verleugnet von dem Manne der mein Vater,
> Missachtet von dem Weib das ich geliebt.—

All passions have left him except that for truth, he cries in maudlin rage:

> Denn wie's nur eine Tugend gibt: die Wahrheit,
> Gibts auch ein Laster nur: die Heuchelei.

The recollection of his hurt pride excites Don Cäsar to such a degree that he is led to say that he would kill his rival, were he still living:

> Die Eifersucht ist Demut, ich bin stolz,
> Verachtung liegt mir naher als der Hass.

He desires to know the truth from Lukrezia at all cost; however, the truth for him is the preconceived opinion that she loved Beglioso, and that she is a hypocrite because she will not admit it to him. Lukrezia flees to an adjoining room in order to pray before a picture of the Madonna hanging side by side with Beglioso's picture. Don Cásar's rage culminates in his shooting Lukrezia. The next moment he is seized by remorse: "Weh mir! —O meine Taten!" (2014)

The manner of Don Casar's death was discussed above.

The scene preceding the killing of Lukrezia resembles the one in Otto's room before Erny's death in *Ein treuer Diener seines Herrn*. Don Cásar and Otto von Meran are ruled by their violent passions; resistance of any sort brings them near insanity. They are characterized by complete lack of moral fibre and they recognize no law except that of their own unbridled nature. Conflict with society is inevitable. However, there is one redeeming feature in the character of Don Cäsar; he is a true friend as he shows in his ardent endeavors to save the life of General Russworm. His punishment seems too harsh. He bears the brunt of the disadvantages of his birth. As the illegitimate child of the emperor, Don Cäsar is not publicly acknowledged by his father, who, nevertheless, should have shown clemency to the young man in whose favor many mitigating circumstances could be urged.

Bishop Melchior Klesel

> Ihr seid der Widerhall von euerm Herrn,
> Wenn nicht vielmehr das Echo er von euch,

says Maximilian to Bishop Klesel during the meeting of the archdukes. We have discussed a number of men who were placed in ruling positions

chiefly by virtue of their birth and have seen that they were not equal to
their high office of responsibility. Neither Rudolf, nor Mathias, nor Ferdinand were able to do what would have been for the best of their subjects,
namely: to prevent the Thirty Years' War. If one of the Habsburgs had had
the ability, energy, wisdom, and foresight of Klesel, he could possibly have
prevented the great disaster which killed off more than half of the popula-
tion of Central Europe.

Klesel, the son of a farmer, had become a churchman. The shrewdness
with which he gained his ends was repeatedly referred to above. Mathias
became the ruler of the German Empire by the grace of Melchior Klesel.
As the right hand man of Mathias and as a high church official he has
attained a rank which places him on a level with kings. His is the candor,
pride, and courage of the self-made man:

> Mich hat umsonst aus meiner Niedrigkeit
> Die Vorsicht nicht gestellt auf jene Stufe
> Zu der sonst nur Geburt und Gunst erhebt.
> Der Kirche Macht bekleidet mit dem Purpur,
> Der mich den Konigen zur Seite stellt.
> Ich werde nicht vor Menschen feig erzittern,
> Und warens Konige—im Land der Zukunft;
> Die nämlich kommen kann, nicht kommen muss.

That Klesel does not forget his own pocket is quite characteristic: "Man
sieht sich vor; die Zeiten schlagen um." (2508)

Which are the measures and policies that—had Klesel been allowed to
carry them out—would have prevented the great war?

> . . . ein fester Plan beherrscht das Ganze
> Und jeder Schritt führt näher an das Ziel,

he says to the fanatic Catholic Ferdinand. Since half of Austria is Protestant, Klesel has wisely occupied many of the offices with Protestants:

> Wir suchen Wissen bei der Wissenschaft,
> Der Glaube wird gelehrt von gläub'gen Meistern,

i. e. Klesel, although a high church official himself, separates science and
religion. He had become rector of the University of Vienna in 1616. Ferdinand refers to this fact when he says:

> Die hohe Schule, deren Rektor ihr,
> Ertont von Worten frecher Kirchenleugner.

Klesel believes in compromise with the Protestants. He means to live
up to the charter of freedom of religion granted to Bohemia by Rudolf and
allows the Protestants to build churches.

It is for these very policies that Ferdinand has Klesel imprisoned at
Kufstein. The latter's prediction as to Ferdinand's fate was quoted above.

Melchior Klesel is a self-made man equipped with unusual intelligence,
shrewdness, pride, foresight, courage, candor, and personal greed. The
word "unscrupulous"[11] seems too harsh a word applied to the character of

the bishop. After all, his goal was peace. He brought about peace with the Turks, and peace was the objective of his domestic policy:

> Erzwungen ist zuletzt ein jeder Friede;
> Der Schwächere gibt nach. Doch soll das Schwert
> Nicht wüten bis zu völliger Vertilgung,
> Muss Friede werden, der nur Friede ist
> Wenn er gehalten wird, ob frei, ob nicht.

History proved that Klesel was right. In 1648—Ferdinand had been dead for eleven years—peace was made and freedom of worship granted to all. Klesel came back to Vienna in 1628, received like a national hero by an enormous crowd while all church bells were ringing.

Archduke Maximilian

The stout, comfortable brother of Rudolf and Mathias had—like the latter—once fought for a crown, that of Poland, and—like Mathias—had been unsuccessful and even suffered imprisonment. Maximilian has been thoroughly cured of all ambition for power. His major concern is a good dinner-table, as is evidenced by the fact that he carries a special kitchen on his travels. He is a master of the order of German Knights and intent on his dignity, for this reason he objects—in the beginning—to the presence of Klesel at the meeting of the archdukes.

Maxilimian has enough common sense and intelligence to see through Klesel's plans. The archduke knows that the bishop is not acting in Rudolf's interest, yet he does not seem to have the strength to remain outside of the plot—as Leopold does. He signs the agreement which places the power in Mathias' hands. —Like Ferdinand, Maximilian realizes his mistake too late and asks Rudolf's pardon on his knees, a ridiculous figure:

> Mir ist das Weinen näher.
> Auch kniet sichs schwer mit meines Körpers Last.

These two lines are sufficient to characterize the last Habsburg of our discussion: a humorless Falstaff who loves his peace, his comfort, and his food.

Grillparzer's dramatic re-interpretation of Rudolf II presents a personality who, although placed on the throne by his high birth, is unfit to be at the head of a vast empire. The spectator is made to feel that Rudolf might have been happy and successful in the quiet and secluded life of a scholar or scientist. While we cannot attribute to Rudolf those traits that characterize "manly men," we must also recognize that Grillparzer succeeds in showing that Rudolf's actions, or lack of them, do not grow out of weakness. Of the other Habsburgs, only Leopold is a man of action who shows courage, initiative, and even dash. Mathias lacks perseverance. Ferdinant is a fanatic; Don Cäsar, a libertine; and Maximilian, a gourmand. Bishop Klesel is a self-made man with unusual intelligence, foresight, and courage. He and Rudolf represent a study in contrasts: Rudolf born to rule, but incapable; Klesel, a capable ruler, but prevented from ruling by dint of his humble birth. In short, the only real men in *Ein Bruderzwist in Habsburg* are Leopold and Bishop Klesel, both minor, but not unimportant, figures.

CHAPTER ELEVEN

DIE JÜDIN VON TOLEDO

Franz Grillparzer's last completed drama is chiefly based on Lope de Vega's *Las paces de los reyes y Judia de Toledo*. Of less influence were Diamante's *La Judía de Toledo* and Cazotte's short story *Rachel ou la belle Juive*. Nevertheless, *Die Judin von Toledo* is Grillparzer's own unique creation. It is an *Erziehungsdrama*[1] by which is meant a play showing what phases a character has to go through before it is definitely stabilized. King Alfonso is the protagonist of this drama.[2] Nevertheless, Grillparzer named the drama after Rahel because she is the active force which initiates the dramatic conflict as well as the development of the play. The *Jüdin*—as well as *Libussa*—is a drama in Hebbel's sense. We might call Rahel a representative of individualism and Alfonso, of collectivism; the latter personifies the concept of the state. Nevertheless, Grillparzer portrayed his characters as human beings first of all. We see how they, as human beings with vastly differing temperaments compromise or conflict with the existing medieval order of the state.

The creation of *Die Judin von Toledo* extends over more than a quarter of a century. Leopold Hradek[3] presents and summarizes the seven stages of Grillparzer's activity as lying between the years 1816 and the middle of the fifties. The first production of this drama, which like *Libussa* and *Ein Bruderzwist* had remained in Grillparzer's desk until his death, took place in the Burgtheater in Vienna on January 23, 1873.[4]

We shall discuss King Alfonso VIII, Count Manrique of Lara, and Don Garceran.[5]

Alfonso

The very first appearance of the King of Castile in a dialogue with his mentor Manrique gives us a complete picture of Alfonso's past life and of his characteristics. Lope de Vega, in the drama we mentioned above, devotes the entire first act to his hero's youth. As such an exposition did not fit into Grillparzer's plan, he surmounted the difficulty of portraying Alfonso by having him reminisce on his early youth, a procedure which does not seem artificial inasmuch as the king had come to Toledo again for the first time after his eventful ascendance to the throne at the age of eleven. —Alfonso's reflections reveal his noble mind, his modesty, his readiness to acknowledge what others have done for him:

> Deshalb, wenn andre Fürsten Väter heissen
> Des eignen Volks, nenn' ich mich seinen Sohn,
> Denn was ich bin, verdank' ich ihrer Treue.

Don Manrique had been severe with his royal pupil; he had tested him again and again with the result that: "Mir blieb der Neid, und er war fleckenlos," little realizing that, in his eagerness to train a perfect ruler, he had made the very understandable mistake of never allowing his ward to come into contact with the temptations of the world. That Alfonso is no light-hearted trifler, in fact, that he is accustomed to think about himself and his relations to the world—a trait which he does not share with his Spanish model—is made manifest in his reply to the Count's flattering remarks:

> Bin ich nicht schlimm, so besser denn fur euch,
> Obgleich der Mensch, der wirklich ohne Fehler,
> Auch ohne Vorzug wáre, furcht' ich fast;
> . . . .
> War einer je gerecht, der niemals hart?
> Und der da mild, ist selten ohne Schwäche.

In the following statement—also made by Alfonso—we see the theme of the drama:

> Besiegter Fehl ist all des Menschen Tugend,
> Und wo kein Kampf, da ist auch keine Macht.
> Mir selber liess man nicht zu fehlen Zeit.

It is significant that Alfonso realizes himself this great truth which Nietzsche once formulated: "Erster Grundsatz: man muss es notig haben, stark zu sein: sonst wird man's nie."[6] As Alfonso says himself, he had not had any time to take a wrong step. His life had been similar to that of a cadet in a military academy: every minute's activity is carefully prescribed. In such a system even a weakling can succeed, for nothing more is required of him than to act promptly on the authority of others. However, the king is no weakling; and he fully realizes the state of affairs.

As for his present life, Alfonso is thoroughly bored. That women existed in the world he had learned when he met the correct and virtuous Englishwoman Eleonore at the altar:

> Die wirklich ohne Fehl, wenn irgend jemand,
> Und die ich, grad heraus, noch wärmer liebte,
> Wár' manchmal, statt des Lobs, auch etwas zu verzeihn.

Alfonso has learned another truth: that it is a much more likable trait to be fallible than to be correct. In this mood he is confronted by Rahel, or more correctly, he is made to realize Rahel's attractiveness not only through his eyes; placing her fear for her life in the service of her coquettish designs, the vivacious young Jewess clings to the leg of the king, pressing herself against it[7] and resting her head on his knee (331).

Alfonso's peace of mind is gone; that he will not without scruples yield to the temptation—as his Spanish model does—seems certain. Grillparzer, in discussing his Alfonso, says about him:[8] "Alles was er ist und war, lehnt sich auf gegen das neue uberwältigende Gefühl (das der Wollust)." His sense of order revolts:

> Allein Gewohnheit ist des Menschen Meister
> Und unser Wille will oft, weil er muss.

Step by step we see him lose his struggle against his senses. Earlier, before he had met Rahel, we had occasion to note his tolerance toward the Jews (288 ff). In the second act he speaks of the great history of the Jews as we know it from the Old Testament. He mentions Ahasverus and Esther. Alfonso envies Garceran, who is about his age, the freedom he enjoys because he is not a king. Alfonso knows of Garceran's experience with wom-

en and asks him for instructions in the "ars amandi," before going to
Rahel in the garden house.

Alfonso, before sending the Jewess and her family home, orders the willful child to return to its place on the wall his picture which she had taken out of its frame and attached to a chair. Rahel, yielding to an odd fancy of the moment, pierces it with a needle; Alfonso believes that he feels a physical pain in his heart and wonders whether she is criminally practicing magic.

> Ist sie nicht schön?
>
> . . . .
>
> Und wie das wogt und wallt und glüht und prangt,

he says to Garceran.

Alfonso's entering the garden house had been the first step on the wrong path, at least in the eyes of the world. The queen and the court are approaching; the fact that he sees fit to hide shows that he is no longer at his ease. The queen might believe, he says, what he himself believes. As Eleonore has learned that he is in the garden house, he becomes defiant:

> Muss ich, noch gestern Vorbild aller Zucht,
> Mich heute scheun vor jedes Dieners Blicken?
> Dann fort mit dir, du Buhlen um die Gunst!
> Bestimmen wir uns selber unsre Pfade.

For a moment he tries to place the blame for his predicament on Garceran; but he sees his injustice at once and gives definite orders to take Rahel and her sister away. Yet the spectator feels that Alfonso is not safe:

> Die höchste Zeit war's, dass sie ging, denn wahrlich
> Die Langeweile eines Fürstenhofs,
> Sie macht die Kurzweil manchmal zum Bedürfnis.
> Doch dieses Mädchen, obgleich schon und reizend,
> Sie scheint verwegner Brust und heft'gen Sinns
> Da sieht sich denn ein Kluger billig vor.

He wishes to go to the border at once where his presence is needed:

> Vier Augen drohen in Toledo mir
> Voll Wasser zwei, und andre zwei voll Feuer.

Rahel, however, "weiss das besser" (724). She has left her picture despite his definite orders; and he cannot resist following her himself to return it:

> Vor allem gilt es sich erobern selbst—
> Und dann entgegen feindlichen Erobrern.
> Retiro heisst das Schloss?—Was wollt ich nur?

It was not in Grillparzer's plan to show Alfonso's affair with Rahel at its height. In the third act Garceran sums up the situation:

> Kommt ihm zum erstenmal das Weib entgegen,
> Das Weib als solches, nichts als ihr Geschlecht
> Und rächt die Torheit an der Weisheit Zögling.

The king himself tells Garceran that he realizes he is doing wrong, and that he is able to drop the affair whenever he wishes. In Garceran he finds a constant admonisher.[9] That Alfonso does not really love Rahel she herself realizes with the sure instinct of a woman (926 ff., 1095). Garceran points out that love and respect go together, knowing that the king does not respect Rahel.

> Verachtung wàr' ein viel zu hartes Wort!
> Nichtachtung etwa, doch bleibt's wunderbar,

Alfonso says, *i.e.* he wonders himself why he could have left his wife and his duties for this woman. Rahel's moods and coquettishness continue to fascinate him. At one moment, when she is playing with his armor, he says to her: "Du albern spielend, töricht-weises Kind," for the very person who holds him back also reminds him of his duties as a soldier.

Then Esther arrives with the news of the plot, and the king rushes to Toledo to call his nobles to account for their disloyalty. He finds the palace deserted—apparently, at least—but he drives himself to action, expressing a thought which might also be called a leading one in this drama:

> Allein was soll das Grübeln und Betrachten,
> Gut machen heisst's; damit denn fang' ich an.

As he finds the queen's door locked, he has her called to him. Eleonore forgives him after he expresses his sincere regret and his good intentions for the future. He wishes to turn over a new leaf and absolves himself of his sins, a thing the queen in her purity does not need to do. he says. When Eleonore confesses her vengeful thoughts, he is pleased:

> Wohl etwa Rachsucht gar? Nun um so besser,
> Du fühlst dann, dass Verzeihen Menschenpflicht
> Und niemand sicher ist, auch nicht der Beste.
> Wir wollen uns nicht rächen und nicht strafen,
> Denn jene Andre, glaub, ist ohne Schuld
> Wie's die Gemeinheit ist, die eitle Schwäche,
> Die nur nicht widersteht und sich ergibt.
> Ich selber trage, ich, die ganze Schuld.

However, the queen goes too far in this early stage of their reconciliation. She believes in the magic of Rahel's picture and insists that he stop wearing it at once. Alfonso does not believe in magic:

> Umgeben sind wir rings von Zaubereien,
> Allein wir selber sind die Zauberer.

Eleonore's attitude and Rahel's picture call forth a comparison: it was Eleonore's cold virtue which had made his lapse possible:

> Dort jenes Mädchen— . . .
> War töricht sie, so gab sie sich als solche
> Und wollte klug nicht sein, noch fromm und sittig.
> Das ist die Art der tugendhaften Weiber,
> Dass ewig sie mit ihrer Tugend zahlen.
> Bist du betrubt, so tròsten sie mit Tugend,
> Und bist du froh gestimmt, ist's wieder Tugend,
> Die dir zuletzt die Heiterkeit benimmt,
> Wohl gar die Sünde zeigt als einz'ge Rettung.
> Was man die Tugend nennt, sind Tugenden,
> Verschieden, mannigfaltig, nach Zeit und Lage,
> Und nicht ein hohles Bild, das ohne Fehl,
> Doch eben drum auch wieder ohne Vorzug.

He becomes embittered at the thought of Eleonore's and Manrique's plotting. The queen withdraws and Alfonso learns too late that the nobles have rushed to Retiro, leaving him without horses. If they have killed Rahel, he prays to God, that he might be enabled to punish the guilty ones not as a tyrant but as a human being.

In the fifth act Alfonso is found weeping not because of love but because of wrath. He wishes to rally the common people in an attempt to punish the nobles. While she was living he wished to leave her, he says, but now that she is dead, Rahel and her picture will never leave him. He idealizes her so that even her sister Esther feels the desire to tell him the truth about Rahel:

> So sehr der Schmerz verlornen Wert verdoppelt,
> Sag' ich euch doch: ihr schlagt zu hoch sie an.

Everybody in the world is the product of his surroundings, he believes, but about Rahel he says:

> Sie aber war die Wahrheit, ob verzerrt,
> All was sie tat ging aus aus ihrem Selbst,
> Urplotzlich, unverhofft und ohne Beispiel.
> Seit ich sie sah, empfand ich, dass ich lebte
> Und in der Tage trübem Einerlei
> War sie allein mir Wesen und Gestalt.

On the day of his coronation he has sworn justice and punishment for all the guilty. Therefore he decides to view Rahel's corpse in order to harden himself against his struggle with himself.

What is going on in Alfonso's heart when he returns? He stands silent for a while, looking at old Isaak. Then Alfonso looks at his hands, rubs them as well as his neck and breast as though he were cleansing himself. Manrique and the queen with her son have come, ready to receive their punishment. No time is to be lost as the Moorish invasion threatens. Alfonso asks Garceran what he thought of Rahel while she was living; after hearing Garceran's answer:

> Herr, sie war schön.
> . . . .
> Doch auch verbuhlt und leicht, voll arger Tücken,

the king cannot understand why he should not have realized it himself during her lifetime. Magic he rejects as a superstition. As the only explanation he has to take Garceran's statement that it was "natural," yet:

> Natürlich ist zuletzt nur was erlaubt.
> Und war ich nicht ein König, mild, gerecht?
> Der Abgott meines Volks und all der Meinen.
> Nicht leer an Sinn, und blind auch nicht vor allem,

he says and insists that Rahel was not even beautiful. He describes the feelings he had when he saw the mutilated corpse. Instead of the voluptuous images of the past he saw, in his mind's eye, his wife and child and his people. He threw Rahel's picture at the corpse, an action symbolizing the fact that she had left his heart completely.

He almost regrets that he has to punish the nobles, the king says.
Indeed, they are all guilty—he himself included—except his son:

> Doch hier mein Sohn. Tritt du in unsre Mitte,
> Du sollst der Schutzgeist sein von diesem Lande,
> Ob uns ein hohrer Richter dann verzeiht.
> Fuhrt Doña Clara, ihr ihn an der Hand,
> Euch hat ein günstiges Geschick verliehn
> In Unbefangenheit bis diesen Tag
> Das Leben zu durchziehn; ihr seid es wert,
> Die Unschuld einzufuhren unter uns.

Alfonso forgives Eleonore, for what she did was done for her son, he claims.
He and the guilty nobles will fight for Castile, for the fatherland imperiled
by the infidels at its borders. Those killed in battle will atone for all. It has
been charged that Grillparzer weakened his drama considerably by allowing the murder of Rahel to go unpunished. However, Alfonso's decision
seems psychologically well motivated on the basis of his character as
portrayed in the drama. His own feeling of guilt and contrition as well
as the danger to the state from without kept him from dealing too harshly
with those whose action had been prompted by their concern for the safety
of the fatherland. That the dramatist personally did not condone this
miscarriage of justice may be seen in the curse pronounced by Esther
immediately after the exit of the nobles. Moreover, the fact that Esther
retracts her curse as soon as she realizes that no one is without guilt, shows
the lofty position of the wise old dramatist who stands above all his creations with the impartiality of a puppet-master, as it were. Any conclusions
on the basis of the play in regard to Grillparzer's own personal attitudes
must remain idle speculation.

Die Judin von Toledo reminds in some respects of Kleist's *Prinz von
Homburg*. Like the latter the king of Castile undergoes a development
which could not have been portrayed more convincingly and psychologically
true. Alfonso, a precocious child who has accidentally remained free from
any strong passion, develops before our eyes into a man who knows the
meaning of real virtue. This word "virtue" can be understood only by him
who knows the meaning of guilt; and only he knows what is meant by
"guilt" who has become guilty himself. —To be sure, that which would have
been little more than play in early youth becomes torture and disgrace
when it appears belatedly.[10] However, we believe that—whatever Grillparzer's intentions, if any—the end of the drama shows a conciliatory
optimism, to wit: not suffering, but activity, not contemplative remorse,
but brave deeds are the best retribution. This view represents a modern
ethical thought: the best form of atonement is the devotion of one's life
to the service of humanity. Alfonso, forced to choose between his private
life and his duties decides for the latter, but not for himself: he abdicates
in favor of his son. His courage and his manliness are shown in the determination with which he makes his final decision and with which he goes to war.

It appears that with the advent of the twenties of this century a view
has been gaining ground to the effect that Grillparzer's end of *Die Judin von
Toledo* represents a gloomy pessimism. Wedel-Parlow's argument in favor

of this pessimism[11] is neither convincing nor based on any tangible element in the drama itself nor on any statement the dramatist may have made on the subject:

> Ihm (Alfonso) bleiben nur trostlose Leere, Misstrauen und Furcht vor neuer Niederlage—der Tod der Seele, wo nicht auch des Leibes. —Grillparzer hat im Drama die letzte Furchtbarkeit verschleiert. Doch wie er es sich dachte, vermag etwa der Seelenzustand von Konig Ahasver zu Anfang von *Esther* zu zeigen, nicht minder aber der Schlussatz von seiner ersten Aufzeichnung zur *Judin von Toledo*: "Alfons ward daruber wahnsinnig."

The fact that Grillparzer states in his earliest notes that Alfonso becomes insane, while in the drama itself, written many years later, he lets the king take such a humble yet dignified and determined stand toward his own guilt and his duties is an argument in favor of the optimism we see in the final scene.

Even less convincing is Joachim Müller[12] who would probably like best to call the dramatist from his grave and dictate to him a correction of the "Halbheiten" as he, the critic, sees them, when he states in his abstruse technical language:

> Leid und Schuld zerstoren ihn (Alfonso) nicht physisch. Dass er trotz der Verzweiflung und des masslosen Schmerzes nicht physisch endet, erscheint als eine letzte Halbheit. Die Menschenauffassung Grillparzers zeigt hier äusserste Paradoxie einer konsequenten Inkonsequenz [!]. Zum letzten Male wird aus dem aktiv sich verzehrenden Menschen der passiv zuruckweichende, aus dem "Unmenschen" (V. 1736), der sich in blinder Rache von sich selbst entfernen will, der Mensch, der der eigenen Unbestandigkeit treu bleibt und auch zuletzt nicht zum Einsatz und zur Überwindung des ursprunglichen Ausgesetztseins kommt. Dies geschieht durch die unheimliche Disillusionierung. Im Konig erlischt beim Anblick der ermordeten und zerstorten Judin jede Liebesregung. Damit ist aber nicht im geringsten der seelische Ausgleich hergestellt, geschweige denn eine echte Wesensentscheidung gefallen.

Count Manrique of Lara

Alfonso's father had died when the child was only four years old. When after considerable confusion in Castile the child was proclaimed king by the people of the country who had tired of the rulership by Fernando, King of Leon and Alfonso's uncle, Count Manrique had made it his duty to rear the child in a way which would make him best suited for his future royal duties. We learn from Manrique himself that he is a severe and critical person (151 ff.). He is less tolerant and less democratic than Alfonso which is made manifest when Lara refers to the Jewish family as "Pöbel." His foremost characteristics are his love for his country and his abhorrence of all unconventional acts, especially on the part of the king. His disappointment is great when he learns the bitter truth about Alfonso in the second act. His son Garceran blocks his way into the room where Alfonso is hiding:

> Sieh mir ins Aug! Er kann es nicht ertragen.
> So raubt mir denn zwei Söhne dieser Tag.

Of course, it was Manrique's blindness in his educational policy that brought about the king's lapse as it was Manrique who had chosen a wife for his ward who happened to be most reserved, correct and almost frigid. But from the portrayal of the stern old mentor it is clear that he could not even be expected to see that he was responsible for the concatenation of events. Nor could he be charged with malicious intent. In Manrique Grillparzer has not only portrayed a viable character but also perfected the motivation in his drama.

The country is in danger through the inactivity of the king. (In Lope de Vega's drama the king spent seven years with Rahel.) It is for his love of country that Lara becomes disloyal to his ruler. He invites the nobles in order to discuss an independent step for the salvation of the country although he is fully aware of the fact that they have no authority for such a meeting. Manrique sees in Rahel the only cause of the king's neglect of his duties; she must be removed; there are two ways of accomplishing this, but both are considered ineffective by the count. As he begins to describe a third way, the queen who is present at the meeting interrupts him with the word "death." She pronounced, the count says, what he did not dare say. Manrique rationalizes on death: after all, many die in battle, others of diseases, and the sacred order which God himself established demands the death of one person. They will ask the king to remove the stumbling-block; should he refuse, they would kill Rahel.

In the fifth act Manrique is the first to submit himself to the king for punishment of his crime:

> Wir haben an dem König uns versündigt,
> Das Gute wollend, aber nicht das Recht,
> Wir wollen uns dem Rechte nicht entziehn.

Thus this representative of the medieval state does not lack a sense of justice, nor does he lack courage. When Esther advises him, the queen, and those who came with him, to flee from the wrath of the king, Manrique proudly lays down his arms voluntarily, ready to atone for the crime which he committed for the good of the country. There is nothing in these lines (1759-1806) to lead the spectator to doubt Manrique's sincerity.

In his portrayal of Manrique Grillparzer improved the historical figure. It is through the Count of Lara that Alfonso is maintained on his throne. Manrique is a proud, strong and conventional character who believes implicitly in the divine order of the medieval state. He places all his ability and courage into the service of his king and his country. He has a strong sense of justice, which, however, does not prevent him from taking direct action when the good of his native land is at stake. In his eagerness to rear a perfect king he adopts a not uncommon but mistaken educational policy which brings the very opposite of the desired results.

Don Garceran

Don Garceran is a minor character who—before the curtain rises—has undergone more or less the same type of development which the king undergoes in the course of the drama. Don Garceran belongs to that vast majority of human beings who, being normal human beings, learn to compromise with the life among their fellowmen. They are never dramatic figures. The dramatic figures come from the ranks of that small minority who refuse, in one way or another, to compromise with life. The follies of his youth and their consequences had made Don Garceran see the error of his ways.

Manrique's son had been ordered from the court to the frontier because—dressed in women's clothes—he had managed to make his way into the room of one of the queen's ladies in waiting, the virtuous Doña Clara. At the beginning of the first act, Don Garceran returns to the court:

> Ein wackrer Mann, Herr, fürchtet keinen Feind,
> Doch schwer drückt edler Fraun gerechter Zorn.

The king is ready to forgive the young knight. Later it is Alfonso who orders Don Garceran to accompany the Jewish family. Having been taught wisdom by his own experience, Don Garceran is filled with apprehension for Alfonso: "Nicht deine Tochter ist's, noch du, für die ich fürchte," (557) he says to Isaak, and his subsequent role is that of a worldly-wise monitor to the young king. He tries his best to persuade Alfonso to leave Rahel and to return to his duties. The king's affair reminds him of his own disssolute earlier life, and he feels ashamed both of himself and his ruler (876-878).

Don Garceran's position between his father and the king is a rather difficult one. He has incurred his father's displeasure, as was mentioned before because the latter wrongly believes that his son has played the role of a procurer. Don Garceran protests his innocence with great eloquence to the assembled nobles and especially to Doña Clara (1280 ff.). Manrique replies that if he is a Castilian and a man who loves his country, he will join the nobles and show the way to the king's mistress. "Nichts gegen meinen König, meinen Herrn," Garceran replies. But he had seen—at the beginning of act three—the worst possible results of nepotism brought about by the fact that Rahel was making the best of her relation to the king and, above all, having just returned from the frontier, he knows better than any one else the danger to the country from the invading Moors. Thus after a short struggle he joins the nobles (1543). He is convinced that Rahel's death is the only solution for the king as well as for Castile. However, the inner struggle between his loyalty to his king and his apprehension concerning the safety of the state might have been shown more clearly.

Later Don Garceran is one of the first to join his father in placing himself at the mercy of Don Alfonso:

> Seht mich bereit. Ich tret' an eure Seite
> Und treffe mich des Königs erster Zorn.

In the final scene the king promises the hand of Doña Clara to Don Garceran, should he purify himself in the impending battle. Concerning this lady Rahel had once remarked mockingly:

> Die viel zu bleich für wangenfrische Liebe,
> Wär' nicht die Farbe, die dem Antlitz fehlt,
> Ersetzt durch stets erneutes Schamerröten.

Now Alfonso gives her good advice out of the depth of his experience:

> Ihr sollt ihn bessern, Doña Clara! doch, um Gott!
> Macht ihm die Tugend nicht nur achtungswert,
> Nein liebenswürdig auch. Das schützt vor Vielem.

Garceran's traits are—generally speaking—taken from Lope de Vega's play. Grillparzer enlarged and deepened his role. Don Garceran knows the world and men better than Alfonso. Above all, Manrique's son—in contrast to the king—is well versed in matters of love. From a sense of loyalty the vassal tries to check the king's fatal passion. He does not tire of warning his superior, but is very reluctant in joining the revolt against him. Don Garceran is neither a philistine, nor a coward, nor a hypocrite, as has been charged. There is nothing in the drama to show that Garceran was not entirely sincere in his reformation under the stimulus of his love for the virtuous Doña Clara (408), in his apprehension concerning the "state of the nation" (cf. the beginning of act III) and concerning the danger from the Moors at the border. While he did betray his king and childhood companion (and was ready to take his punishment for his disloyalty), he is as little or as much a traitor to his country as are his father and the other nobles.

It has been demonstrated that Alfonso, the protagonist, as well as Manrique and Garceran, the minor male characters, are men with courage and determination. All three readily admit their human failings and face the consequences like men. In contrast to Rudolf II, Grillparzer's Alfonso is a capable ruler despite his shortcomings.

CHAPTER TWELVE

As we view, in retrospect, the long line of dramatic figures analyzed in these pages, we are impressed, first of all, by the infallible psychological insight that enabled Austria's foremost dramatic artist to create so many widely different living and viable human types and individuals. Franz Grillparzer was, indeed, blessed with a super-sensitivity that aided his powerful urge to explore, and interpret correctly, the human soul whenever and wherever he came into contact with it. He himself strikingly describes this remarkable empathy:

> Ich glaube, dass das Genie nichts geben kann, als was es selbst in sich gefunden und dass es nie eine Leidenschaft oder Gesinnung schildern wird, als die es selbst als Mensch in seinem eigenen Busen trägt. Daher kommen die wichtigen Blicke, die oft ein junger Mensch in das menschliche Herz tut, indes ein in der Welt Abgearbeiteter, selbst mit scharfem Beobachtungsgeist Ausgerusteter nichts als hundertmal gesagte Dinge zusammenstoppelt. Also sollte Shakespeare ein Mörder, Dieb, Lügner, Veräter, Undankbarer, Wahnsinniger gewesen sein, weil er sie so meisterlich schildert? Ja! Das heisst, er musste zu dem allen Anlage in sich haben.

Little wonder, then, that he showed himself a master in the creation of women characters, a fact which has been determined and repeated by so many critics and most comprehensively discussed by Francis Wolf-Cirian in her book GRILLPARZERS FRAUENGESTALTEN. It has now been shown that he was equally masterful in the creation of men. The range and variety of his portraiture of men becomes apparent when we compare, for instance, Phaon with Zawisch or Don Cäsar; Rustan with Leon or Don Garceran; Aietes with Ottokar or Alfonso; Rudolf II with Primislaus or Rudolf I; or Phryxus with Bancbanus or Manrique. —That on the basis of Grillparzer's creative ability "manly men" would not be lacking among his dramatic figures is self-evident.

We have frequently differed with the critics quoted for various reasons. At times our differences rested on errors of fact, in which cases our corrections need no further explanation. But on a number of other occasions our differences grew out of a matter of definition. Those differences might be succinctly summarized in conclusion in a clear statement of what is understood by "manly."

Of all the critics who by direct statement or by implication find Grillparzer's dramas lacking in "manly" characters only two define their terms. We shall turn first to Volkelt who, as we have seen, is chiefly responsible for this widely quoted view regarding our dramatist. Volkelt's definition of what he considers "spezifisch männlich" is as follows:

> Das wahrhaft männliche Wollen geht in dem klaren Lichte des Bewusstseins vor sich, es hat zu Bedingungen weiten und freien Blick, bewegliche, gewandte Reflexion, kritisches, ungeniertes, bis zu gewissem Grade respektloses Denken. Dagegen steht ihm stilles Sinnen, eingeschränkte Gemütstiefe, helldunkles Bewusstsein wenn dies vorherrschend auftritt, hindernd gegenüber.[1]

From some of these words, e. g. "critical," "unabashed," "disrespectful," it would appear that Volkelt's "man" must to some extent be revolutionary, and that conservative qualities, even faithfulness and loyalty, which certainly do characterize numerous heroes of dramas and epics, have no place in his scheme. On the negative side "quiet reflection" and "fixed depth of feeling" are mentioned as unmanly. Consistently enough, Volkelt considers Hamlet as not "manly." Volkelt may, of course, define words as he chooses; but it must be pointed out that his definition varies widely from the generally accepted usage; and if his strictures on Grillparzer are quoted apart from his context, the term "manly" naturally takes on its usual meaning and a great injustice is done our dramatist.

The other critic to define his terms is E. J. Williamson with whose characterizations we have frequently differed in the preceding chapters. Williamson's purpose is to discover elements of romanticism in Grillparzer's works. He points out[2] that the "romantic idea of a perfect character was that of a person who combined within himself the best features of both sexes," as Schlegel put it: "sanfte Männlichkeit" and "selbständige Weiblichkeit;" and Williamson comes to the conclusion that "Grillparzer's characters correspond excellently to Schlegel's demand." He then divides the dramatist's characters into three classes: I, the instinctive type who follows blindly uncontrollable impulses; II, the quietistic type who turns away from life and seeks happiness in retirement and solitude; III, commonplace characters drawn from ordinary life.

Naturally enough a certain artificiality results from Williamson's efforts to fit the characters into these classes. Furthermore, it might be added, when he states[3] "most of the men whom he [Grillparzer] portrayed have something feminine in their nature" and calls this feminine element "instinctive," his definition and Volkelt's become to some extent contradictory. The latter certainly considers "quiet reflection" an element that is not manly, while Williamson calls it "feminine" to be "instinctive."

We have throughout used the term "manly" in the sense in which the average reader would understand it, that is, in conformity with, say, Webster's definition: "brave, resolute, noble." It goes without saying that such bravery includes moral as well as physical courage.

A brief review of a number of the men analyzed in these pages will suffice to show Grillparzer could portray—and did not shun the portrayal of—men whose manliness conforms to the generally accepted definition of the term. Whatever the defects in the portraiture of Jaromir, the protagonist in Grillparzer's early drama *Die Ahnfrau*, we recognize in this rather phantastic figure a man of strength, courage, and strong passion. His lot is an unspeakably cruel one; but he perishes through his own excess of passion. Excess of passion in quite a different situation also leads to the death of Leander whom we see develop into a man in the course of the drama. In weak men one never encounters the overpowering passions of a Jaromir or a Leander. —Ottokar is a tragic hero in Schiller's sense. To a degree also Phryxus belongs into this category; both are the protagonists in the tragedies in which they play a role. —Among the other dramatic figures who play major roles, if not necessarily the leading role, mention should be made, first of all, of Rudolf I of *Konig Ottokars Gluck und Ende* and of Primislaus of *Libussa* who are equipped with all the "Regententugenden" one could desire —not the least among them strength, courage, and nobility of spirit—even though the one is a nobleman, the other—like Bishop Klesel—of humble beginnings. There is another man among Grillparzer's rulers, Alfonso of *Die Judin von Toledo*, who is chastened in the course of the plot after a moral lapse made possible by a faulty, though well-meant, education. Not the least among these manly men is Bancbanus, the faithful vassal. Although he represents Grillparzer's dramatic personification of Kant's categorical imperative, Bancbanus is a living human being with normal human emotions who by dint of his loyalty and the wisdom and patience of his old age manages to suppress his personal desire for revenge in the interest of the welfare of the state. Mention should be made, further, of Leon— like Bancbanus a leading figure—who, despite his youth, delights the spectator with his courage, wit, and humor; of Phaon, the naive and unsophisticated young Greek, who learns a few facts of life and performs heroic deeds for his lady-love. Here, too, belongs the Jason of *Die Argonauten*, the fearless adventurer and impetuous suitor, although he shows later —in *Medea*—that he lacks moral stamina.

Of the manly men among the minor figures Count Borotin, the victim of a malicious fate which brings him many misfortunes and finally death, never loses his zestful love of life. Von Merenberg, the father, a medieval knight in the best sense of the word, perishes in a just cause. The brave barbarian Absyrtus finds death because he allows lust for gold to get the better of him. Seyfried von Merenberg, who has much in common with Schiller's Max Piccolomini, is a tragic hero although his unhappy role does not end in death. Grillparzer's Bishop Klesel, a self-made man with the ability of a wise and strong ruler, might have prevented the Thirty Years' War, had he been in a position to carry out his ideas. It is fitting to end the list of courageous men portrayed by Austria's greatest dramatist with three loyal servants, friends, or vassals: Rhamnes, the teacher-slave of Greece's greatest poetess, her staunch defender to the end; Naukleros, Leander's brave monitor and friend in life and death; and Leopold, the only Habsburg of *Ein Bruderzwist in Habsburg* who demonstrates his continued devotion to Rudolf II by word and deed.

NOTES

Notes for Introduction

[1] Nördlingen, 1888, second edition Munchen, 1909.

[2] *Op cit.*, pp. 2, 3, 197.   [3] *Op cit.*, p. 3.   [4] *Op cit.*, p. 28.

[5] Reich, Emil, *Franz Grillparzers Dramen*, Funfzehn Vorlesungen gehalten an der Universität Wien, Dresden, E. Pierson, 1909, p. 262.

Bulthaupt, Heinrich, *Dramaturgie des Schauspiels; Grillparzer, Hebbel, Ludwig, Gutzkow, Laube*, Oldenburg & Leipzig, Schulzesche Hof-Buchhandlung, 1908, p. 39.

Kaderschafka, Karl, in Franz Grillparzer, *Samtliche Werke*, Historisch-kritische Gesamtausgabe, Im Auftrage der Bundeshauptstadt Wien, hrsg. von August Sauer, Wien, Kunstverlag Anton Schroll & Co., 1909ff, referred to as "W. A.", I vol. VI, p. XXV.

[6] Williamson, Edward John, *Grillparzer's Attitude Toward Romanticism*, Chicago, The University of Chicago Press, 1910, pp. 24, 25.

Klarmann, Adolf D., "Psychological Motivation in Grillparzer's *Sappho*," *Monatshefte fur deutschen Unterricht, deutsche Sprache und Literatur*, vol. XL, (1948), p. 272, repeats, essentially, what Volkelt and the rest have said in regard to Grillparzer's men. In contrast to Williamson, Klarmann links Grillparzer with the impressionists.

[7] Williamson, *op cit.*, looks at Grillparzer's works from the point of view of romanticism. Muller, Joachim, *Grillparzers Menschenauffassung*, Weimar, Hermann Bohlaus Nachfolger, 1934, reads into Grillparzer the very pessimistic philosophy that mere existence is tragic suffering.

[8] Curme, G. O., Edition of Franz Grillparzer's *Libussa*, New York, Oxford University Press, 1913, p. XV.

Notes for Chapter One

[1] For influences and sources of *Die Ahnfrau* cf.:

Komorzynski, Egon von, "*Die Ahnfrau* und die Wiener Volksdramatik," *Euphorion*, IX (1902), pp. 350-360.

Wyplel, Ludwig, "Ein Schauerroman als Quelle der *Ahnfrau*, Ein Beitrag zur Entstehungsgeschichte der Tragodie," *Euphorion*, VII (1900), pp. 725-758.

Lessing, O. E., *Schillers Einfluss auf Grillparzer*, Bulletin of the University of Wisconsin, No. 54, Madison, Wis., 1902.

Kohn, Joseph, "Zur Charakteristik der *Ahnfrau*," *Jahrbuch der Grillparzer-Gesellschaft*, XI (1900), pp. 22-76.

Backmann, Reinhold, "Entwicklungsgeschichtliches zu Grillparzers *Ahnfrau*," *Jahrbuch der Grillparzer-Gesellschaft*, XXVIII (1926), 22-43.

Arlt, Gustave O., "A Source of Grillparzer's *Ahnfrau*," *Modern Philology*, XXIX (1931), pp. 91-100.

Zucker, A. E., "An *Ahnfrau* Scene in Schiller's *Wallenstein*," *Modern Language Notes*, LI (1936), 97-98.

Wolff, Hans M., "Zum Problem der *Ahnfrau*," *Zeitschrift für deutsche Philologie*, LXII (1937), pp. 303-317.

For the history of this drama cf. the exhaustive study by Minor, J., "Zur Geschichte der deutschen Schicksalstragodie und zu Grillparzers *Ahnfrau*," *Jahrbuch der Grillparzer-Gesellschaft*, IX (1899), pp. 1-85.

For a brief account, in English, cf. Douglas Yates, *Franz Grillparzer. A critical Biography*, vol I, Oxford, 1946, pp. 25-30.

[2] Note the points of similarity between the ancestress and Elga of Grillparzer's master-*Novelle, Das Kloster bei Sendomir*.

Notes for Chapter Two

1 For influences see:

Sauer, August, in introduction to *Sappho*, W. A, I, 1, pp. LXXXVIII ff.

2 Schwering, Julius, *Franz Grillparzers hellenische Trauerspiele, auf ihre literarischen Quellen und Vorbilder gepruft*, Paderborn, 1891. A discussion of this book by August Sauer, *Anzeiger fur deutsches Altertum*, XIX (1893), pp. 308 ff.

Lessing, O. E., "Sappho-Probleme," *Euphorion*, X (1903), pp. 592-611.

————, *Grillparzer und das Neue Drama*, München, Piper, 1905. Reviewed by Robert Petsch, *Euphorion*, XIV (1907), pp. 160-179.

Lessing, O. E., *Schillers Einfluss auf Grillparzer*, Bulletin of the University of Wisconsin, No. 54, 1902.

Pachaly, Paul, *Erlauterungen zu Grillparzers Sappho*, 4th ed., Leipzig, 1926 (W. Königs Erläuterungen zu den Klassikern, Bdch. 52).

Yates, Douglas, *Der Kontrast zwischen Kunst and Leben bei Grillparzer*, Berlin, 1929 (Germanische Studien, E. Eberling, Heft 75).

Münch, Ilse, *Die Tragik in Drama und Personlichkeit Franz Grillparzers*, Berlin, Junker & Dunnhaupt, 1931.

Volkelt, Johannes, *op. cit.*, 39-49.

Root, Winthrop H., "Grillparzers *Sappho* and Thomas Mann's *Tonio Kroger*," *Monatshefte*, XXIX (1937), pp. 59-64.

Klarmann, Adolf D., *op. cit.*

Cf. especially the interesting and deep discussion of the Sappho "problem" in Douglas Yates, *Franz Grillparzer*, 1946, Chapter II, pp. 31-58.—A future Grillparzer scholar who becomes fascinated by the Sappho "problem" will probably begin by examining the terms "subjective and "objective" (which are already becoming suspect) and then give *his* opinion of the Sappho "problem."—The often quoted statement by Grillparzer (Yates, page 36) permits, of course, a number of interpretations.

3 Ehrhardt, August, *Franz Grillparzer, sein Leben und seine Werke*, München, O. Beck, 1910. p. 69, gives this estimate of Phaon: "er kann gut mit Pferden umgehen."

4 E. J. Williamson, *op. cit.*, p. 25, refers to Phaon as the "männlich-weiblich" type of man which was the ideal of the romanticists (the Schlegels, Novalis, and others). However, he gives no evidence to support his statement.

Notes for Chapter Three

1 Backmann, Reinhold, *Die ersten Anfange der Grillparzerschen Medeadichtung*, Diss., Leipzig. Weida, i. Th., Thomas & Hubert, 1910. Cf. also vol 1, 2, of *W. A.*, edited by Backmann.

Kohm, Josef, *Grillparzers Goldenes Vlies und sein handschriftlicher Nachlass*, Vienna, Kommissionsverlag von Karl Gerolds Sohn, 1906. Reviewed by Reinhold Backmann, *Euphorion*, XVI (1909), pp. 203-219, 555-579.

Radermacher, Ludwig, "Grillparzers Medea," *Jahrbuch der Grillparzer-Gesellschaft*, XXXII (1923), pp. 1-10.

Milrath, Max, "Das goldene Vliess, Libussens Geschmeide und Rahels Bild," *Jahrbuch der Grillparzer-Gesellschaft*, XX (1911), pp. 226-258.

Lesch, H. H., "Der tragische Gehalt in Grillparzers Drama 'Das goldene Vliess,'" *Jahrbuch der Grillparzer-Gesellschaft*, XXIV (1915), pp. 1-55.

Kilian, Eugen, "Miscelle zum zweiten Teil der Vliess-Trilogie," *Jahrbuch der Grillparzer-Gesellschaft*, III (1893), pp. 366-369.

Lessing, O. E., *Schillers Einfluss auf Grillparzer*, Bulletin of the University of Wisconsin, No. 54 (1902).

Idem, "Motive aus Schiller in Grillparzers Meisterwerken," *Journal of English and Germanic Philology*, V (1903-1905), pp. 33-43.

Hart, H., "Grillparzers Medea und Ibsens Nora," *Tag*, N. 407 (1901), discussed in *Jahresberichte fur neuere deutsche Literaturgeschichte*, XIII (1902) p. 496.

Yates, Douglas, *Franz Grillparzer*, 1946, Chapter III, pp. 59-75.

Dunham, T. C., "Medea in Athens and Vienna," *Monatschefte*, XXXVIII (1946), pp. 217-225.

[2] Volkelt, Johannes, *op. cit.*, p. 35.

[3] *Op. cit.*, p. 15.

[4] *Ibid.*, p. 15.

[5] *Qp. cit.*, p. 25.

[6] *Ibid.*, p. 24.

[7] *Op. cit.*, p. 35.

[8] The "männlich-weiblich" type of male of the romanticists is not capable of such wooing.

[9] *Op. cit.*, p. 80.

[10] Ilse Münch, *op. cit.*, p. 36.

[11] Also his figure disproves Volkelt's statement (*op. cit.*, p. 35), quoted above, to the effect that Grillparzer shunned the "specifically manly in man" in the portraiture of his characters.

[12] *Op. cit.*, p. 43.

[13] *Ibid.*, p. 43.

[14] Ilse Münch, *op. cit.*, p. 43.

Notes for Chapter Four

[1] *Neue Freie Presse*, February 2, 1872, as quoted by O. E. Lessing, *Grillparzer und das neue Drama*, *cit.*, p. 35.

[2] "German Playwrights," *Critical and Miscellaneous Essays*, London, Chapman & Hall, 1899, I, 355-395, p. 365.

[3] *Franz Grillparzer, Vortrage und Aufsatze zur Geschichte des geistigen Lebens in Deutschland und Oesterreich*, Berlin, Weidmann, 1874, pp. 193-307.

[4] Seemüller, Joseph, Ausgabe der *Oesterreichischen Reimchronik* (written between 1300 and 1320), in the *Monumenta Germaniae historica*, vol. V of the *Deutschen Chroniken*. Of the 98,595 verses, about 13,000 deal with the deeds of King Ottokar (Ehrhard, *op. cit.*, p. 195).

[5] For the sources, history, and influence of this drama see also: Glossy, Carl, "Zur Geschichte des Trauerspiels 'König Ottokars Glück und Ende,'" *Jahrbuch der Grillparzer-Gesellschaft*, IX (1899), pp. 213-247.
Collison, W. E., Körner, A. M., and Triebel, L. A., "Notes on Grillparzer's 'Konig Ottokar's Gluck und Ende,'" *Modern Language Review*, V (1910), pp. 454-472.
Eggert, C. E., Edition of Franz Grillparzer's *Konig Ottokars Gluck und Ende*, New York, Henry Holt, 1910, p. LV.
Strich, Fritz, *Grillparzers Aesthetik*, Berlin, A. Duncker, 1905.
Redlich, Oswald, *Grillparzers Verhaltnis zur Geschichte*, Vortrag gehalten in der feierlichen Sitzung der Kaiserlichen Akademie der Wissenschaften in Wien, am 1. Juni 1901. Almanach der Kaiserlichen Akademie, 57.
Klaar, Alfred, *"Konig Ottokars Glück und Ende." Eine Untersuchung uber die Quellen der Grillparzerschen Tragodie*, Leipzig, 1885.
Farinelli, Arturo, *Grillparzer und Lope de Vega*, Berlin, E. Felber, 1894.
Littroff-Bischoff, Auguste von, *Aus dem persönlichen Verkehre mit Franz Grillparzer*, Wien, Rosner, 1873.
Salinger, Herman, "Shakespeare's Tyranny of Grillparzer," *Monatshefte*, XXXI (1939), pp. 222-229.

[6] *Op. cit.*, p. 303.

[7] *Op. cit.*, p. 246.

[8] Meyer, R. M., *Die deutsche Literatur des 19ten Jahrhunderts*, Berlin, Bondi, 1906. Meyer holds that. Ottokar "eigentlich nur wegen einiger

Privatsunden zugrunde geht" (p. 100).

[9] *Op. cit.*, p. 246.

[10] *Op. cit.*, p. 14.

[11] *Op. cit.*, p. 246.

[12] *Op. cit.*, p. 246.

[13] *Op. cit.*, p. 25.

[14] *Op. cit.*, pp. 9, 13.

[15] *Op. cit.*, pp. 52, 53.

[16] *Grillparzer und das neue Drama*, München & Leipzig, Piper, 1905, p. 40.

[17] *Op cit.*, p. 247.

[18] *Op. cit.*, p. XLVII.

[19] This has also been recognized by Emil Reich (*Franz Grillparzers Dramen*, Dresden, E. Pierson, 1909, p. 127) and by Ehrhard (*op. cit.*, p. 202).

[20] *Op. cit.*, p. 128.

[21] From the *Oesterreichische Reimchronik, cit.*, as quoted by Ehrhard, *op. cit.*, p. 206.

[22] Act I, scene 5.

[23] So fine is this point that it was misinterpreted by two critics: Adolf Lichtenfeld, *Schulausgabe von "Konig Ottokars Gluck und Ende,"* Stuttgart, Cotta, 1900, p. 91; and Gustav Waniek, *Schulausgabe von Grillparzers "Konig Ottokars Gluck und Ende,"* Wien-Prag, Tempsky, 1903, p. 150, who believed that the "ocean of suspicion" was to be created in the addressee of the letter, the Archbishop of Mayence. Also Alois Bernt, "Splitter zur Erklarung von Grillparzers 'König Ottokar,'" *Euphorion*, XI (1904), pp. 518-520, called attention to this misinterpretation.

[24] R. M. Meyer (*op. cit.*, p. 100) to the contrary notwithstanding, in whose opinion the episode "verdirbt doch den grossen Gegensatz zwischen Ottokar . . . und Rudolf."

[25] *Op. cit.*, p. 208.

[26] R. M. Meyer's statement does not seem warranted: "auch Seyfried Merenberg, ein von Ottokar wie Max Piccolomini von Wallenstein enttäuschter edler Jungling, und sein uninteressanter Vater nehmen zu viel Raum ein: Grillparzer haftete noch zu sehr an den Urkunden, an den 'dankbaren Stellen' der alten Chroniken" (*op. cit.*, p. 100).

Notes for Chapter Five

[1] "Grillparzer und Byron, Zur Entstehungsgeschichte des Trauerspiels 'Ein treuer Diener seines Herrn,'" *Euphorion*, IX (1902), pp. 677-698; X (1903), pp. 159-180.

[2] For other sources, influences, and the history of the play we refer to:
Sauer, August, "Ein treuer Diener seines Herrn," *Jahrbuch der Grillparzer-Gesellschaft*, III (1892), 1-40.
Rosenberg, F., "Zur Quelle von Grillparzers 'Ein treuer Diener seines Herrn,'" *Archiv fur das Studium der neueren Sprachen*, 124, pp. 291-299. (Loyal subject motive in Fletcher's "Loyal Subject.")
Weilen, A. von, "Zu Grillparzers 'Ein treuer Diener seines Herrn,'" *Euphorion*, XVIII (1911), pp. 136-142. (Parallels in George Lillo's "Elmerick or the justice triumphant.")
Reich, Emil, *op. cit.*, VII.
Roselieb, Hans, "Grillparzer und die Barocke," *Jahrbuch der österreichischen Leo-Gesellschaft;* referred to in *Jahresberichte über die wissenschaftlichen Erscheinungen auf dem Gebiete der neueren deutschen Literatur*, VIII (1910), p. 202.
Katann, Oskar, "Grillparzers 'Ein treuer Diener seines Herrn,'" *Der Kunstgarten*, VI, pp. 121-128.
Scherer, Wilhelm, *op. cit.*, pp. 247-254.
Cf. also the, in part, highly conjectural chapter on "Ein treuer Diener seines Herrn" in Douglas Yates, *op. cit.*, pp. 121-135.

[3] *Cf.* also Reichert, Herbert W., "The Characterization of Bancbanus in

Grillparzer's 'Ein treuer Diener seines Herrn,' " *Studies in Philology,* XLVI (1949), pp. 70-78.

4 *Op. cit.,* 251, 252.

5 *Op. cit.,* p. 19.

6 *The German Drama of the Nineteenth Century,* translated from the German edition (1906) by L. E. Horning, New York, Holt, 1909, p. 30.

7 *Op. cit.,* p. 84.

8 *Grillparzers Personlichkeit in seinem Werk,* Zürich, Leipzig, Verlag der Münsterpresse, 1928, p. 100.

9 *Op. cit.,* p. 25.

10 Über das künstlerische Problem in Grillparzers 'Ein treuer Diener seines Herrn,' " *Euphorion,* VII (1900), 541-547; pp. 543, 544.

11 *Op. cit.,* pp. 101, 102.

12 *Op. cit.,* p. 159.

13 *Dramaturgie des Schauspiels,* Oldenburg und Leipzig, Schulzesche Hofbuchhandlung, 1918, III, p. 102.

14 With *Ein treuer Diener seines Herrn* Grilparzer becomes a forerunner of Hebbel.

15 Beriger evidently thinks that wise ruling depends on physical strength.

16 *Cf.* also Bulthaupt as quoted above (note 13).

17 A careful re-reading of the third act will show that the reasons for Erny's suicide lie in the character of the prince, in the queen's foolish indulgence toward her spoiled brother, and, of course, in Erny's character, who is the very opposite of Kunigunde. The motivation is flawless. It also becomes clear that Bancbanus could not have prevented the catastrophe in view of the conditions so clearly presented in the first two acts.

18 *Op. cit.,* p. 102.

19 *Op. cit.,* p. 159.

20 "Bemerkungen zu Grillparzers Bancbanus," *Euphorion,* VIII (1901), pp. 685-700.

21 *Op. cit.,* p. 544.

22 Ludolf von Wedel-Parlow, *Grillparzer,* Wertheim am Main, E. Bechstein, 1932, p. 96, says: "Das heroische Verhalten Bancbanus zieht die Blicke des Zuschauers auf sich, die aufreizende Wirkung (des Aufruhrs) wird dadurch unwillkürlich gemildert; auch halten die Fehler der Aufständischen den Fehlern der Fürstenfamilie die Waage und nehmen ihnen die Schärfe des Vorwurfs."

23 *Op. cit.,* p. 547.

24 *Op. cit.,* p. 156.

25 *Jahrbuch der Grillparzer-Gesellschaft,* I (1890), p. 214.

26 *Op. cit.,* pp. 214-215.

27 O. E. Lessing, *Grillparzer und das neue Drama, cit.,* p. 56, states erroneously that Simon and Peter are exiled; he evidently confused them with the two men of Otto's retinue who were deported (1915-1927).

28 *Op. cit.,* p. 238.

Notes for Chapter Six

1 "Aus dem Grillparzer-Archiv, Tagebuchblätter," *Jahrbuch der Grillparzer-Gesellschaft,* III (1893), 95-268; pp. 177ff.

2 For the influences, sources, and history of this drama *cf.*:
Scherer, W., *op. cit.,* 254-260.
Farinelli, A., *op. cit.,* 88-103.
Reich, Emil, *op. cit.,* 164-185.
Bulthaupt, H., *op. cit.,* 76-93.
Schütze, M., Edition of *Des Meeres und der Liebe Wellen,* New York, Henry Holt, 1930.
Ehrhardt, A., *op. cit.,* 272-294.
Sauer, A., "Grillparzer und das Königliche Schauspielhaus in Berlin, Mit

einem ungedruckten Briefe des Dichters," *Euphorion*, XXVII (1926), 112-114.

Yates, D., "Grillparzer's Hero and Shakespeare's Juliet," *Modern Language Review*, XXI (1926), 419-425.

Schwering, J., *Franz Grillparzers hellenische Trauerspiele, auf ihre literarischen Quellen und Vorbilder geprüft*, Paderborn, 1891, 151-183.

Sauer, A., review of Schwering, J., *op. cit., Anzeiger für deutsches Altertum*, XIX (1893), 334-338.

Dunham, T. C., "The Monologue as Monodrama in Grillparzer's Hellenic Dramas," *Journal of English and Germanic Philology*, XXXVII (1938), 513-523.

Yates, D., *op. cit.*, 151-188.

[3] Cf. Meyer, R. M., *op. cit.*, 106; and Scherer, W., *op. cit.*, 258.

[4] Act II, 2, 79ff.

[5] M. Schütze, *op. cit.*, LXXIX, finds it difficult to believe in Leander's accomplishments.

[6] M. Schütze, *op. cit.*, LVIII, asserts: "Leander is not a man in love; he is a spoiled boy crying for the object of a sudden hysterical appetite."

Notes for Chapter Seven

[1] *Op. cit.*, 147.

[2] For the sources, influences, and history of *Der Traum ein Leben cf.*:
Franz Grillparzer, Sämtliche Werke, W. A., I, 5 (1936), edited by Wilhelm, Gustav. [For the literary parallels *cf.* the extensive notes, pp. 272-329.]

Hock, Stefan, *"Der Traum ein Leben," Eine literarhistorische Untersuchung*, Stuttgart and Berlin, J. G. Cotta'sche Buchhandlung Nachfolger, 1904.

Meyer, R., "Grillparzers 'Traum ein Leben,'" *Weimarer Vierteljahrsschrift für Literaturgeschichte*, V (1892), 438.

Payer, R. v., "Grillparzers 'Traum ein Leben,' Ein Beitrag zur vergleichenden Literaturgeschichte," *Oesterreichisch-Ungarische Revue*, N. F., X, 53 ff.

Hock, Stefan, "Zum 'Traum ein Leben,'" *Jahrbuch der Grillparzer-Gesellschaft*, XIII (1903), 75-122.

Wurzbach, Wolfgang, "Eine unbekannte Opernbearbeitung von Grillparzers 'Der Traum ein Leben,'" *Jahrbuch der Grillparzer-Gesellschaft*, XXIX (1930), 100-107.

Benzinger, A., "Handlung und Charaktere in Grillparzers 'Der Traum ein Leben,'" *Studium und Leben*, II, 264-276, 329-336, 390-394.

[3] *Op. cit.*, 75.

[4] *Op. cit.*, 72.

[5] *Op. cit.*, 188.

Notes for Chapter Eight

[1] For a brief discussion of Grillparzer's approach to the writing of comedies and the extent of his occupation with the comedy problem *cf. Franz Grillparzer, Sämtliche Werke, W. A.*, I, 5 (1936), edited by Gustav Wilhelm, pp. 335 ff.

[2] *Op. cit.*, 264.

[3] For the history, the sources, influences and problems in *Weh dem, der lügt!* we refer to:
W. A., I, 5 (1936), edited by Gustav Wilhelm.

Minor, Jacob, "Grillparzer als Lustspieldichter und 'Weh dem, der lügt!,'" *Jahrbuch der Grillparzer-Gesellschaft*, III (1893), 41-60.

Volkelt, Johannes, "Grillparzer als Dichter des Komischen," *Jahrbuch der Grillparzer-Gesellschaft*, XV (1905), 1-30.

Jerusalem, Wilhelm, *Grillparzers Welt- und Lebensanschauung*, Vienna, J. Eisenstein, 1891. (Festrede, Ehrhard, *op. cit.*, 326).

Goedecke, Karl, *Grundriss zur Geschichte der deutschen Dichtung*, VIII, Dresden, L. Ehlermann, 1903, 324-325; 436.

Katann, Oskar, " 'Weh dem, der lugt!' und das Problem der Wahrhaftigkeit," *Grillparzer-Studien*, Vienna, Gerlach & Wiedling, 1924, 184-220; 310-315.

Farinelli, Arturo, *op. cit.*, 122-134.

[4] Scherer, *op. cit.*, 263.

[5] Müller, Joachim, *op. cit.*, 90.

[6] *Op. cit.*, 90.

[7] *Samtliche Werke*, XVII, 197.

Notes for Chapter Nine

[1] For the sources, influences, and history of *Libussa* cf.:
Franz Grillparzer, Samtliche Werke, W. A., I, 6 (1927), edited by Karl Kaderschafka, and especially the bibliography, 341-344.

Goedecke, Karl, *Grundriss*, VIII, 438 f.

For a minute outline of the drama in the English language we refer to G. O. Curme's edition of *Libussa*, Oxford University Press, American Branch, 1913, XL-XCVII, and to P. M. Campbell's review of this work in the *Modern Language Notes*, XXVIII (1913), 255-257.

[2] *Op. cit.*, 273.

[3] *Op. cit.*, 137.

[4] *Op. cit.*, 272-273.

[5] *Cf.* the quotation by E. J. Williamson, in the introduction, above.

Notes for Chapter Ten

[1] Wedel-Parlow, Ludolf von, *op. cit.*, 164-165, regrets that Grillparzer has not restricted himself to Rudolf alone, *i. e.* to the first, third, and fourth acts. This critic also asserts that Grillparzer failed to invigorate the drama by adding the second and fifth acts. Our character study will show that Wedel-Parlow's assertion lacks foundation. Careful source studies do not necessarily prove that Grillparzer was in this play a victim of inhibitions ("innere Hemmungen," *op. cit.*, 165).

[2] For a complete history of *Ein Bruderzwist in Habsburg* cf. Kaderschafka, Karl, *op. cit.*, W. A., I, 6, XXV-XLII, and for the sources and influences *cf.* the bibliographies, 341-342, 412f.

Goedecke, Karl, *Grundriss*, VIII, 458 ff.

[3] For the stage productions of this drama *cf.* Kaderschafka, Karl, "Ein Bruderzwist in Habsburg auf der Bühne," *Grillparzer Studien*, edited by Oskar Katann, Vienna, Gerlach & Wiedling, 1924; 221-243, 315-325.

[4] As quoted by Scherer, *op. cit.*, 284.

[5] *Die Geburt der Tragodie aus dem Geiste der Musik*, in *Nietzsches Werke*, II, Leipzig, Reclam, 1931, 55.

[6] *Op. cit.*, 68.

[7] *Op. cit.*, 275.

[8] *Op. cit.*, 86-98.

[9] *Cf.* also lines 2473 ff., 2485 ff., 2560 ff., 2613 ff., and 2769 ff.

[10] *Op. cit.*, 255.

[11] Reich, Emil, *op. cit.*, 276.

Notes for Chapter Eleven

[1] Berger, Alfred von, *Dramaturgische Vorträge*, Vienna, Carl Konegen, 1890, 34-60.

Ehrhardt, *op. cit.*, 386.

Lessing, O. E., *Grillparzer und das neue Drama*, 131.

[2] *Cf.* Lasher-Schlitt, Dorothy, *Grillparzer's Attitude Toward the Jews*, New York, G. E. Stechert & Co., 1936, p. 80: ". . . nor is she [Rahel] the most important, despite the fact that the drama is named after her. She is there more as a foil for the unfolding of the story of King Alphons, of his transgression and final repentance. After the third act she does

not even appear on the stage, not even as a corpse at the end."

[3] Introduction to this drama in *W. A.*, I, 7, p. XV.

[4] Detailed information concerning the sources, influences, and the history of the drama can be found in:

Berger, Alfred von, "Das, 'Glück' bei Grillparzer," *Jahrbuch der Grill-parzer-Gesellschaft*, X (1900), 70-79.

Wurzbach, Wolfgang von, " 'Die Jüdin von Toledo' in Geschichte und Dichtung," *Jahrbuch der Grillparzer-Gesellschaft*, IX (1899), 86 ff.

Lambert, Elie, "Eine Untersuchung der Quellen der 'Jüdin von Toledo,' " *Jahrbuch der Grillparzer-Gesellschaft*, XIX (1909), 61 ff.

Lambert, Elie, "La Juive de Grillparzer: étude sur la composition et les sources de la pièce," *Revue de Littérature Comparée*, Paris, Champion, 1922 II, 238 ff.

Aschner, S., "Zur Quellenfrage der Jüdin von Toledo," *Euphorion*, XIX (1918), 297-301.

Glossy, Carl, "Aus Bauernfelds Tagebüchern," II (1849-1879), *Jahrbuch der Grillparzer-Gesellschaft*, VI (1896), 85-223.

Sauer, August, "Oesterreichische Dichter; Ausgaben und Forschungen," *Euphorion*, XXVII (1926), 264-274.

Farinelli, A., *op. cit.*, 143-171.

[5] For the grotesque figure of Isaak *cf.* Dorothy Lasher- Schlitt, *op. cit.* 90 ff.

[6] Nietzsche, Friedrich, *Gotzendammerung*, as quoted by Ernst Bertram, *Nietzsche, Versuch einer Mythologie*, Berlin, Georg Bondi, 1921, 50.

[7] Grillparzer's "Plan zur Jüdin von Toledo," *Sämtliche Werke*, IX, 220.

[8] *Samtliche Werke*, IX, 220.

[9] Cf. lines 913, 989 ff., 1285 ff.

[10] Wedel-Parlow, L. v., *op. cit.*, 181.

[11] *Op. cit.*, 189.

[12] *Op. cit.*, 118.

Notes for Chapter Twelve

[1] *Op. cit.*, 35.

[2] *Op. cit.*, 24.

[3] *Op. cit.*, 24.

APPENDIX

Die Ahnfrau

The ghost of an ancestress has been haunting the castle of Count von Borotin for centuries. This she must do until the last of the accursed family is dead. At the beginning of the play the line seems to be near extinction. Count Borotin has had a son besides his daughter Bertha. But Jaromir had been kidnapped by robbers when only three years old and later he became the captain of this same robber band. One day Bertha, while walking in the woods, is attacked by a group of these robbers. Jaromir frees her, as the girl thinks, at the risk of his life. They fall in love and meet secretly. The band of robbers is defeated by soldiers and Jaromir flees to the castle. Under the name of Jaromir von Eschen he obtains the count's consent to his engagement to Bertha. Though the young man had decided to change his mode of living, yet the robber awakens in him when he sees his companions in danger. He rushes out to help them. The count joins the soldiers of the king. Jaromir and his father meet in the darkness of the night, not recognizing each other. The youth stabs the count with the dagger that had killed the adulterous ancestress centuries ago. To Bertha he discloses his real identity and persuades her to elope with him to his castle on the Rhine. From an old robber he hears that he is the count's son and Bertha's brother. But, blaming fate for the horrible position into which it has led him, he is unwilling to give up the girl he loves. Bertha, learning of the real relationship, takes poison and dies. Jaromir is awaiting Bertha in the family vault in order to flee with her. The "Ahnfrau" appears and kills him through her embrace. The old malediction has been fulfilled and now the ghost of the "Ahnfrau" can finally find rest and peace in the grave.

Sappho

Adorned with the wreath of victory, Sappho, the greatest poetess of Greece, has returned from Olympia to Lesbos, her island home. Her countrymen rush out to meet her in order to celebrate her triumph. She is accompanied by a Greek youth, Phaon, whom the poetess loves for his beauty and whom she offers all the treasures of her soul. Phaon had become intoxicated with his enthusiasm for the songs of Sappho. At the Olympic games he had fallen at her feet in worship. Sappho listens happily to his description of his veneration for her; however, what Phaon feels for her is only an enthusiastic admiration, not real love. Oppressed by the greatness of her mind, Phaon must admit to himself, that he, the insignificant one, can never reach her greatness. An affection develops in him quite spontaneously for a lovely young slave of Sappho, Melitta, who is spiritually on the same level with him. Sappho, who witnesses accidentally an amorous scene between the two lovers, suffers all the tortures of hurt pride and gnawing jealousy. She gives orders to remove Melitta to the island of Chios. Phaon flees with Melitta in order to protect his beloved. However, the fugitives are captured. Melitta subjects herself humbly; Phaon, however, reproaches Sappho for her action, and, reminding her of her position and reputation, inquires what she proposes to do. Sappho overcomes her passion and realizes that she was about to become faithless to her high calling for the sake of sensual love, and that she, the poetess crowned with laurels, must renounce human love. She gives up the world. Transfigured, like a priestess, she chooses death and throws herself into the ocean from the Leucadian rock. She returns, in the words of her teacher Rhamnes, to her home that is not of this earth.

Das goldene Vliess

Grillparzer gave the subtitles *Der Gastfreund, Die Argonauten,* and *Medea* to the subdivisions of his trilogy.

Der Gastfreund

To demand hospitality upon divine order, Phryxus comes to King Aietes of the barbarian country of Colchis. He carries with him the golden fleece of a ram. Aietes, greedy for the rare treasure, murders the guest. Invoking the revenge of heaven upon the barbarian, Phryxus prophesies that the golden fleece would witness the death of Aietes' children. Medea, the defiant daughter of the king, who is proud of her ancestry and her freedom and who has been enjoying her carefree life of hunting and fighting, sees with horror the furies of crime rise, and—turning suddenly clairvoyant—announces approaching disaster.

Die Argonauten

Act 1. Since that fateful hour Medea has retreated to a lonely tower, devoted to her magic. Greeks, the Argonauts, under the leadership of Jason, have arrived to claim the golden fleece. Boldly Jason forces his way into the tower of Medea. Infatuated by his handsome appearance, she prevents his death. Act 2. Afraid, the Argonauts—left without a leader—await the return of Jason. The hypocritical Aietes invites the Greeks to his house. Medea is to give Jason the poisoned cup, but upon discovering the identity of the hero, the Colchian princess warns him. Act 3. Filled with fear, the wild child of nature fights against the unknown power of love. Chance decrees that she fall into the hands of the Argonauts. Jason, to whom she seems divine in this gloomy land of barbarians, woos her impetuously; however, she hides her love. When Aietes approaches to destroy the stranger, Medea throws herself between the combatants with the confession that she loves Jason. The barbarian king curses her: her love shall be her punishment. Medea, however, renounces her father, her brother, and her home. To Jason, the egotist, she is only the means of obtaining his ardently longed-for goal, the golden fleece. Not even her threat to end her own life in case he should attempt to wrest the treasure from the death-dealing dragon restrains him. Horrified, Medea suspects that Jason will never love her as she loves him. Act 4. Very reluctantly yielding to his determination to secure the treasure even at the cost of her life, Medea makes use of her magic to narcotize the dragon which guards the treasure. Jason finally gains the fleece, whereupon he is momentarily seized with horror; he feels that this symbol of vain glory will some day bring ruin to him also. Medea's brother throws himself into the ocean; Aietes, her father, ends his own life. Laden with crime, Jason and Medea sail for Greece.

Medea

Act 1. Four years have passed. The Greeks have returned. Jason is weary of Medea. In barbarian Colchis the princess was the most beautiful; in sunny Hellas she seems ungracious to Jason. He fears, hates, and despises her; she is a burden to him. In addition, the unjust suspicion of murder rests upon her. The play begins at this point. Jason and Medea have had to leave Jason's home. Kreon, the king of Corinth, receives Jason; also he grants protection to Medea and her children with the stipulation that she show herself willing to conform to Greek customs. Act 2. Medea is still a loving wife and a loving mother. Wishing to be a Greek woman, she endeavors to learn from the lovely Princess Kreusa a Greek song that she hopes will please Jason, but this proves to be in vain, for Jason does not heed her striving for femininity, her gentleness, and her patience. A new misfortune approaches: the ban of the Amphictyonic League persecutes Jason and Medea at Corinth. Now Kreon grants shelter only to Jason and advises him to repudiate Medea. The king intends to give his daughter to Jason in marriage; and the latter, filled with duplicity, is not averse to the plan. Full of ill will, Medea separates from Jason, the hero whom she formerly admired and loved, but whom she now thinks weak and hypocritical. As an only condition she claims her children from him, yet even this request is refused. She leaves, thirsting for revenge. Act 3. Medea is to leave Corinth before evening. Jason's conversation with her reveals the smooth-tongued hypocrite completely. Only as a favor Jason allows her to take with her one of her sons, if he will go of his own free will. However, both children, frightened by Medea's threatening speech, wish to remain with Jason and the gentle Kreusa. Most horribly disappointed, deprived of her children, overpowered by the feeling of the wrong she is suffering, Medea collapses. Act 4. Kreon demands from Medea a final sacrifice, the golden fleece. She had buried it together with her instruments of magic; now, however, irritated to the utmost, Medea discards all consideration and composure, thinking only of revenge. As a bridal gift she sends Kreusa a magic cup from which flames issue forth and burn Kreon's daughter to death. In a blind rage Medea murders her own children, that through them she may revenge herself on Jason for his treachery. Act 5. Despair and horror resound throughout the palace; King Kreon, recognizing too late the danger of the guilty Jason's presence, banishes him. Depressed by the realization of his guilt and his contemptibleness, Jason lies on the bare ground in a lonely region. Medea, on her way to Delphi, takes leave of him forever. At Delphi she intends to return the golden fleece to the god. All earthly desires have vanished. "Was ist der Erde Gluck?—Ein Schatten! Was ist der Erde Ruhm?—Ein Traum!" Jason and Medea, who found each other in ardent love, separate in misfortune, and Medea's last words sound horrible to the ears of Jason: "Bear! Endure! Atone!"

Konig Ottokars Gluck und Ende

Act 1: Ottokar, in his boundless arrogance, wishes to separate from his noble wife on invalid pretexts in order to marry Kunigunde, the granddaughter of the king of Hungary. Ottokar's presumptuousness is such that he disregards all laws. Margaret accepts the injustice done to her and even presents her faithless husband with her lands, Austria and Styria, although they are fiefs of the Empire. To date, the successful king's exuberance and arbitrariness have been boundless; he dreams of ruling Poland, Silesia, and Hungary. His lands do him homage; envoys of the Electors arouse in him hopes for the crown of the German Empire. He only makes game of them all, however, not suspecting that his violations of the law have made him innumerable enemies. Act 2: Ottokar is secretly deserted by the Austrian and Styrian knights since he has repudiated Margaret and married Kunigunde. The young queen, who is in no wise attracted by the much older Ottokar, listens to the bold advances of the adroit Zawisch von Rosenberg. To Ottokar's surprise, news arrives that not he but Count Rudolf of Habsburg has been chosen German Emperor by the Electors; the envoys of the new head of the Empire appear promptly to reclaim in the name of the Emperor the vacant fiefs of Austria, Styria, and Carinthia, demanding that Ottokar surrender them; at the same time they insist upon his doing homage for Bohemia and Moravia. Act 3: Rudolf, the representative of the imperial dignity, the guardian of the law, has concentrated his army at the Bohemian border. When he invites Ottokar to Vienna for a friendly discussion, the latter accepts in order to impress with his pompous retinue the poor Habsburg whom he despises. However, matters take an unexpected turn for Ottokar. Justice is shown to be stronger than arrogance. Clad in a simple doublet, but vested with the dignity of an Emperor, Rudolf approaches him. While Ottokar is kneeling in the Emperor's tent to do homage for the purpose of the reenfeoffment—without witnesses, as he supposes—the tent curtains fall to the ground, for the revengeful Zawisch had cut the strings in order to expose Ottokar to public gaze as he kneels before his rival. Act 4: In despair over this humiliation, Ottokar returns to Prague. Seated on the steps of his own royal castle in disguise, he hears himself discussed by the burghers of his capital. He learns of the mockery of the defiant noblemen; he endures the poignant scorn of the young Queen Kunigunde. Furious and blinded by these humiliations, Ottokar resolves to restore his honor by violence. He tears up the treaty with Emperor Rudolf, has the older Merenberg, one of the hostages, killed, and prepares for war. Act 5: Ottokar, however, no longer possesses his former energy. He hesitates when he ought to advance, and there are traitors in his army. At Götzendorf, where his headquarters are situated, his first wife, Margaret, has died. Penitently he prays at her bier, forgetting battle and enemy. Not so Emperor Rudolf; with quiet determination he gives his orders. The Bohemians fight only half-heartedly; Rudolf is victorious, and Ottokar is killed—despite Rudolf's order that his life be spared—by the hand of young Merenberg, who is eager to avenge the death of his father.

Beside the body of Ottokar Rudolf invests his son Albrecht with the duchy
of Austria, and thus the dynasty of the Habsburgs in Austria is initiated.

Ein treuer Diener seines Herrn

The Hungarian Count Bancbanus swears to the King Andreas of Hungary to maintain peace and order as vicegerent during the latter's absence.
However, Queen Gertrude is hostile to the Count, also her brother, the passionate Duke Otto von Meran. The over-conscientious, pedantic vicegerent
of the Empire finds himself overloaded with political affairs. The courtiers
rail at the old man whose honest objective is the good of the country. His
noble, virtuous wife Erny seems neglected by him on account of many affairs of state; in the whirl of the profligate court she is exposed to the advances of the Duke of Meran which become bolder and bolder. Although
the words of the tempter do not fail to make some impression, she remains
firm; in fact, she even goes so far as to show the Duke her contempt. Otto
von Meran who cannot bear this humiliation demands of the queen that she
secure for him a private talk with Erny in order to enable him to call
her to account. However, when Otto wishes to abduct the resisting Erny
she kills herself. Alarmed by the long absence of Erny, Bancbanus breaks
into the room of the queen who—in order to protect her brother—takes the
responsibility for the bloody deed upon herself. An open revolt breaks out,
stirred up by the relatives of Erny and the Count. Bancbanus more than
anyone else seems to have just cause for joining the rebels; but he, mindful
of the oath he had sworn to his master and king, suppresses all thoughts
of vengeance. He even protects his enemies, the Queen and the Duke of
Meran, against the revolt which threatens their lives. Duke Otto falls into
deep despair that borders on insanity. The Queen is accidentally killed by
one of the rebels. When the King returns, Bancbanus resigns his post which
he had held so faithfully. Otto von Meran on emerging from his stupor testi-
fies to Erny's marital faithfulness, which Bancbanus had never doubted.
Then the venerable old man, broken and deprived of the dearest he had
possessed, retires to end his days in solitude.

Des Meeres und der Liebe Wellen

Hero had left the house of her parents in order to become a priestess
of Aphrodite in the temple of Sestos. She voluntarily renounces society and
wishes to belong to herself and her service to the goddess. As she goes to the
altar in order to take the binding vow, her glance falls on a young stranger
who has come to the festivity from Abydos on the other shore of the Hellespont. She realizes then that the happiness of woman does not lie in the service for the gods, but in love and devotion to a man. Leander, who hereto-
fore had been shy and timid, falls violently in love with her. During the
following night it is with terror that Hero sees Leander climb her tower
by the side of the ocean, but she consents to permit the exhausted swimmer a brief rest before his return through the channel. When the watch-
man approaches, Leander hides in Hero's bedroom. After the temple-
guard has gone, Leander reënters, protests his love, and happens to touch
Hero's shoulder in the dark. He asks the shuddering girl to place the lamp

in the window so that it may serve him on a future occasion as a guide when he swims across the sea. Hero permits him to stay that very night. The happiness of the lovers, however, is short-lived. The secret tryst of the priestess with a young stranger is discovered by Hero's uncle, the High-priest. On the day after that eventful night he sends Hero on long tiring errands. Upon her return, having placed the lamp in the window, the ex-hausted Hero falls asleep. The priest changes the position of the flame so that the storm extinguishes it; and the youth, robbed of the guiding beacon, is thrown on the rocks of the shore by the storm. Hero, matured to womanhood through love, makes no secret of her grief. Hero's heart breaks and she sinks lifeless from the arms of the servants who are hold-ing her.

Der Traum, ein Leben

We are taken to the Orient, into the plains of Samarkand. Rustan, a fervid and ambitious youth, lives with his uncle, the peaceful farmer Massud, and the latter's daughter Mirza. The colored slave Zanga excites Rustan's longing for adventure and travel. Determined to depart on the next day, Rustan falls asleep while outside of the hut the music of a song— sung by an old dervish—is heard. The song treats the theme that the world is a shadow and that there is truth only in thought. In a dream Rustan lives a life filled with wild ambition. His experiences unroll before our eyes with an uncanny speed. Rustan—so he dreams—is honored as the man who saved the life of the King of Samarkand although another person had really done it. This other, the "Mann vom Felsen," demands a reward from Rustan and is murdered by the latter. However, the dagger in the wound of the dead man betrays Rustan as the murderer. Meanwhile Rustan has won and married the king's daughter Gülnare; he proceeds to commit crime after crime. When the king dies of poison Rustan becomes his suc-cessor, but a successful revolt against him breaks out. Death at the hands of the executioner is to be his lot. His only choice is to throw himself into a river. At this turn Rustan wakes up. He realizes what he might have been capable of if the experiences which he dreamed had been reality. Shaken to the core and cured of his longing for glory and power, Rustan ends by seeking happiness in his peaceful hut at Mirza's side:

> Eines nur ist Glück hienieden,
> Eins: des Innern stiller Frieden
> Und die schuldbefreite Brust.

Weh dem, der lugt

The pious Bishop Gregor of Chalons considers the lie as the source of all evil: "Woe to him who tells a lie!" His amiable and adroit young cook, who is very devoted to his master, offers to free the bishop's nephew Atalus from captivity in the castle of the heathen Count Kattwald of the Rhine district (Rheingau). Gregor enjoins upon his loyal servant never to lie or to deceive on his dangerous mission. Leon does this with exquisite humor, telling the truth in the conviction that the people will not believe him, and, later, in the belief that God will help him who is truthful. Thus he returns safely with Atalus and Edrita, the daughter of Count Kattwald. The devout bishop on hearing Leon's adventures confesses humbly that it is impossible for man to solve by a simple formula the puzzle of this confused world. Every one considers it a great virtue to speak the truth and yet all deceive themselves as well as their fellowmen.

> Das Unkraut, merk' ich, rottet man nicht aus,
> Gluck auf, wächst nur der Weizen etwa drüber.

Libussa

King Krokus of Bohemia has died after a strenuous reign. He had been able to force obedience from his powerful chiefs, Lapak, the wise, Domaslav, the rich and influential, and Biwoy, the strong, and to subjugate the people under a wise but firm rulership. As none of the three noblemen feels confident to take the government, they approach the three daughters of the king, Kascha, Tetka, and Libussa, with the request that one of them be their sovereign. As the daughters of a divine mother, the three have been leading a secluded life of contemplation, devoted to divination, a power inherited from their mother. Scornfully Kascha and Tetka refuse to occupy themselves with material cares. Libussa, the youngest, however,—not satisfied with the life of inactive contemplation—wishes to be human among humans and—in order to be able to help her fellowmen—accepts the crown. There are two other determining factors in her decision. She had gone into the woods in order to find an herb which would cure her father. As she came too late, however, she felt that she was to blame for her father's death and that she should carry on his work for his and her people. During her search in the woods she had fallen into a river from whose waves she had been rescued by a simple farmer, Primislaus, who had taken her to his house where she spent the night. Dressed in the simple peasant clothes of the latter's deceased sister, she had returned the next day. An awakening love for the strong and wise farmer is a second reason for her dissatisfaction with her former inactive life.

The form of government Libussa has introduced at the beginning of the second act calls to mind Rousseau's ideals of government in conformity with nature. As may be expected, difficulties soon arise. The people clamor for their "right"—a concept which is most distasteful to Libussa. In her view on justice we readily recognize Hegel's philosophy of justice:

> Dass du dem Dürft'gen hilfst, den Bruder liebst,
> Das ist dein Recht, vielmehr ist deine Pflicht,
> Und Recht ist nur der ausgeschmückte Name
> Für alles Unrecht das die Erde hegt.

Libussa finds that the task she has set for herself is too difficult. Moreover, her people prefer to be ruled by a man. The three noblemen suggest marriage to Libussa, each in the hope that she would choose him. The proud daughter of a powerful king and a descendant of the gods desires to marry a man who would combine the good qualities of the trio, namely wisdom, strength, and influence. She thinks of Primislaus, but her immense pride prevents her from sending for him. To rid herself of the bothersome suitors, Libussa gives them a riddle to solve of which only

Primislaus knows the solution. Secretly she hopes that the latter may hear
of it and come to woo her. During her stay in his humble house he had
taken a jewel with the picture of her mother which had formed part of a
chain belt. Thus she words her riddle as follows:

Wer mir die Kette teilt,
Allein sie teilt mit Keinem dieser Erde,
Vielmehr sie teilt, auf dass sie ganz erst werde;
Hinzufugt was, indem man es verlor,
Das Kleinod teurer machte denn zuvor:
Er mag sich stellen zu Libussas Wahl,
Vielleicht wird Er, doch nie ein Andrer ihr Gemahl.

The three noblemen happen to meet Primislaus and—at a loss for a
solution—ask him to help them. Cleverly the farmer manages to obtain the
chain in exchange for the jewel and intentionally misinterprets the riddle
in order to send the three duped ones back to Libussa. His pride has been
hurt as he believes that the latter has left the fate of their love entirely to
chance. Disappointed he returns to his plow. —As the need of a strong ruler
becomes more and more evident to Libussa, she sends for Primislaus, but
she is determined not to compromise her pride.

The third and fourth acts are devoted to the long struggle between the
pride of Libussa and that of Primislaus. She who at first had established
an almost Communistic government meets the simple farmer as a sovereign.
She is determined to make him say the decisive word, but fails as Primislaus
is too proud to propose to one so much higher in station. Now she puts
him to a number of tests in order to discover a weak trait in his character; Primislaus, however, does not allow himself to be overwhelmed by her
regal display; he shows that he is wise, noble, and a man. When later he
discovers that she no longer stands before him as a princess, but as a woman,
his tone changes to humility and solicitude. Speaking in modern terms,
we would say that he is a born psychologist who always does the right thing
at the right time, and thus wins the woman Libussa. The latter proclaims
Primislaus King of Bohemia, kneeling before him and thereby expressing her
voluntary submission to her husband and king. She has become the ideal
woman of whom Primislaus had spoken earlier to Wlasta, one of Libussa's assistants in her amazon-government:

So ist das Weib der Schönheit holde Tochter,
Das Mittelding von Macht und Schutzbedürfnis,
Das Hochste was sie sein kann nur als Weib,
In ihrer Schwäche siegender Gewalt.

In the fifth act Primislaus has taken over the government with a firm
hand; yet he always makes Libussa feel that he is only her regent; she,
on the other hand, has made his will her own as she realizes that his
measures are for the good of her people. At the time of the action they
are making their stay in a simple farm house.

Primislaus' next step is the foundation of a city. In search for a con-
venient site, the energetic king and his assistants had met a man felling
a tree. When questioned for what purpose he would use the timber, the
worker replied "Prah," which means "threshold." Since this seemed to them

a good omen they decided to build the city there. Primislaus comes to Libussa with the request to bless the new undertaking by dedicating it to the gods. Libussa expresses her doubts concerning the merits of city life which —in her estimation—makes people onesided and puts them out of touch with nature. However, after hearing Primislaus' reasons for the necessity of "progress," she consents, although she feels that she does not have the strength:

> Doch glaub ich, Primislaus, mehr als die Seh'rin
> Liebst du dein Weib. Ich will sie dir erhalten.

Despite Primislaus' objections she proceeds with the dedication. The gift of clairvoyance, which had left her since she separated from her sisters, returns to her once more. In her vision she predicts that the era of irrationalism and idealism will be followed by that of rationalism and realism only to be followed by a return to idealism. She predicts the coming of Christianity. The gods will merge into one God, and this God will expand and individualize until there are as many gods as there are thinking beings. The beautiful and the good will be identical. Enthusiasm will no longer be foreign to cold utility, but—emanating from the latter—it will derive its ardor from it. The distinguished individual will no longer assert himself. But the goal and the destination of the whole will be the happiness and equality of all.

The strain of the trance proves too much for the weakened woman; she collapses and dies. It seems to be a vain task to search for her "tragic guilt." Libussa lives and dies for her people. Determining factors in her death are her assumption of the rulership, the summoning of Primislaus, matrimony, motherhood, her consent to the new form of gvernment, the dedication of the city foundation. Libussa's entire life is one of sacrifice and resignation with but a short period of happiness.

Ein Bruderzwist in Habsburg

The first act—as well as the third and fourth—plays in Prague. The scene opens on the "Kleinseiler Ring." General Russworm is to be executed for the slaying of Belgioso who happened to be a rival of Don Cásar, the natural son of the Emperor Rudolf II. Don Cäsar has been pursuing the daughter of the citizen Prokop, Lukrezia, to whom he expresses openly his satisfaction over his rival's death. The next scene takes place in the imperial castle in Prague. Archduke Mathias, the younger brother of the emperor, accompanied by his clever adviser Melchior Klesel, tries to obtain an audience. Mathias is rather discouraged; he has failed in everything he has ever attempted to undertake. However, his mood changes quickly when Klesel hints at some plans he has for him and begs him to ask his brother for the command of the Hungarian army engaged in a war with the Turks. The emperor appears, leaning on a cane. He inspects two portraits, chooses one silently, and directs his chamberlain Wolf Rumpf to pay for it. Rudolf disregards all business affairs and buries himself in a new book by Lope de Vega "Sotija del olvido." When approached by Mathias, the emperor ignores him completely and tells his chamberlain in more and more impassioned

tones that he desires to be alone. However, although the imperial treasury
is exhausted, he is ready to see precious stones which are being brought by
a merchant from Florence. Don Cásar comes to plead for the life of his
friend Russworm, but in vain; the death sentence is already signed. Angri-
ly the emperor threatens Don Cásar's life, should he—the libertine who
associates with mutineers and Lutherans—dare to plead for his friend. He
also orders Don Cäsar to leave Lukrezia in peace. Rudolf's wrath flares up
once more when Don Casar hints that he knows himself to be the son of the
emperor; for it reminds the latter of the prediction of Tycho Brahe, the
famous Danish astronomer, that a close relative would be his greatest
enemy. Archduke Ferdinand of Styria, Rudolf's nephew, appears to urge
action against the Protestants. Counter to his own better convictions, the
emperor appoints Mathias commander of the Hungarian army, expecting
that he will listen to the advice of his able general Mansfeld. Rudolf is
horrified when Ferdinand reports that in Styria, Carniola, and Carinthia
sixty thousand people have been converted to Catholicism, that twenty thousand who refused to be converted by force have been driven from their
homes, and that he has given up the idea of marrying the Protestant widow
of the Elector of Saxony whom he loves in order to woo the deformed daughter of the Catholic King of Bavaria. Rudolf sends his nephew away. The
otherwise unsociable ruler suddenly wishes to be surrounded by human beings. Ferdinand is reminded of the fact that he wished to introduce his
younger brother Leopold to the emperor who eagerly sends for the young
man: "Allein er ist ein Mensch." The church service is announced. All those
present group themselves for the procession to the chapel. Leopold, who
comes rushing in, is given a very friendly greeting by Rudolf.

The second act plays in the Hungarian camp of Mathias near Raab;
Mathias' army has been defeated again. He himself, however,—a very accomplished fighter—has battled his way out with remarkable bravery.
He is proud of his art. In the midst of his defeat he thinks of future victory which he expects to obtain through a rather hazy plan taken from
Vegetius' *Rei Militaris Instituta*. Mathias is opposed to making peace; yet
he follows the talented Klesel who has higher plans for Rudolf's brother. In
a family counsel to which the Archdukes Maximillian, the brother of Rudolf
and Mathias, Ferdinand, and Leopold have been invited, the clever bishop
contrives to persuade the Habsburgs to make peace with the Turks and
to form an alliance against Rudolf II.

In the third act Rudolf learns of the development of the uprising. In
his immediate vicinity the estates of Bohemia revolt against him. The act
closes with Mathias' victorious march into Prague. Leopold, the only one
of the Habsburgs who has remained loyal to the emperor, wrests from the
latter the fateful order which summons the army gathered at Passau. Thus
renewed civil war is brought on.

This struggle—Leopold's army is defeated—begins the fourth act. Don
Cäsar, who had been captured when he attempted to kidnap Lukrezia and
later freed by the rebels, kills Lukrezia in a fit of rage over her alleged
hypocrisy. Recaptured and imprisoned, the mad criminal has been bled by
the doctors. In a second attack of insanity Rudolf's natural son has torn

the bandages off his arms and is about to bleed to death in his cell unless a physician can come to his aid. In a most dramatic scene the emperor—himself a prisoner in his castle—pronounces and executes judgment over the culprit by refusing to surrender the key to Don Cäsar's cell and by dropping it into a well. Then follow Rudolf's long monologues containing the historic curse which he pronounces over the city of Prague, but which he later retracts. Maximillian and Ferdinand come to beg his pardon for their disloyalty, which he readily gives. Rudolf resigns the throne voluntarily, and collapses. We do not learn until the next act whether he has died or merely swooned.

In the fifth act—which plays in Vienna—Klesel has virtually taken over the reign for Mathias who proves himself to be as inactive as Rudolf II. Archduke Ferdinand—backed by the Catholic countries—has Klesel taken to Kufstein and imprisoned. In the anteroom the departing bishop meets, Colonel Wallenstein—the spirit of the approaching Thirty Years' War— who brings the report of the revolt in Prague ("Fenstersturz"). News of Rudolf's death arrives. [Grillparzer placed this event (1612) and the beginning of the great war (1618) on one and the same day.] We are made to feel that Ferdinand is rising above Mathias, just as Mathias rose above Rudolf. The former is overwhelmed by the feeling of guilt toward his deceased brother whose spirit seems to hover about him. Penitently Mathias kneels and beats his breast, pronouncing the Catholic phrase of the confession of sins: "Mea culpa, mea culpa, mea maxima culpa," while the crowd outside greets its new emperor: "Vivat Mathias."

Die Judin von Toledo

The young King Alfonso of Castile had not had a normal youth. Deprived of his kingdom when a mere child, he had later risen to power with the help of the strong Manrique, Count of Lara, who had educated Alfonso for his difficult royal duties. For reasons of state the young king had been, married early to the virtuous but ungraceful Eleonore of England, the daughter of Henry II. —Alfonso governs as a good and wise king; however, his wisdom has not been derived from experience. After many years of absence he has come to Toledo again where—at the beginning of the first act—he welcomes the queen for whose sake he has arranged his gardens in English style; however, he finds no appreciation on the part of the queen. In a mood of listless vexation Alfonso is confronted by a woman who in every respect is the extreme opposite of the queen. The flighty, vivacious, aggressively coquettish, and beautiful Jewish girl Rahel turns to him for protection when the keepers are trying to drive her, Isaak, her father, and Esther, her sister, from the gardens. For the first time in his life the king experiences a great passion. With the hand of a master Grillparzer shows us the stages by which Alfonso gradually succumbs to the snares of the willful siren. At the beginning of the third act Alfonso has spent some time in seclusion with Rahel at his castle Retiro although he should have been at the head of his army on the frontier which is threatened by an invasion of the Moors. He is repeatedly warned by the worldly-wise Don Garceran, the son of Count Manrique. Alfonso is fully aware of his shortcomings and regrets them; he also knows that he does not love Rahel. When Esther appears with the news that the nobles and the queen are plotting against Rahel's life, the king leaves, ready to assert his royal authority. A reconciliation with Eleonore is almost brought about when her cold virtuousness causes him to compare her with the woman he has left at Retiro. The queen leaves, and the nobles, guided by Garceran, hurry to Retiro to remove what they consider the obstacle in the way of the safety of Castile. In the greatest anger and intent on revenge, Alfonso rushes back to Retiro; however, it is too late; he finds Rahel murdered. The indignant king takes the first step to punish the nobles. Before executing his plans to avenge the murdered woman, however, Alfonso wishes to see her body. The sight of the mutilated lifeless body and the distorted features serves to free him completely from his infatuation. He wonders why he could ever have been attracted by this woman. In deep contrition Alfonso VIII proclaims his little son king of Castile, while he will be his marshal. Alfonso forgives Eleonore; he and the guilty nobles will fight for Castile against the Moors. Those who will be killed in battle will atone for all.

BIBLIOGRAPHY

I. Collective Editions of Grillparzer's Works

Grillparzer, Franz, *Briefe und Tagebucher*, Eine Ergänzung zu seinen Werken, hrsg. von Glossy, Carl, und Sauer, August, Stuttgart, J. G. Cotta, n.d.

Grillparzer, Franz, *Gesammelte Werke*, Auf Grund der von der Gemeinde Wien veranstalteten kritischen Gesamtausgabe, hrsg. von Rollet, Edwin, und Sauer, August, 9 Bde. Kunstverlag Anton Schroll & Co., Wien, n.d.

Grillparzer, Franz, *Grillparzers samtliche Werke*, hrsg. von Sauer, August, Stuttgart, Cotta, Ed. 5. 20v. 1893.

Grillparzer, Franz, *Grillparzers Werke*, hrsg. von Franz, Rudolf, Leipzig und Wien, Bibliographisches Institut, 5 v. (preface 1903)

Grillparzer, Franz, *Grillparzers samtliche Werke*, hrsg. von Necker, Moritz, Leipzig, M. Hesse, 16 v., 1903.

Grillparzer, Franz, *Grillparzers Meisterdramen*, hrsg. von Necker, Moritz, Leipzig, M. Hesse, 4 v. in 1, 1903.

Grillparzer, Franz, *Grillparzers Gesprache und die Charakteristiken seiner Personlichkeit durch die Zeitgenossen*, hrsg. von Sauer, August, Wien, Verlag des Literarischen Vereins, 6 v., 1904-1916.

Grillparzer, Franz, *Grillparzers Werke*, hrsg. von Hock, Stefan, Berlin, Bong, 16 v. in 6 (1912?)

Grillparzer, Franz, *Samtliche Werke*. Historisch-kritische Gesamtausgabe. Im Auftrage der Bundeshauptstadt Wien, hrsg. von Sauer, August, fortgef. v. Backmann, Reinhold, Kunstverlag Anton Schroll & Co., Wien, (1909-   ).

Grillparzer, Franz, *Selbstbiographie, Erinnerungen*, hrsg. von Hock, Stefan, Berlin, Bong (1912?). (In his *Werke.* 14 [1912?].)

Grillparzer, Franz, *Studien zur Literatur*, hrsg. von Stein, Fritz, Wien I, Carl Stephenson Verlag, n.d.

Grillparzer, Franz, *Grillparzers Werke*, hrsg. von Castle, Eduard, Wien, Oesterreichische Staatsdruckerei, 6 v., 1924.

Grillparzer, Franz. *Schau und Sammlung*, ausgewählt und eingeleitet von Muller, Joachim, Jena, E. Diederichs, 1938.

Grillparzer, Franz, *Grillparzers Werke*, hrsg. von Kindermann, Heinz, Leipzig, Reclam, 6 v., 1941.

Grillparzer Franz, *Der arme Spielmann, Das Kloster bei Sendomir, Selbstbiographie*, hrsg. v. Mell, Max, Wien, Verlag Albrecht Durer, 1947.

Grillparzer, Franz, *Ein Lebensbild in Selbstzeugnissen*, hrsg. von Rintelen, Fritz Martin, Munchen, B. Funck, (c. 1947).

Grillparzer, Franz, *Der innere Orden, ein Brevier*, hrsg. von Meyer, Christoph, Munchen, R. Piper, (c. 1947).

Grillparzer, Franz, *Autobiographisches; Studien*, [Kritische Ausgabe], hrsg. von Nadler. Josef, Wien, R. M. Rohrer, 1949.

Grillparzer, Franz, *Spuren des Lebens* (Teils.) *Erzahlungen und Aufzeichnungen*, hrsg. v. Langenbucher, Hellmuth, Bayreuth, Gauverlag, 1944.

Grillparzer, Franz, *Grillparzer im Bilde*, hrsg. von Payer von Thurn, Rudolf, and Reuther, Hermann, Wien, Wiener Bibliophilengesellschaft, 1930.

II. Grillparzer Bibliographies

Goedecke, Karl, *Grundriss zur Geschichte der deutschen Dichtung*, VIII, Dresden, L. Ehlermann, 1905.

Weilheim, A., *Katalog einer Wiener Grillparzer-Sammlung, mit bibliogra-

*phischen Anmerkungen, einem Verzeichnis der Bildnisse des Dichters
und Proben aus der Übersetzungsliteratur,* Wien und Leipzig, 1905.
Vancsa, Kurt, *Germanisch-Romanische Monatsschrift,* XIX (1931); *Euphorion,* XXXVI (1935); *Jahrbuch der Grillparzer-Gesellschaft,* XXXIV (1938).
Körner, Josef, *Bibliographisches Handbuch des deutschen Schrifttums,* Bern, A. Francke A. G. Verlag, 1949, pp. 383-386.
Petry, Karl, *Handbuch zur deutschen Literaturgeschichte,* Cologne, Balduin Pick Verlag, 1949, pp. 782-785.

III. Individual Editions of Grillparzer's Dramas
(alphabetical according to editors)

Grillparzer, Franz, *Weh dem, der lügt!* edited by Bell, Clair Hayden, New York, etc., Oxford University Press, 1928.
Grillparzer, Franz, *Family Strife in Hapsburg,* transl. by Burkhard, Arthur, Yarmouth Port, Mass., 1940.
Grillparzer, Franz, *A Faithful Servant of His Master,* transl. by Burkhard, Arthur, Yarmouth Port, Mass., 1941.
Grillparzer, Franz, *Medea,* transl. by Burkhard, Arthur, Yarmouth Port, Mass., 1941.
Grillparzer, Franz, *The Golden Fleece: A Dramatic Poem in Three Parts,* transl. by Burkhard, Arthur, Yarmouth Port, Mass., 1942.
Grillparzer, Franz, *Libussa,* edited by Curme, George O., New York, Oxford, Univ. Press, 1913.
Grillparzer, Franz, *The Jewess of Toledo,* transl. by Danton, Henry, and Danton, Annina Periam. (In Francke, Kuno, ed., *German Classics of the 19th and 20th centuries* [c. 1913-1914] v. 6.)
Grillparzer, Franz, *Der Traum, ein Leben,* hrsg. von Dlaske, Eduard, Wien, Oesterreichischer Bundesverlag, 1946.
Grillparzer, Franz, *Konig Ottokars Gluck und Ende,* ed. by Eggert, C. E., New York, Henry Holt & Co., 1910.
Grillparzer, Franz, *Sappho,* ed. by Ferrell, Chiles Clifton, Boston, Ginn and Company, 1899.
Grillparzer, Franz, *Sappho,* transl. by Frothingham, Ellen, Boston, Roberts Brothers, 1876.
Grillparzer, Franz, *Konig Ottokars Glück und Ende,* hrsg. von Findeis, Richard, Wien, Mainz, 1911 (neuere Dichter).
Grillparzer, Franz, *Die Ahnfrau,* ed. by Heuser, Frederick W. J., and Danton, George H., New York, Henry Holt & Co., 1907.
Grillparzer, Franz, *Ein Bruderzwist in Habsburg,* Leipzig, Insel-Verlag, 1941.
Grillparzer, Franz, *Medea,* Wiesbaden, Kesselring, 1948 (Kesselringsche Schulausgaben, 10. Bd.)
Grillparzer, Franz, *Des Meeres und der Liebe Wellen,* ed. by Kind, John, Louis, and Purin, Charles Maltador, New York, Oxford University Press, 1916.
Grillparzer, Franz, *Sappho,* ed. by Kind, John Lewis, New York, Oxford University Press, 1916.
Grillparzer, Franz, *Correggio:* a tragedy by Oehlenschläger. *Sappho:* a tragedy by Grillparzer, transl. from the German by Lee, Mrs. Eliza (Buckminster), Boston, Phillips and Sampson, 1846.
Grillparzer, Franz, *Ein Bruderzwist im Hause Habsburg,* hrsg. von Lichtenheld, A., Wien, Gräser, 1926. (Gräsers Schulausgaben klassischer Werke, Heft 62.)

Grillparzer, Franz, *Libussa*, hrsg. von Lichtenheld, A., Leipzig, Teubner, n.d. (Gräsers Schulausgaben klassischer Werke, Heft 63.)

Grillparzer, Franz, *Les vagues de la mer et de l'amour*, traduit par Loiseau, Hippolyte, Paris, Aubier, Éditions Montaigne, 1942.

Grillparzer, Franz, *Sappho*, transl. by Middleton, Edda, New York, D. Appleton and Company, 1858.

Grillparzer, Franz, *König Ottokars Gluck und Ende*, hrsg. von Prosch, Franz, Wien, Graser, n.d. (Gräsers Schulausgaben klassischer Werke, Heft 64.)

Grillparzer, Franz, *Sappho*, hrsg. von Prosch, Franz, Wien, Gräser, n.d. (Gräsers Schulausgaben klassischer Werke, Heft 61.)

Grillparzer, Franz, *Sappho*, ed. by Rippmann, Walter, London, Macmillan, 1901.

Grillparzer, Franz, *Die Ahnfrau*, hrsg. von Schreyvogel, Joseph, Wien, J. B. Wallishausser, 2nd ed., 1819.

Grillparzer, Franz, *Des Meeres und der Liebe Wellen*, ed. by Schütze, Martin, New York, Henry Holt & Co., 1912.

Grillparzer, Franz, *Hero and Leander; King Ottokar, His Rise and Fall; Thou Shalt not Lie*, transl. by Stevens, Henry H., Yarmouth Port, Mass., 1938.

Grillparzer, Franz, *Thou Shalt not Lie* transl. by Stevens, Henry H., Yarmouth Port, Mass., 1939.

Grillparzer, Franz, *Libussa*, transl. by Stevens, Henry H., Yarmouth Port, Mass., 1941.

Grillparzer, Franz, *A Dream Is Life: Dramatic Phantasy in Four Acts*, transl. by Stevens, Henry H., Yarmouth Port, Mass., 1946.

Grillparzer, Franz, *The Ancestress*, transl. by Spahr, Herman L., Hapeville, Georgia, USA, Tyler & Company, (c. 1938).

Grillparzer, Franz, *Die Ahnfrau*, hrsg. von Streinz, Franz, Wien, Gräser, 1901. (Gräsers Schulausgaben klassischer Werke, Heft 66.)

Grillparzer, Franz, *Der arme Spielmann*, hrsg. von Walheim, Alfred, Wien, Gräser, 1926. (Gräsers Schulausgaben klassischer Werke, Heft 77.)

Grillparzer, Franz, *Sappho*, Wien, J. B. Wallishausser, 1819, 2nd ed.

Grillparzer, Franz, *Das goldene Vliess*, Wien, J. B. Wallishausser, 1822.

Grillparzer, Franz, *Ein treuer Diener seines Herrn*, Wien, J. B. Wallishausser, 1830.

Grillparzer, Franz, *Weh' dem, der lügt!* ed. by Waterhouse, Gilbert, Manchester, University Press; London, New York, etc., Longmans, Green & Co., 1923.

Grillparzer, Franz, *Weh dem, der lugt*, hrsg. von Wilhelm, Gustav, Wien, Gräser, n.d. (Gräsers Schulausgaben klassischer Werke, Heft 101.)

Grillparzer, Franz, *König Ottokars Gluck und Ende*, hrsg. von Zaunbauer, Alois, Wien, Amandus-Edition, 1946. (Oesterreichische Lesehefte für Schule und Haus.)

Grillparzer, Franz, *Der Traum ein Leben*, hrsg. von Zimmert, Ferdinand, Wien, Gräser, 1925. (Gräsers Schulausgaben klassischer Werke, Heft 65.)

IV. Books

Alker, Ernst, *Franz Grillparzer; Ein Kampf um Leben und Kunst*, Marburg a. L., N. G. Elwert, 1930.

Auernheimer, Raoul, *Franz Grillparzer, Der Dichter Oesterreichs*, Wien, Ullstein, 1948. Reviewed by Horvay, Frank D., *German Books*, II, 4 (September, 1949), 154-156.

Backmann, Reinhold, *Die ersten Anfange der Grillparzerschen Medeadichtung*, Weida, i. Th., Thomas & Hubert, 1910. Dissertation (Ph.D.), Leipzig.

Baldrian, Rudolf, *Grillparzer in Bad Hall*, Bad Hall, Verlag: Kurdirektion Bad Hall, (194-).

Bellaigne, Camille, Études musicales, (2. série), Paris, C. Delagrave, 1903.

Berger, Alfred von, *Dramaturgische Vortrage*, Wien, Carl Konegen, 1890, 34-60.

Beriger, Leonhard, *Grillparzers Personlichkeit in seinem Werk*, Horgen-Zürich, Verlag der Münsterpresse, 1928.

Bertram, Ernst, Nietzsche, *Versuch einer Mythologie*, Berlin, Georg Bondi, 1921.

Blaze de Bury, Ange Henri, *Goethe et Beethoven*, Paris, Perrin et Cie., 1892.

Bock, Alfred, *Deutsche Dichter in ihren Beziehungen zur Musik: Klopstock, Wieland, Lessing, Schiller, Goethe, Herder, Jean Paul, Romantiker, Hoffmann, Lenau, Heine, Grillparzer*, Neue Ausg., Giessen, J. Ricker'sche Verlagsbuchhandlung, 1900.

Braun, Hans, *Grillparzers Verhaltnis zu Shakespeare*, Nurnberg, Lotter, 1916.

Bücher, Wilhelm, *Grillparzers Verhältnis zur Politik seiner Zeit*, Marburg, N. G. Elwert, 1913.

Bulthaupt, Heinrich, *Dramaturgie des Schauspiels*. Grillparzer, Hebbel, Ludwig, Gutzkow, Laube; Oldenburg und Leipzig, Schulzesche Hof-Buchhandlung, 1908.

Collijn, Gustaf, *Franz Grillparzer, Hans lif och verk*, Stockholm, G. Lindstrom, 1902.

De Walsh, Faust Charles, *Grillparzer as a Poet of Nature*, New York, The Columbia University Press, 1910.

Ebner-Eschenbach, Marie von, *Meine Erinnerungen an Grillparzer*. (In Ebner-Eschenbach, *Sämtliche Werke*, Bibliotheksausgabe, Leipzig, Schmidt & Co., 1928, v. 12.)

Ehrhard, Auguste, *Franz Grillparzer, sein Leben und seine Werke*, Deutsche Ausgabe von Necker, Moritz, 2., umgearbeitete Auflage, München, O. Beck 1910.

Farinelli, Arturo, *Grillparzer und Lope de Vega*, Berlin, E. Felber, 1894.

Farinelli, Arturo, *Lope de Vega en Alemania*, traducción de la obra alemana "Grillparzer und Lope de Vega," por Enrique Massaguer, Barcelona, Bosch, 1936.

Fäulhammer, Adalbert, *Franz Grillparzer, eine biographische Studie*, Graz, Leuschner & Lubensky, 1884.

Foglar, Adolf, *Grillparzers Ansichten uber Literatur, Buhne, und Leben*, 2te und vermehrte Auflage, Stuttgart, Goschen, 1891.

Fries, Albert Rudolf, *Intime Beobachtungen zu Grillparzers Stil und Versbau*, mit Exkursen zu Klopstocks, Goethes und Shakespeares Stil, Berlin, E. Ebering, 1922. (Germanische Studien, hrsg., von Dr. E. Ebering, Hft. 18).

Geissler, H. W., *Grillparzer und Schopenhauer*, Weimar, Uschmann, 1915. Dissertation (Ph.D.), K. Ludwig-Maximilian-Universitat zu München.

Herrmann, Elizabeth Adelaide, *Histrionics in the dramas of Franz Grillparzer*, Berkeley, University of California Press, 1912. Thesis (M.A.), University of California.

Hock, Erich, *Das Schmerzerlebnis und sein Ausdruck in Grillparzers Lyrik*, Berlin, Eberling, 1937.

Hock, Erich, *Franz Grillparzer: Besinnung auf Humanitat*, Hamburg, Hoffmann und Campe, 1949.

Hock, Stefan, *Der Traum, ein Leben,* eine literar-historische Untersuchung, Stuttgart, Cotta, 1904.

Hohlbaum, Robert, *Grillparzer,* Stuttgart, Cotta, 1938.

Hradek, L., *Studien zu Grillparzers Altersstil und die Datierung des Estherfragmentes,* Prag, Koppe-Bellmann, A. G., 1915.

Jerusalem, Wilhelm, *Grillparzers Welt- und Lebensanschauung,* Festrede zur Grillparzerfeier, gehalten im Wissenschaftlichen Club am 12. Januar 1891. Wien, J. Eisenstein & Co., 1891.

Katann, Oskar, ed., *Grillparzer-Studien,* Wien, Gerlach & Wiedling, 1924.

Kind, Friedrich, *Der Freischutz,* Friedrich Kinds Operndichtung und ihre Quellen, hrsg. von Hasselberg, Felix, Anhang: Franz Grillparzer, Der wilde Jager (Parodie der Wolfsschlucht), Berlin, Domverlag, 1921.

Klaar, Alfred, *Grillparzer als Dramatiker,* Wien, Bauer, 1891.

Kleinberg, Alfred, *Franz Grillparzer, der Mann und das Werk,* Leipzig und Berlin, B. G. Teubner, 1915.

Kosch, Wilhelm, *Oesterreich im Dichten und Denken Grillparzers,* Nymwegen, Wächter-Verlag, 1946.

Krauske, Marie, *Grillparzer als Epigrammatiker,* Berlin, A. Duncker, 1906.

Küchling, (Eduard) Hermann, *Studien zur Sprache des jungen Grillparzer mit besonderer Berucksichtigung der "Ahnfrau,"* Diss., Leipzig, Druck von K. H. Scheithauer, 1900.

Kuh, Emil, *Zwei Dichter Oesterreichs: Franz Grillparzer-Adalbert Stifter,* Pest, G. Heckenast, 1872.

Kuranda, Peter, *Grossdeutschland und Grossosterreich bei den Hauptvertretern der deutschösterreichischen Literatur, 1830-1848,* Wien und Leipzig, Oesterreichischer Bundesverlag für Unterricht, Wissenschaft und Kunst, 1928.

Lange, Edmund, *Franz Grillparzer: sein Leben, Dichten und Denken,* Gutersloh, C. Bertelsmann, 1894.

Lasher-Schlitt, Dorothy, *Grillparzer's Attitude Toward the Jews,* New York, G. E. Stechert & Co., 1936.

Laube, Heinrich, *Franz Grillparzers Lebensgeschichte,* J. G. Cotta, 1884.

Leitich, Ann Tizia, *Zwolfmal Liebe; Frauen um Grillparzer,* Wien, G. Fromme, (c. 1948).

Lenz, Harold, F. H., *Franz Grillparzer's Political Ideas and "Die Jüdin von Toledo,"* New York, 1938.

Lessing, O. E., *Grillparzer und das neue Drama,* eine Studie, München, Piper, 1905.

Lessing, Otto E., *Schillers Einfluss auf Grillparzer,* Madison, Wis., 1902. Thesis (Ph.D.), University of Michigan, 1901.

Lex, Michael, *Die Idee im Drama bei Goethe, Schiller, Grillparzer, Kleist,* Munchen, Beck, 1904.

Littrow-Bischoff, *Aus dem personlichen Verkehre mit Franz Grillparzer,* Wien, Rosner, 1873.

Ludwig, Alfred Josef, *Der klassische Wiener, Franz Grillparzer,* Wien, Amandus-Edition, 1946.

Lux, Joseph August, *Grillparzers Liebesroman, die Schwestern Fröhlich,* Roman aus Wiens klassischer Zeit, Berlin, A. Bong, 1912.

Mahrenholtz, R., *Franz Grillparzer und das spanische Drama,* Herrigs Archiv, 86 (1890), 369-382.

Mettin, Hermann Christian, *Grillparzer; Dramaturgische Essays,* Berlin, v. Hugo, 1944.

Minor, Jakob, *Rede auf Grillparzer,* gehalten am 15. Januar 1891 im Festsaale der Universität, Wien, Selbstverlag der K. K. Universität, 1891.

Müller, Joachim, *Grillparzers Menschenauffassung,* Weimar, Verlag Hermann Bohlaus Nachf., 1934.

Müller-Guttenbrunn, Adam, *Im Jahrhundert Grillparzers,* Literatur- und Lebensbilder aus Oesterreich, 3. unveränderte Auflage, Leipzig, G. H. Meyer, 1895.

Münch, Ilse, *Die Tragik in Drama und Persönlichkeit Franz Grillparzers*, Berlin, Junker & Dünnhaupt, 1931.

Nadler, Josef, *Franz Grillparzer*, Vaduz, Liechtenstein Verlag, 1948.

Nietzsche, Friedrich, *Die Geburt der Tragödie aus dem Geiste der Musik*, in *Nietzsches Werke*, II, Leipzig, Reclam, 1931.

Nolte, Fred O., *Grillparzer, Lessing, and Goethe in the Perspective of European Literature*, Lancaster, Pa., 1938.

Pachaly, Paul, *Erlauterungen zu Grillparzers Sappho*, Leipzig, W. Königs Erläuterungen zu den Klassikern, Bdch. 52, 1926.

Pollak, Gustav, *Franz Grillparzer and the Austrian Drama*, New York, Dodd, Mead & Co., 1907.

Pollak, Gustav, *International Perspective in Criticism; Goethe, Grillparzer, Sainte-Beuve, Lowell*, New York, Dodd, Mead & Co., 1914.

Pollak, Gustav, *International Minds and the Search for the Restful*, New York, The Nation Press, Inc., 1919.

Puttmann, Max, *Franz Grillparzer und die Musik*, Langensalza, H. Beyer & Söhne, 1910.

Quiller-Couch, Arthur, editor, *The Oxford Book of English Verse*, Oxford, At the Clarendon Press, 1924.

Redlich Oswald, *Grillparzers Verhaltnis zur Geschichte*, Vortrag gehalten in der feierl. Sitzung der Kaiserlichen Akademie der Wissenschaften am 1. Juni 1901, Issued as part of the *Almanach der Kaiserlichen Akademie der Wissenschaften*, 51. Jahrgang, 1901.

Reich, Emil, *Franz Grillparzers Dramen*, Funfzehn Vorlesungen gehalten an der Universitat Wien, 3te vermehrte Auflage, Dresden, E. Pierson, 1909.

Reich, Emil, *Grillparzers dramatisches Werk*, (Vierte, völlig neu bearbeitete Auflage des Buches 'Franz Grillparzers Dramen'), Wien, Saturn-Verlag, 1938.

Reich, Emil, *Grillparzers Kunstphilosophie*, Wien, Manz, 1890.

Saverio, Emil Francis, *The musical element in the Viennese Volksstück and in the dramas of Grillparzer*, Richmond, Va., G. W. Herndon Co., 1925. Thesis (Ph.D.), University of Texas.

Schaefer, Albert E., *Grillparzers Verhaltnis zur preussisch-deutschen Politik*, Berlin, E. Ebering, 1929. (Germanische Studien, Hft. 69).

Scherer, Wilhelm, *Vortrage und Aufsatze zur Geschichte des geistigen Lebens in Deutschland und Oesterreich*, Berlin, Weidmannsche Buchhandlung, 1874. VIII, *Franz Grillparzer*, 193-307.

Schneider, Reinhold, *Im Anfang liegt das Ende; Grillparzers Epilog auf die Geschichte*, Baden-Baden, H. Buhler Jr., 1946.

Scholz, Wilhelm von, *Kleists, Grillparzers, Immermanns, und Grabbes Dramaturgie*, München und Leipzig, Georg Müller, 1912.

Schreyvogl, Friedrich, *Franz Grillparzer, Einsamer unter Geniessern*, Roman, Berlin, etc., P. Zsolnay, 1940. ("Jubiläumsausgabe;" first published 1935 under Title: *Grillparzer*.)

Schubert, Franz Peter, *Mirjam's Siegesgesang, Kantate fur Sopran-Solo und gemischten Chor mit Klavier*, [Gedicht von Franz Grillparzer], Op. 136, hrsg. von Hoppel, Hubert, Wien, A. Robitschek, (c. 1946).

Schwering, Julius, *Grillparzers hellenische Trauerspiele*, Paderborn, 1891.

Sittenberger, Hans, *Grillparzer, sein Leben und Wirken*, Wittenberg bez. Halle, A. Ziemsen, 1903.

Sprengler, Joseph, *Grillparzer, der Tragiker der Schuld*, Lorch, Württ., A. Bürger, 1947.

Störi, Fritz, *Grillparzer und Kant*, Frauenfeld, Leipzig, Huber & Co., 1935.

Strich, Fritz, *Franz Grillparzers Aesthetik*, Berlin, A. Duncker, 1905.

Vancsa, Kurt, *Franz Grillparzer, eine Studie*, Wien, Amandus-Edition, 1946.

Volkelt, Johannes Immanuel, *Zwischen Dichtung und Philosophie*, gesammelte Aufsätze (darunter: "Grillparzer als Dichter des Komischen"), München, C. H. Beck, 1908.

Volkelt, J. I., *Franz Grillparzer als Dichter des Tragischen*, 2ter unveränderter Abdruck, München, Beck, 1909. (1. Druck: Nördlingen, 1888.)

Wartburg, Helmut von, *Grillparzers dramatische Fragmente*, Affoltern am Albis, J. Weiss, 1945.

Wartenegg, Wilhelm von, *Erinnerungen an Franz Grillparzer*, Fragmente aus Tagebuchblattern, Wien, C. Konegen, 1901.

Wedel-Parlow, Ludolf von, *Grillparzer*, Wertheim am Main, E. Bechstein, 1932.

Weigand, Hermann J., *The modern Ibsen*, New York, Holt, 1925.

Williamson, Edward John, *Grillparzer's attitude toward Romanticism*, Chicago, The University of Chicago Press, 1910. Thesis (Ph.D.), University of Chicago.

Wolf-Cirian, Francis, *Grillparzers Frauengestalten*, Stuttgart und Berlin, Cotta, 1908.

Wutzky, Anna Charlotte, *Grillparzer und die Musik*, Regensburg, G. Bosse, 1940.

Yates, Douglas, *Der Kontrast zwischen Kunst und Leben bei Grillparzer*, Berlin, Germanische Studien, E. Eberling, Heft 75, 1929.

Yates, Douglas, *Franz Grillparzer; A Critical Biography*, Vol. I, Oxford, Basil Blackwell, 1946. Reviewed by Drake, Patricia, *German Quarterly*, XXII (1949), 55-56.

Zausmer, Otto, *Grillparzers Lyrik als Ausdruck seines Wesens*, Wien-Leipzig, Deutscher Verlag für Jugend und Volk, (c. 1933).

Zimmermann, Hans Gerold, *Die dichterische und technische Behandlung von Kampf und Krieg im dramatischen Werk Franz Grillparzers*, Diss.— Fribourg, Willisau, Buchdr. Willisauer Bote, 1945.

Zipper, Albert, *Franz Grillparzer*, neue durchgesehene Ausgabe, Leipzig, P. Reclam jun., 1923. (Dichterbiographien, 9. Bd.)

V. Articles and Reviews

Arlt, Gustave O., "A Source of Grillparzer's *Ahnfrau*," *Modern Philology*, XXIX (1931), 91-100.

Aschner, S., "Zur Quellenfrage der Jüdin von Toledo," *Euphorion*, XIX (1918), 279-301.

Backmann, Reinhold, "Entwicklungsgeschichtliches zu Grillparzers 'Ahnfrau.' " *Jahrbuch der Grillparzer-Gesellschaft*, XXVIII (1926), 22-34.

Backmann, R., "Kohm, J., Grillparzers Goldenes Vliess," *Jahrbuch fur neuere deutsche Literaturgeschichte*, 1903, N. 1889-1890, Rezension, *Euphorion*.

Berger, Alfred von, "Das 'Glück' bei Grillparzer," *Jahrbuch der Grillparzer-Gesellschaft*, X (1900), 70-79.

Bernt, Alois, "Splitter zur Erklärung von Grillparzers 'König Ottokar,' " *Euphorion*, XI (1904), 518-520.

Campbell, P. M., Review of "Curme, G. O., edition of *Libussa*," New York, Oxford University Press, 1913, *Modern Languages Notes*, XXVIII (1913), 255-257.

Carlyle, Thomas, "German Playwrights," in *Critical and Miscellaneous Essays*, London, Chapman & Hall, 1899, I, 355-395.

Collison, W. E., Korner, A. M., Triebel, L. A., "Notes on Grillparzer's 'König Ottokars Glück und Ende,' " *Modern Language Review*, V (1910), 454-472.

Drake, Patricia, "Grillparzer's Self-Identification with Rousseau," *Modern Language Notes*, LXIV (1949), 398-399.

Dunham, T. C., "Medea in Athens and Vienna," *Monatshefte für deutschen Unterricht*, XXXVIII (1946), 217-225.

Dunham, T. C., "The Monologue as Monodrama in Grillparzer's Hellenic Dramas," *Journal of English and Germanic Philology*, XXXVII (1938), 513-523.

Glossy, Carl, "Aus Bauernfelds Tagebüchern, II (1849-1879)," *Jahrbuch der Grillparzer-Gesellschaft*, VI (1896), 85-223.

Glossy, Carl, "Zur Geschichte des Trauerspiels 'König Ottokars Glück und Ende'," *Jahrbuch der Grillparzer-Gesellschaft*, IX (1899), 213-247.

Griffith, B. E., "Grillparzer and the London Theatre," *Germanic Review*, VIII (1933), 246-264.

Hart, H., "Grillparzers Medea und Ibsens Nora," *Tag*. N. 407, 1901, discussed in *Jahresberichte fur neuere deutsche Literaturgeschichte*, XIII (1902), 496.

Hock, Stefan, *"Zum 'Traum ein Leben,'"* *Jahrbuch der Grillparzer-Gesellschaft*, XIII (1903), 75-122.

Horvay, Frank D., "Goethe and Grillparzer," *The Germanic Review*, XXV (1950), 85-94.

Kaderschafka, Karl, " 'Ein Bruderzwist in Habsburg' auf der Bühne," in *Grillparzer Studien*, hrsg. von Katann, Oskar, Wien, Gerlach & Wiedling, 1924, 221-243, 315-325.

Kaufmann, F. W., "Grillparzer's Relation to Classical Idealism," *Modern Language Notes*, LI (1936), 359-363.

Kaufmann, F. W., "Grillparzer's Position in Nineteenth-Century Thought," *Modern Language Notes*, LIII (1938), 347-351.

Killian, Eugen, "Miscelle zum zweiten Teil der Vliess-Trilogie," *Jahrbuch der Grillparzer-Gesellschaft*, III (1893), 366-369.

Klarmann, Adolf D., "Psychological Motivation in Grillparzer's *Sappho*," *Monatshefte für deutschen Unterricht*, XL (1948), 271-278.

Kohn, Joseph, "Zur Charakteristik der 'Ahnfrau,' " *Jahrbuch der Grillparzer-Gesellschaft*, XI (1900), 22-76.

Komorzynski, Egon von, " 'Die Ahnfrau' und die Wiener Volksdramatik," *Euphorion*, IX (1910).

Lambert, E., "Eine Untersuchung der Quellen der 'Jüdin von Toledo,' " *Jahrbuch der Grillparzer-Gesellschaft*, XIX (1909), 61 ff.

Lambert, E., "La Juive de Grillparzer: Étude sur la composition et les sources de la pièce," *Revue de Littérature comparée*, Paris, 1922, II, 238 ff.

Lasher-Schlitt, Dorothy, "Hebbel, Grillparzer, and the Wiener Kreis," *PMLA*, LXI (1946), 492-521.

Lasher-Schlitt, Dorothy, "Josef Schreyvogel, Grillparzers väterlicher Freund," *Germanic Review*, XXI (1946), 268-305.

Lesch, H. H., "Der tragische Gehalt in Grillparzers Drama 'Das goldene Vliess.' " *Jahrbuch der Grillparzer-Gesellschaft*, XXIV (1915), 1-55.

Lessing-Dilg, O. E., "Bemerkungen zu Grillparzers Bancbanus," *Euphorion*, VIII (1901), 685-700.

Lessing, O. E., "Motive aus Schiller in Grillparzers Meisterwerken." *Journal of English and Germanic Philology*, V (1903-1905), 33-43.

Lessing, O. E., "Sappho-Probleme," *Euphorion*, V (1903), 592-611.

Milrath, Max, "Das goldene Vliess, Libussas Geschmeide und Rahels Bild," *Jahrbuch der Grillparzer-Gesellschaft*, XX (1911), 226-258.

Minor, Jakob, "Grillparzer als Lustspieldichter und 'Weh dem, der lügt,' " *Jahrbuch der Grillparzer-Gesellschaft*, III (1893), 41-60.

Minor, Jakob, "Zur Geschichte der deutschen Schicksalstragödie und zu Grillparzers 'Ahnfrau' " *Jahrbuch der Grillparzer-Gesellschaft*. IX (1899), 1-85.

Paulsen, Wolfgang, "Grillparzers Erzählungskunst," *Germanic Review*, XIX (1944), 59-68.

Petsch, Robert, "Review of Lessing, O. E., Grillparzer und das neue Drama," *Emphorion*, XIV (1907), 160-179.

Radermacher, Ludwig, "Grillparzers Medea," *Jahrbuch der Grillparzer-Gesellschaft*, XXXII (1923), 1-10.

Reichert, Herbert W., "The Characterization of Bancbanus in Grillparzer's 'Ein Treuer Diener seines Herrn,'" *Studies in Philology*, XLVI (1949), 70-78.

Richter, Helene, "Review of Wiegand, Hermann J., The modern Ibsen. A Reconsideration," New York, Henry Holt & Co., 1925, *Euphorion*, XXVII (1926), 615-619.

Root, Winthrop H., "Grillparzer's *Sappho* and Thomas Mann's *Tonio Kroger*," *Monatshefte fur deutschen Unterricht*, XXIX (1937), 59-64.

Salinger, Herman, "Shakespeare's Tyranny of Grillparzer," *Monatshefte fur deutschen Unterricht*, XXXI (1939), 222-229.

Sauer, August, "Ein treuer Diener seines Herrn," *Jahrbuch der Grillparzer-Gesellschaft*, III (1893).

Sauer, August, "Grillparzer und das Königliche Schauspielhaus in Berlin," Mit einem ungedruckten Brief des Dichters, *Euphorion*, XXVII (1926), 112-114.

Sauer, August, "Oesterreichische Dichter, Ausgaben und Forschungen," *Euphorion*, XXVII (1926), 264-274.

Sauer, August, "Review of Schwering, J., Franz Grillparzers hellenische Trauerspiele," *Anzeiger fur deutsches Altertum*, XIX (1893), 334-338.

Schütze, Martin, "Toward a Modern Humanism," *Publications of the Modern Language Associations of America*, LI, (No. 1, March, 1936), 284-299.

Speier, Max, "Ueber das künstlerische Problem in 'Ein treuer Diener seines Herrn,'" *Euphorion*, VII (1900), 541-547.

Volkelt, Johannes, "Grillparzer als Dichter des Komischen," *Jahrbuch der Grillparzer-Gesellschaft*, XV (1905), 1-30.

Whitaker, Paul K., "The Concept of 'Sammlung' in Grillparzer's Works," *Monatshefte fur deutschen Unterricht*, XLI (1949), 93-103.

Weilen, A. von, "Zu Grillparzers 'Ein treuer Diener seines Herrn.'" *Euphorion*, XVIII (1911), 136-142.

Wenger, N., "An Introduction to the Aesthetics of Literary Portraiture," *Publications of the Modern Language Association of America*, L, (No. 2, June, 1935), 515-629.

Wolff, Hans M., "Zum Problem der Ahnfrau," *Zeitschrift fur deutsche Philologie*, LXII (1937), 303-317.

Wurzbach, W. von, "Die Judin von Toledo in Geschichte und Dichtung," *Jahrbuch der Grillparzer-Gesellschaft*, IX (1899), 86 ff.

Wurzburch, W. von, "Eine unbekannte Opernbearbeitung von Grillparzers 'Der Traum, ein Leben,'" *Jahrbuch der Grillparzer-Gesellschaft*, XXIX (1930), 100-107.

Wyplel, Ludwig, "Ein Schauerroman als Quelle der 'Ahnfrau,' Ein Beitrag zur Entstehungsgeschichte der Tragödie," *Euphorion*, VII (1900), 725-758.

Wyplel, Ludwig, "Grillparzer und Byron, Zur Entstehungsgeschichte des Trauerspiels 'Ein treuer Diener seines Herrn,'" *Euphorion*, IX (1902), 159-180.

Yates, Douglas, "Grillparzer's Hero und Shakespeare's Juliet," *Modern Language Review*, XXI (1926), 419-425.

Zeydel, Edwin H., "Tieck und Grillparzer," *Germanisch-Romanische Monatsschrift*, XXIV (1936), 372-379.

Zucker, A. E., "An *Ahnfrau* Scene in Schiller's *Wallenstein*," *Modern Language Notes*, LI (1936), 97-98.

CPSIA information can be obtained at www.ICGtesting.com
Printed in the USA
BVOW09s0027071014

369774BV00019B/224/P

9 781258 407308